SILVER AGE SENTINELS
CRIMINAL INTENT
THE VILLAIN'S ALMANAC

WRITTEN BY
Dale Donovan, Jason Durall, Peter Flanagan, Michelle Lyons, Stan!

ADDITIONAL WRITING BY
Bruce Ballon, Matt Keeley, Jesse Scoble

TRI-STAT SYSTEM™ DESIGNED BY
Mark C. MacKinnon

LINE DEVELOPING BY
Jesse Scoble

EDITING BY
Michelle Lyons, Mark C. MacKinnon, Jesse Scoble

ART DIRECTION AND GRAPHIC PRODUCTION BY
Jeff Mackintosh

COVER BY
Matt Harpold

INTERIOR ARTWORK BY
Uko Smith and Udon with Eric Kim and Attila Adorjany

SPECIAL THANKS TO
John Davies, James Lowder

PLAYTESTERS
John Fiala, Peter Flanagan, Tom Miskey, Anthony Roberson

NOTES ABOUT GAME CONTENT

The game stats presented herein are for both the Tri-Stat System and the d20 System. Values presented on the left side of a character sheet are for the Tri-Stat System while numbers presented on the right side of the character are for the d20 System. Also, information presented outside of double square brackets, before a slash are for the Tri-Stat System while text presented within {[double square brackets]}, after the slash are for the d20 System. Any reference to the "Level" of an Attribute also refers to the Attribute's "Rank" when using *Silver Age Sentinels d20*. Furthermore, unless specified otherwise, "Stat" also refers to "Ability Score" when using *Silver Age Sentinels d20*. For example, "Relevant Stat" also means "Relevant Ability Score." Also "Health Points" and "Hit Points" are often used interchangably.

For the character entries, some of the d20 System point costs are presented in parantheses. This is done to indicate the number of Points a character spent to acquire the given Attribute although the Attribute rank listed is higher than the Point cost would suggest. This difference is due to the "special" bonuses gained from class Level progression for the character's selected class(es).

GUARDIANS OF ORDER, TRI-STAT SYSTEM, and SILVER AGE SENTINELS are trademarks of GUARDIANS OF ORDER, INC.

'D20 SYSTEM' and the 'D20 SYSTEM' logo are Trademarks owned by WIZARDS OF THE COAST and are used according to the terms of the D20 System License version 3.0. A copy of this License can be found at www.wizards.com/d20.

DUNGEONS & DRAGONS® and WIZARDS OF THE COAST® are Registered Trademarks of WIZARDS OF THE COAST, and are used with Permission.

WATCHMEN written by Alan Moore (DC Comics 1986), BATMAN: THE KILLING JOKE written by Alan Moore (DC Comics 1988), GOLDFINGER screenplay by Richard Maibaum and Paul Dehn (MGM Studios, 1964)

First Printing — September 2003 Printed in Canada

ISBN 1-894525-64-7 • Production Number 13-009

GUARDIANS OF ORDER, INC. • P.O. Box 25016, 370 Stone Road, Guelph, Ontario, CANADA, N1G 4T4
Phone: (519) 821-7174 • Fax: (519) 821-7635 • info@guardiansorder.com • http://www.guardiansorder.com

TABLE OF CONTENTS

793.93 CRI 9

JUSTICE

SECURITY

PEACE

INTRODUCTION

Any fan of four-colour heroes knows that villains come in all shapes, sizes, and demeanours. Some want to take over the world, others want to blow it up, and quite a few just want to get rich quick. There are even one or two who have truly noble intentions — their methods, however, do not meet with public approval. A villain can be an individual who gained superpowers through any number of odd circumstances: an alien with abilities far beyond those of mortals, a time traveller using future technology, or even just an ordinary human with the money or power to command (or even create) vast armies.

But what is a villain, really? What is he or she good for in your campaign? The obvious answer is that the villain (or villains) is the antagonist in your story. He or she acts as a foil for your heroic characters, testing and challenging them so that they will grow in both power and personality. He or she is the focus, indeed the personification of whatever problems the player characters face, enabling them to defeat by proxy the other demons in their lives through superior valour, virtue, and teamwork. Villains have a special place in superhero stories, for they are the lynchpin of the whole endeavour — the central point around which everything else revolves, holding it all together by their mere presence.

Heroes are measured by the power, capabilities, determination, and competence of the foes they battle. Therefore, as a GM, it is imperative to present engaging, effective, well-thought-out opponents with whom your characters can struggle. This book is designed to help you envision and present these crucial, yet often unappreciated, individuals in a way that will enthral your players and give a sense of realism to your most important creations: the bad guys.

"When were you planning to do it?"

"'Do it?'

"Dan, I'm not a republic serial villain. Do you seriously think I'd explain my masterstroke if there remained the slightest chance of you affecting its outcome?

"I did it thirty-five minutes ago."

— Ozymandias, *Watchmen*

"You see, it doesn't matter if you catch me and send me back to the Asylum ... Gordon's been driven mad. I've proved my point. I've demonstrated there's no difference between us and everyone else!

"All it takes is one bad day to reduce the sanest man alive to lunacy. That's how far the world is from where I am. Just one bad day.

"When I saw what a black awful joke the world was, I went crazy as a coot! I admit it! Why can't you? I mean, you're not unintelligent! You must see the reality of the situation."

— The Joker, *The Killing Joke*

Man has climbed Mount Everest, gone to the bottom of the ocean. He's fired rockets at the Moon, split the atom, achieved miracles in every field of human endeavour ... except crime!

— Auric Goldfinger, *Goldfinger*

assesses what is necessary for a group of backstabbing black-hearted individualists to pull together for the greater evil. Chapter Four discusses criminal organisations, those dastardly groups bent on world domination (or some other appropriately nefarious goal). It gives guidelines on how to create your own organisation of villainy, as well as an example organisation set in the heart of Empire City.

Chapter Five finishes off the book with a Most Wanted list of *Silver Age Sentinel*'s most feared villains, including the Artificer and Green Ronin, and several brand new faces. It also devotes a section to taking the rough sketch of a supervillain's personality and breathing life into it to make them a unique individual, as well as exploring a villain's role in a campaign and how he or she may interact with the heroes.

Villains can be found in all manner of places, from back alleys to underground complexes, from dingy attics to skyscraper penthouses and everywhere in between. They work alone, in packs, and in organisations both large and small. This chapter will cover the basic requirements of the criminal mind, what a bad guy needs in order to be truly formidable, and the seven most common strategies for highly effective villains. Chapter Two focuses on solo villains, those sometimes-difficult-to-handle individuals who must be strong enough to pose a threat to a group on their own, yet weak enough to be soundly defeated by a determined effort. It covers the whys and hows of those who choose that lifestyle, along with tips on their favourite types of crimes and helpers. Having looked at villains on their own, Chapter Three is devoted to the study of criminal teamwork. It

File   Edit   View   Insert   Format   Font   Tools   Windo

Docun

Font: **Times New Roman**   Size: 11 pt   Colour: ■   Style: Normal

12.21.00

We are born into a world of pain and blood. What choice do we have but to rail against the injustice, the madness of it all? All of us wake from peaceful slumber to a place haunted by hunger, fear, and sickness — a world beyond comprehension and bereft of meaning, a world where we are alone. Is there some grand design? Some ineffable mystery? A passion play of karma and free choice? If there is a meaning hidden between the lives then I have yet to discern it, and should I awake with such clarity of sight to pierce the thunderous heavens, I would refuse them and cut my strings, for I am no marionette.

My first memory that I can acutely recall is of the gutters of Munich. A young woman and her babes were huddled there beneath a thin coat, in the filth. A mangy dog was at her feet, less pitiful than she, for it knew to lie there was death. It came to me, while she could only plead mutely with her eyes. My father let me take the dog home. I may have been five. Every week when we passed by the square she was still there, but her dog was now at my heels. He knew where life lay, and where death squatted. I do not know what happened to her children — taken for sale or by death, I suppose — but I remember seeing her weaken, and diminish. My father's lesson was well learned. One must be more than hungry to survive, you must always be ready to step forward, and leave death behind you.

Even then I knew that a thousand traps waited for the unwary and the foolish. Would I succumb, lost to the pursuit of pennies like my father, frozen by the looking glass like my mother, or raging mindlessly against the cruel world like so many of my countrymen, turned apoplectic as they watched their homeland torn down around them. Now that I have the perspective of a second lifetime, I realise the young Mister Matthews has too much of my former countrymen in him. He makes himself the ever-enduring victim, spitting futilely into the storm of the world order. His pets are raised to be slavishly dependent on him — while mine are taught to taste of the apple of knowledge for themselves.

Matthews is ever-hungry, but cannot shed his past. It chains him down worse than a Dickensonian ghost. Yet in contrast, the lovely assassin, Alice, the self-styled Queen of Hearts, has but one direction — forward. She is consumed with her survival, but has no deep seated hunger to satisfy. "I play for the thrill," she says, purring with her cat-like cruelty. Yet the game she plays is pedestrian — there is no scope. She burns brightly against the darkness, but in the end she is only a single candle, with no ability to spread like wildfire. Not so hard to snuff.

And that is what the righteous, self-aggrandising champions of bedlam do with frightening regularity. They were born blind, believing themselves "blessed" into their coddled, illusionary lives of home and hearth. I say their lives do disservice to them, for they are unprotected against the pain and blood that drenches everyone's time on this planet. They have forgotten the horror of waking from the dream, and believe their egotistical propaganda; they desperately sit atop Pandora's box, never realising the bottom has long dropped out, spilling travesty and abomination upon the earth. Do these self-proclaimed protectors of justice not realise the very notion is absurd? What is justice or truth in a society that propagates lies, abuse, and exploitation? When Maxwell Liberty became a victim of war, it should have dropped the scales from his eyes. Tragically, he succumbed to the sinister lure of unachievable hope — Pandora's most malicious demon. What sane man would throw himself to the nuclear fire? Liberty is not a stupid man. It is clear he sought an end to life, laughing at God in his choice. There was not one single possibility of survival — yet he accomplished the impossible. I must repeat: He accomplished the impossible. This singular moment should have destroyed all of the world's preconceived notions. He alone broke through man's potential, and rewrote humanity's destiny. If the impossible could be reached, then literally ANYTHING could happen. He set the mark of high water. And this, then, is the Sentinel's great failure. Infinite opportunity was revealed, and he embraced the old way; he did nothing new. The paltry lives he saves are nothing, wasted drops of blood in the roaring stream of life. He could have diverted the course, creating a glorious new path of man's own choosing. Instead, he let the small minds trap him within a house of cards. He could shatter it with a breath, but is too scared and pitiful to even open his eyes.

Help   Sat 3:26 PM   **Text Editor**

1

125% ▲▼

LIBERTY

JUSTICE

SECURITY

PEACE

INTRODUCTION

12.21.01

I look back at the notes of yesteryears. The world spirals ever faster towards oblivion. A few of us are prophetic enough to stave off the entropy, but we are labelled madman, villain, monster. Even poor, lost Isambard Brunel, the Iron Duke, knows the world is innately wrong, and the borders of reality must be shored up. Leaving our direction in the hands of the masses, or their hyperbolic protectors, will only doom us all. What does a Red Phoenix offer other than Amazonian fantasy? Or a Mother Raven, offering blind devotion to sanctimonious spirits — is this not the modern era? Have we descended back into the annals of ignorance? Science can master the occult in the 21st century, and harness it for the betterment of mankind. How can these pathetic wretches hope to lead us through the dangerous of tomorrow and tomorrow?

We will die in pain and blood, alone in the darkness, always alone. My desire and legacy is to empower man, to set him free to chart his own course, free of Old Testament Gods and New Age Morons. The Iron Duke feels my frustration, but sadly can no longer see the grand design. He has traded the invaluable gift of sight for the prosaic strength of Atlas — not unimpressive, but hardly inspiring. Should he ever recover his adroit and profound intellect, then together we may forge a way out of this hell.

Strangely enough, the murderous Janus shares my vision. Although he has no wish to remake the world into paradise, he too is witness to the falsity of the world's paragons — icons of stasis and lifelessness. Janus defies them in their glory and power, kicks them in the groin and gouges them in the eyes. He is an angel of death, sweeping away the detritus, to make way for something better. He is no smith, no craftsman, only a harbinger of destruction, yet his purpose is cleaner than the shattered mask of Caliburn, whose wrath twists within like a corkscrew, or the xenospawn, Slipstream, who next to Sentinel is the world's greatest aberration.

This is not to say I have never respected the Guard. The power they command is nearly unimaginable in scope. I weep for their wastefulness, however. They could be godkings and queens,

heralding in a golden age of paradise. Instead, they sit in their Olympian Tower, a sign of hubris and self-declared apotheosis, and call us criminal. They are a beacon of pointlessness, shepherding the sheep onto their fruitless path. They wish to cage us and break our wills, convincing us their system of punishment leads to redemption, that their wars makes peace, and their vengeance is merciful.

We will not go quietly. A legion of individuals — each driven to shatter the chains of stagnation, and storm forward to a better future. We will strike like nature's hammer, smashing today's inert paradigms, as a thunderous chorus, the voices of the empowered, scream for a new day. The forces of nihilism — from the mundane Janus to the demigod Requiem — will clean the slate, burning away the dross, then falling aside themselves for the vanguard of change. My passion for our collective tomorrow will carry us forward, over all hurdles and obstacles. My forces will be deployed as pawns upon heaven's board, sacrificed for the good of the many. We must not only destroy the godlike, but must defend ourselves from outside threats like the Parousians, the Haud, and the dimensional armies of the Dark Queen or Dark Empire. The White Rooks are a hundred times more influential than any pawn, but at the end of the game they are still but pieces on the road to victory. Thule will rise behind me like a modern Alexander, sweeping over the lands until there is no place left bereft of order and infinite possibility. I will gladly martyr myself for man's ascension, but I will not lay down until my heir's kingdom is secure.

Ordo Ab Chao

— excerpted from the journals of Kreuzritter, King of Thule

THE ANATOMY OF A VILLAIN

| CRIMINAL INTENT INTRODUCTION | CRIMINAL INTENT ANATOMY OF A VILLAIN | CRIMINAL INTENT THE LONE VILLAIN | CRIMINAL INTENT SUPERVILLAIN TEAMS | CRIMINAL INTENT ORGANISATIONS | CRIMINAL INTENT MOST WANTED | CRIMINAL INTENT APPENDIX |
| INTRODUCTION | CHAPTER 1 | CHAPTER 2 | CHAPTER 3 | CHAPTER 4 | CHAPTER 5 | APPENDIX |

LIBERTY

JUSTICE

SECURITY

PEACE

PLAYING THE VILLAIN

For the most part, this chapter speaks about the process of creating villains and their backgrounds and nefarious schemes. In *Silver Age Sentinels*, however, that is only half the battle. Because this is a role-playing game, you must also be able to bring your villains to life at the gaming table — to portray them so that the players hate them as deeply as their heroes do.

From time to time, sidebars like this one will be used to present role-playing-specific tips and suggestions to help toward that end.

FREEDOM FIGHTERS OR TERRORISTS?

The world is a complicated place, even more so with the addition of metahuman abilities added into the mix. Not every fight has a clear-cut good guy and bad guy. Or, more correctly, those roles can be reversed quite quickly given only a minor adjustment to the perspective from which one views a conflict.

Take, for example, a fictional country run by a powerful metahuman noblewoman. Her rule is absolute, her laws are strict (though fairly applied), but she provides a high standard of living and protection for all citizens. Some citizens, though, oppose her rule because they want freedoms she does not grant (free speech, open borders for trade and emigration, etc.), and they form a rebellion. They begin by publishing a subversive newspaper, but soon find themselves actually engaging in combat with the national police.

Who is the villain in this example? Is it the ruler a benevolent monarch or an evil despot? Is the rebellion a collection of noble freedom fighters or a group of violent terrorists?

BASIC DEFINITIONS

The best places to begin answering the questions posed above are the What Are Villains Made Of? (right column) and Villain's Checklist (page 99) sections of this chapter. Examining all sides in a conflict from those perspectives should provide a basic idea of how many (if any) of the combatants are villains. It is completely possible, one should remember, that two non-villainous forces could be fighting one another simply because of misunderstandings, stubbornness, or habit (if the sides have a long history of being antagonistic toward each other). Of course, it is also possible for two villainous forces to fight one another.

For the purposes of a *Silver Age Sentinels* game, consider that a villain or villainous group must have some goal that is not in the interest of the general populace. In other words, doing good things does not make a cause right or just. For example, even though a group is fighting against an invasion from outer space, if its ultimate goal is to defeat the aliens and then install themselves as dictators, the group is evil.

A more difficult assessment must be made when a group is performing questionable acts — destroying public property, for example. If the group is doing so because these structures contain mind control devices that are sapping free will from the citizens, then the group is probably heroic. If, however, they take no care in who gets hurt or killed during their raids, they have probably crossed the line into villainy.

Situations like these are difficult to adjudicate. GMs should have a clear idea exactly on which side of the moral line different groups and characters in their campaigns stand. Being very clear about which side (if any) of a conflict is the "good guys" helps the players to define what actions are acceptable for their characters to perform. GMs should be wary of sending mixed messages to the players, lest the heroes begin acting in unacceptable manners.

WHAT ARE VILLAINS MADE OF?

Lots of people do things they shouldn't. We all cross the street between corners if we're in a hurry or park in questionable places if the parking lot is too full. It's even rumoured that the Sentinel was caught fudging a line item or two on his tax returns.

Still, simply doing a bad thing does not make someone a villain — there's more to it than that. It's a choice, made somewhere between wishing for something and acting upon it, but it's almost always a deliberate decision. The title of villain is one earned through deliberate and unmistakable actions. But what differentiates a confused or self-serving individual from a true out-and-out villain?

CRIMINAL INTENT

The most basic test of a character's potential villainy is whether he or she actually breaks the law. This is not a hard and fast rule for villains, but it is a good starting point. The law may not always be right or fair, but it is the law; it must be upheld until such time as it is repealed.

For the most part, the law is pretty plain. It's easy to know when one has stepped on the wrong side of it. Hurting someone is wrong, taking something that doesn't belong to you is wrong, destroying things that don't belong to you (and, in certain instances, even things that do belong to you) is wrong — of these facts are terribly difficult to understand.

Anyone who purposely and knowingly sets out to break the law risks being perceived as a villain, by the police if no one else. There are, of course, situations where completely righteous people use civil disobedience to point out the injustice of a particular law or ruling. These individuals are certainly performing criminal activities, but one would be hard pressed to call them "villains." Obviously, there has to be more to the definition of "villain" than simply one who breaks the law.

ENDS AND MEANS

The next thing to be taken into consideration is why a character is breaking the law. Is it a political or social statement? Is he or she seeking the most expedient way to achieve a particular goal? Desperate times require desperate actions. In those situations, good people will occasionally find themselves with no alternative but to choose between an immoral act and an illegal one. Making that choice does not make them villains — in fact, it often makes them heroes.

A person who breaks a law with a heartfelt belief that he or she is doing the right thing and a willingness to accept the consequences of those actions is perhaps someone to be lauded. On the other hand, someone who breaks a law in order to save time, avoid difficult tasks, or because he or she can't be bothered to do things the legal or moral way is almost certainly a villain of one stripe or another. The belief that all paths are equal if they accomplish the same result is characteristic of a criminal mindset, though the degree to which this belief is possessed may vary.

A character who truly believes that the ends justify the means is walking the razor-thin line of radical activism, at best. At worst, he or she is engaging in villainy at its most unrepentant. The best way to tell the difference between the two is the character's reaction to the thought that innocent people may be harmed by his or her actions. True villains are unfazed by the thought of an innocent's suffering if it will accomplish their stated goal.

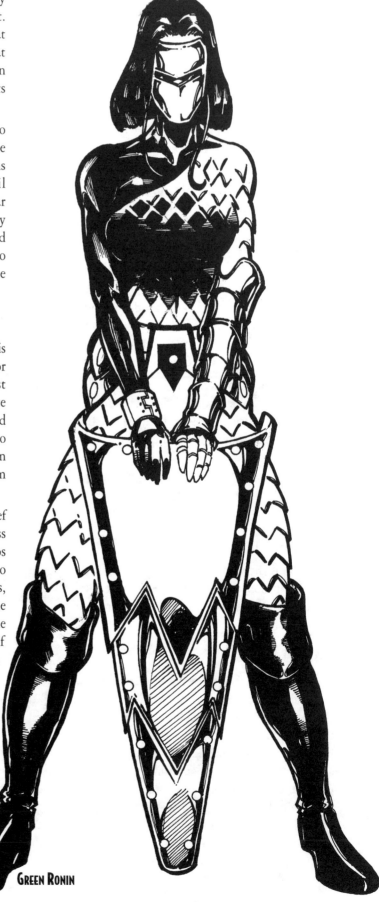

GREEN RONIN

SILVER AGE SENTINELS

ATTENTION, EARTHLINGS!

A *Silver Age Sentinels* campaign may feature characters from other worlds, or even other dimensions. It may include bizarre races from the bottom of the sea or the centre of the Earth. When dealing with races and cultures so alien to our own, how does one measure the term "villain" against them?

In grand superheroic tradition, "humanity" is a condition granted to all sentient creatures, no matter what their skin colour (or consistency). Tiny, blind, subterranean thralls are "human." Little green folk from Mars are "human." Furry, talking marmots from the 8th Dimension are human as well, with all of them deserving the same inalienable rights as the people of Earth.

Rulers and warriors from these various locales are held to the same standards as Earthly heroes. Therefore, the same measures of villainy can be applied to any race as well, no matter how alien. A creature who injures or endangers others, who takes that which doesn't belong to him or her, or who breaks the law and tries to force the world to bend to his or her whim is a villain, no matter what cultural moral-relativism he espouses.

THE NEEDS OF THE WHO?

If a character holds his or her wants and desires to be more important than what anyone else thinks or needs, then he or she is well on the way to ruin. Even the most noble goals and intents can lead to villainous actions if the effects on innocent bystanders are not considered. As beings of power, it is incumbent upon metahumans to protect the interests of society as a whole. The needs of the many, as they say, outweigh the needs of the few. Anyone who forgets that has stepped into the realm of villainy beyond a doubt. Worse still is a character who does not even take into consideration the idea that ordinary folk might have an opinion on such matters. It is a rare villain, indeed, who is so power hungry that he or she no longer considers humanity to be worth concern.

THE WEIGHT OF EVIDENCE

Looking over the history of the *Silver Age Sentinels* campaign setting as well as the history of all comic book heroes, one sees that the villainous status of characters is almost never an absolute. Bad guys often spend years acting in the common good, and even the most shining beacons of justice occasionally wander to the wrong side of the law (if only for a few issues).

The best way to determine if your concept for a prospective adversary is sufficiently villainous it to look at how well they suit the above categories. Once that has been determined, apply the final criteria: would the public approve of his or her actions if the true nature of his or her deeds was made public?

If the answer is a resounding yes, the character is clearly a hero in villain's clothing: not a complete loss as an antagonist, but definitely not a truly evil individual whom the heroes can trounce without guilt. If the answer is a qualified yes, then the character lives on the border between heroism and villainy, and could perhaps be redeemed — someone the authorities will try to capture, but whom the public will support. If there is no way anyone in their right minds would support his or her actions, then the concept has the makings of a true bad guy! Congratulations!

THE VILLAIN'S CHECKLIST

There are some things that all villains need — goals, justification, power, and opposition. With these, villains have more than a mere plot or scheme; they have a complex collection of motivations that allow them honest reactions to the heroes' interference. Once the GM has these aspects firmly in mind, he or she will have a much better insight into how the villains might alter their master plans and still remain true to their purposes and personal visions. Best of all, understanding these items will help the GM develop distinctive personalities for the villains, and create a deeper sense of conflict between them and the heroes.

In truth, all well-conceived characters should be defined in these four areas. The motivations and backgrounds of the heroes, however, are the concern of the players. It is also a good reason to not become too detailed with non-villainous NPCs, so that these characters do not challenge the heroes for dominance in the story. While villains should be complete, well-rounded, self-sustaining characters in order to best challenge the heroes, other characters should be specialised to a fault. Non-villainous NPCs function best if they serve only specific supporting roles with one-dimensional personalities and motivations. This allows the heroes (or villains) to be the ones who string together complex actions that require a breadth of knowledge, experience, and skill. Using this "checklist"

LIBERTY

JUSTICE

SECURITY

PEACE

CHAPTER ONE
ANATOMY OF A VILLAIN

as an aid in villain creation will help assure that you have a well-rounded, internally consistent concept from which to build.

GOALS

What does the villain want? This can be as simple as gaining possession of a specific item or as complex as a philosophical change in a culture's belief system. This is the villain's motivation in a nutshell. If the goal is achieved, his or her days as a villain will probably be over.

To make matters more complicated, though, it is often true that what a villain thinks he or she wants and what will actually satisfy him or her are two entirely different things. For example, a villain might claim to have a goal of stealing enough money to live like a king for the rest of his or her life. After outwitting heroes on a number of successful robberies, however, the villain finds that it was defeating the heroes that really provided the most satisfaction. Despite having secured a fortune in ill-gotten gains, he or she continues the crime spree in order to fulfil his or her true goal — to publicly humiliate the heroes as often as possible.

When setting a villain's ultimate goals, make sure they are not too easily achieved. The best villains are ones who can succeed and still have a motive to reappear later on in your campaign.

The goals of criminals fall naturally into one of two categories: intangible and tangible. Intangible goals are things like fame, or revenge. They cannot be concretely tallied most of the time, but nonetheless provide an impact in the villain's life as well as on those around him or her. The tangible category covers items such as wealth or destruction. Power can fall into either category, depending on the specific incarnation of power the criminal is seeking. The power of ruling a nation and having an army at your beck and call is tangible. Being able to pull strings and call in favours around the world is far less so, but can still be equally effective. Tangible goals have the advantage that since they can be measured, there is theoretically a point at which the villain might say "enough." Intangible goals are typically an ongoing struggle to achieve or maintain, and are likely to continue throughout the villain's life.

DESTRUCTION

There are some villains who truly can be said to have no motivation other than the visceral joy they get from breaking things — the bigger, the better. In many cases this longing is an aspect of a greater desire for revenge or power. In these instances, once the root goal is sated, the need for destruction will vanish as well.

There are others, however, with either extraordinarily simple intelligence or exceedingly deep psychoses, who desire destruction for destruction's sake. They simply enjoy the act of taking something that is whole and rendering it useless. There is no way to reason with such a villain — his or her desire is too primal. Destruction of a specific item or type of item is a tangible goal, while the need for general destruction is intangible (and thus less likely to be sated). GMs designing characters motivated by a need for destruction should decide aspect of destruction is more central to the villain's concept.

FAME

As a look at primetime television proves any night of the week, there are some people who desire fame just because it appeals to them. They have no desire to create something worthy of discussion or to possess skills that others find admirable; they merely wish to be well known among the general population. This is as true for metahumans as it is for ordinary folk.

Some villains who begin their careers seeking money or power find instead that notoriety is really what they desired all along. They get a thrill from seeing the light of recognition in a victim's eyes — all the better if it is laced with an undercurrent of fear. Seeing their exploits in newspaper headlines gives them a joy that is exceeded only by hearing newscasters pronounce their names at the top of a broadcast.

Fame is a slippery goal, and one that is never fully achieved. While fame itself is not necessarily all that difficult to acquire, maintaining "famous" status takes an extraordinary amount of work, especially in this day and age of constantly updated news reports and sensational entertainment. Those villains who set their sights on remaining in the public eye will have to work hard to do so, and are unlikely to ever consider themselves "famous enough."

Of course, some villains are a little more discriminating than that. They wish to be famous for achieving a specific goal. Some may want to set a criminal record of one sort or another (perhaps stealing a larger diamond or more money than anyone ever has). Others may want to be the person to finally defeat a hero who has protected the city for years. In any case, simply getting mentioned on the news isn't enough for these criminals; they will not be satisfied until the world

CHAPTER ONE
ANATOMY OF A VILLAIN

LIBERTY

JUSTICE

SECURITY

PEACE

recognises them for a specific act or achievement. Villains who set this sort of goal often retire from the public eye after achieving it — at least until some upstart criminal threatens to out-do them and obliterate their status in the history books.

Metahuman villains, being as unstable a lot as they are, they can often take fame to bizarre extremes. Based on some inner logic that psychologists may never be able to explain, they will often undertake theme crimes in the hopes that they will make better headlines. These themes can be simple (such as stealing items in alphabetical order) or incredibly intricate (such as stealing an item whose market value can be used to determine the GPS co-ordinates of the next intended target). The crazier the theme, though, the more deranged and dangerous the villain is likely to be.

POWER

Power is an addiction to some and an aphrodisiac to others, but it is something that many villains crave above all other things. Of course, power comes in many forms. This goal may often be hidden by or confused with a desire for money or fame (both of which have the side effect of granting enormous social and political clout).

This goal manifests in a wide range of villains. Some desire power over people — they imagine themselves "kings among men" and want the world to recognise them as superior beings. These characters often try to take control of famous buildings, structures, and sites (sometimes even countries), thriving on the sense of power that comes with holding the fate of innocents in their hands.

Other villains desire power in a more naked form. The sanest of this breed plan crimes like seizing control of an electrical plant or weapons of mass destruction. The more unstable ones, though, desire ways to increase their own metahuman abilities — they seek out experimental procedures or dangerous natural phenomena in the hopes of increasing the amount of power literally at their fingertips.

The most insidious ones, however, are those that desire power over life and death. These can be grandiose would-be world conquerors or bone-chilling serial murderers. The worst thing about these villains is that they seek to steal the one thing that can never be replaced or repaired.

REVENGE

Some characters enter into criminal pursuits without any form of personal gain in mind. They do not want money, fame, or power, and may reject such things even if they are made available. Instead, these villains are interested in taking some form of vengeance on a person or institution they feel has wronged them in the past.

The casual observer can also easily confuse this motivation for something else. For instance, if a villain were seeking revenge against a millionaire who made a fortune on stolen patents, the villain's actions might well be mistaken as being motivated by a desire to gain wealth. The end result is the same for the victim, but a hero who jumped to the wrong conclusion would have a difficult time predicting the villain's future plans.

Revenge is clearly a powerful motivation, but it is a dangerous one as well. It leaves no room for pity or exceptions. Those bent on it often are uncaring (or at best unaware) of the effects they may have on innocent bystanders. A metahuman seeking revenge on the president of a company may attack the corporate headquarters regardless of the number of uninvolved (and potentially sympathetic) workers who may be hurt in the process. Revenge is typically a process with a definite end. Revenge can be ongoing, but there is usually a set goal that the villain considers final — even if it is the heroes' deaths.

WEALTH

The root of all evil, the thing that makes the world go round — money may not be a terribly original or noble reason to commit crimes, but it is the single most common motivator for villainy. The world is full of banks to knock over, millionaires to extort, art and jewellery to fence, and companies to control. Money is an example of a tangible goal, something that can be measured concretely, with a set "goal" amount (though very few villains find the concept of "enough" something they use with any regularity).

The odd thing is that although lack of money is often the thing that starts characters in lives of crime, gaining a significant amount of it is usually not enough to get them to walk the straight and narrow again. One might think that once a villain had gotten clean away with several million untraceable dollars, he or she would hang up the costume and just live the good life. This, however, rarely turns out to be the case.

LIBERTY

JUSTICE

SECURITY

PEACE

CHAPTER ONE
ANATOMY OF A VILLAIN

The reason is a phenomenon as prevalent among average citizens as it is among supervillains — the misapprehension that lack of money is what prevents them from being happy with their lives. In many cases, villains discover the fame or power that they garner in their crime sprees is infinitely more satisfying than the money they collect.

JUSTIFICATION

One of the toughest tricks in effective Game Mastering is the ability to project the inner thoughts of unrepentantly evil characters convincingly. The most difficult part of that task is learning to understand how those characters perceive themselves. Despite the fact that the world knows them as villains, even the most reviled people in history believed in their hearts that they were doing good work (or at least doing the best thing possible in their given situations). Nobody thinks he or she is a villain. With the possible exception of deeply sociopathic individuals, no one ever wakes up in the morning and says, "I wonder what terrible thing I can inflict upon the world today?"

In order to understand the villains in a game, the GM must understand why they are performing evil acts and how they rationalise these actions. The GM must know what the villain believes about him or herself in order to consistently portray that character to the players.

ANTI-SOCIAL

There are some villains who primarily want to cause mayhem and inspire fear in the populace. These characters revel in seeing themselves portrayed as "bad guys" in the popular press, and will often go to great lengths to make each of their crimes successively more outrageous and offensive than the last.

PLAYING THE VILLAIN: GOALS

Keeping a villain's goals in mind will help the GM create a more convincing opponent. They provide insight into what the character wants and what he or she will do in order to succeed, making it easier for the GM to make decisions for the villain during battles and fast-paced role-playing encounters. More importantly, however, knowing the villain's goals allows the GM to determine what the character would or would not do in a given situation. Metahumans are as capable of being distracted or side-tracked as anyone, yet they will not generally allow themselves to be goaded into doing things that will make it more difficult for them to reach their ultimate objectives.

By way of example, let's revisit a villain described under the goal of revenge — the one seeking vengeance on the man who made a fortune from stolen patents. If the millionaire incorrectly surmises that the villain is after money alone, he might try to appeal to the villain's baser instincts by offering to buy his way out of trouble. Depending on the amount of money, the villain might accept that offer (especially if it causes the businessman to lose his entire fortune). If, however, the millionaire offered a joint venture, one that would make money for both the villain and himself, the villain would reject it out of hand. This villain can have no interest in any solution from which his enemy will benefit in the slightest.

PLAYING THE VILLAIN: BLIND SPOTS

This chapter reduces some very complex parts of the human psyche into manageable chunks. In specific, goals and justifications have been described in fairly absolute terms. This is fine when speaking in generalities, but it is a very rare person whose motives are so pure and whose self-understanding is so accurate that he or she will fit neatly into only a single category.

When portraying villains in *Silver Age Sentinels* games, try to give them foibles and thematic blind spots — things about their behaviour or motives that seem slightly at odds with their basic beliefs. Some small bit of hypocrisy is part and parcel of being human.

For example, imagine a noble villain who acquired his or her powers due to exposure to illegally dumped toxic waste, but was horribly disfigured in the process. This villain executes a series of attacks against the company responsible, planning to destroy their factories and prevent this same thing from happening to anyone else. This villain might very well have a "blind spot" to the fact that blowing up factories full of toxic material actually has a pretty good chance of causing other people to suffer the same fate. On the other hand, the villain might be so focused on this crusade against the company that he or she is willing to destroy innocent lives in fires, explosions, and other violent acts as long as they also cause some damage to the hated company.

Anti-social villains act from many subtle motivations, but only rarely do they believe that they are evil at core and have no choice but to behave this way. Many of them have extraordinarily low self-esteem, possibly accompanied by other mental or physical problems. They commit crimes as a means of forcing society to validate their inner hatred. Others believe they have committed some offence for which they must be eternally punished, using their violent behaviour to ensure that world at large heaps the abuse on them they feel they deserve. Anti-social behaviour and its common appearance among solo villains are discussed in more depth on page 41.

Only an extremely rare individual is so consumed with rage and hatred that he or she commits acts of violence simply for their own sake. Such characters are often mindless (or at least uncommonly childlike), and lash out because it is the only means of expression they know.

ENTITLED

There are those who think that the world owes them every conceivable advantage or opportunity, simply by virtue of their birth. They don't accept any responsibility for making things happen in their lives, and expect to be given all the necessities (and many of the luxuries) the world offers. In the ordinary world, such people are called spoiled brats, egomaniacs, or robber-baron industrialists — if they happen to be metahumans, however, they invariably become villains. Metahumans who feel entitled very often also labour under the belief that they are innately better and more important than ordinary folk, simply by virtue of having superpowers. In extreme cases, they may even consider baseline humans as an inferior race — making them less than human in the villains' eyes.

Someone who feels entitled does not perceive his or her actions as bad or wrong. After all, he or she is only taking what is owed — and anyone who opposes him or her is clearly in the wrong. In fact, this villain is likely to consider the heroes to be "bad guys" and cast him or herself in the role of "hero." It would surprise this villain to know that the rest of the world fails to share this interpretation — at least it would if he or she cared at all about what other people thought.

TORQUE

LIBERTY

JUSTICE

SECURITY

PEACE

CHAPTER ONE
ANATOMY OF A VILLAIN

SILVER AGE SENTINELS

NOBLE

Many villains see themselves as magnanimous individuals performing services that will benefit others ("If only the fools could see!"). They believe that they have solutions to problems that plague their neighbours, country, or even all of mankind, but that people are too short-sighted (or jealous of the plan's perfection) to allow these solutions to be implemented.

The truly noble villain has pity in his heart for those who oppose or are frightened by him or her. This villain will usually go out of his or her way to avoid hurting others, and may even abort a scheme if innocents become endangered by their own foolishness. A noble villain may hold the same compassion for the heroes who oppose him or her. On the other hand, the villain may hold them to a higher standard, rationalising that their superpowers and experiences ought to provide them with a greater insight into the ways of the world.

Some villains, however, are more despotic than noble. Such a character knows that his or her vision is true while all others are tainted, myopic, or simply wrong. He or she believes that when all is said and done, the world will comprehend and appreciate the services rendered; therefore it is imperative to achieve these goals as quickly as possible so the world can begin making amends for its short-sightedness. This villain doesn't care in the least how many innocents are hurt in the process of actualising his or her vision, and is especially vicious when dealing with opposing metahumans.

REBELLIOUS

Some villains have an inborn aversion to obeying the rules and laws of society. Sometimes these are idealistic individuals hoping to change the world; other times they are lawless mavericks who simply march to a different beat (and have superpowers with which to bolster their rebelliousness). In any case, these villains generally hold no particular grudge against the world — they just want to be free to do whatever they like, whenever they like.

Rebellious villains typically understand that they are acting against the dictates of society — they know that they are breaking laws and acting in ways that others find inappropriate. They do not think, however, that such small-minded notions should bind them. Their views typically manifest as an extreme form of libertarianism (though most would never use such fancy terminology to describe themselves). Their rebellious nature expresses an inner need for attention in much the same way that many adolescents do.

Villains with a rebellious attitude are not necessarily dangerous to innocent bystanders. Many of them simply want to be free to pursue their lives, and are more than willing to let others do the same. Other rebels, however, express their desires in violent and destructive ways. For the most extreme among them, their wish to be unfettered by anyone else can even extend to the right to hurt or kill anyone they wish — an ambition destined to clash with the duties laid upon both heroes and authority figures in general.

POWER

This category focuses on how the villain is able to attain his or her goals. What sort of resources can he or she draw upon? What is his or her source of power?

In the final analysis, power is the ability to get people to do what one wants them to. Once villains have goals and a sense of their place in the world, they need ways to enact their plans. In other words, they need power. Power comes in many different forms, from the obvious to the very subtle. One does not have to possess metahuman abilities in order to wield power. In fact, some of the most memorable villains in any setting are those who pose credible threats without the benefit of enhanced strength or laser vision.

It is worth noting that this use of "power" is different than power as a goal, as listed above. In the previous section, the pursuit of power is earlier. Here, it is the ability and means to reach beyond normal limitations and acquire the goals the villain has set forth.

MILITARY

Not everyone has metahuman abilities, but it is relatively easy for someone to get a firearm of some description in most of the Western world. It is not wildly inaccurate to consider guns and explosives as the common man's superpower — a single person with a gun wields the power of life and death over half-a-dozen or more individuals. When this is combined with more unusual personal powers, the result can be enough to strike fear into any organisation. Just about every other form of power has the ability to either build or destroy. Firearms, on the other hand, exist for the sole purpose of causing harm to the target against which they are used.

Military power can be handled on anything from personal (pistols, rifles) to international (armies, special

forces). The use of a revolver is only a microcosm of using an armed division — the only difference between them is how big the target of the attack is. As with all forms of power, firearms can be used wisely or foolishly. If one uses them well (that is, sparingly if at all), then one is much less likely to be considered a villain. The unrestrained use of military might, however, is almost certain to gain the wielder a reputation as a bad guy, no matter how noble his or her intentions or goals may be.

POLITICS

Some have called politics "the purest form of power," because it can be found in every area of human endeavour. Whether you're on a schoolyard playground, roaming the mean streets with youth gangs, sitting in the plush boardrooms atop skyscrapers, or walking the hallowed halls of government — politics is the force that makes things happen.

People who can master the intricacies of politics — who have the ability to gather public opinion behind the causes they support (or, perhaps more importantly, to focus public outrage against the causes they oppose) — make the most potent foes. No matter how many robbers a hero captures or how many would-be conquerors he or she defeats, there is no defence against an opponent who can turn public opinion on a whim. While some say "you can't fight City Hall," the truth is that one cannot fight public opinion. It just so happens that the people who occupy City Hall (or any other governmental office) are typically masters of manipulating the public.

There are others who have similar powers — religious leaders, popular actors, writers, and even a rare few who have no claim to fame other than this ability to influence popular sentiment. Any of them can be villains if their goals are selfish enough. The problem is, a hero can never attack them directly — to do so would only exacerbate the problem of negative public opinion. The only hope one has to beat a political villain is to excel at his or her own game — a task truly fit for a hero.

SUPERPOWERS

In any *Silver Age Sentinels* game, the most obvious form of power is metahuman abilities. The players, by virtue of placing themselves in the role of heroes, have guaranteed that this is the kind of power they will most frequently encounter. Superpowers set one apart from the masses from the moment they express themselves. Seemingly impassable barriers (social, financial, or physical) seemingly melt away into insignificance. A character with these powers suddenly finds him or herself living outside the rest of society simply by virtue of the things he or she can do that others cannot. For some, this sort of change inspires a desire to protect the world in which they grew up. In villains, however, it instead leads them to try to take everything they can from a society in which they can no longer function.

A villain's powers influence nearly every other aspect of his or her persona — including his or her goals and justifications, which heroes he or she chooses to harass most frequently, and what crimes he or she commits. A street-level thug rarely tries to become the despotic ruler of the world. Likewise, one almost never sees an international supervillain robbing the local savings and loan office.

If the GM wants a villain that will strike fear into the hearts of millions, he or she has to have suitably awe-inspiring powers. The citizens of an archetypal metropolis such as Empire City have seen quite a lot — they're notoriously hard to impress.

WEALTH

The most common brand of power in the modern world is money. Although it is most often wielded by the extremely rich, one does not need a fortune in order to get a particular task accomplished. Money is also the most versatile form of power that a villain can possess. When spent in the right amounts and in the right places, wealth can be exchanged for just about anything. The pros and cons of money in its varied forms are discussed in Chapter Two, page 51.

Villains who use money as their main source of power are difficult to beat. While individual obstacles can be readily overcome, confronting and defeating the source of the trouble is another matter entirely. In fact, it is often impossible to definitively prove that the person supplying the money is involved at all — the payoffs and purchases made by financially canny villains are typically made through untraceable intermediaries.

It should be noted that money could come into play even with foes who prefer more direct forms of power. Janus is a dangerous villain to begin with; if his recent robberies have provided enough cash to buy improvements and unique modifications to his personal arsenal, he is even deadlier.

CHAPTER ONE
ANATOMY OF A VILLAIN

LIBERTY

JUSTICE

SECURITY

PEACE

PLAYING THE VILLAIN: POWER

One of the most powerful aspects of any villain is, quite simply, their status as a bad guy. Villains have all the advantages in a role-playing game. They have active goals, while the heroes must be reactive: they have to stop the criminals. Villains are rarely bound by social or legal restraints (they are, after all, the "bad guys"), while the heroes must beat them while always upholding society's laws and principles. Perhaps most importantly, the villains have the GM and his or her insights into the plot and the heroes' foibles to guide their actions. As a GM, don't limit the villain too heavily and thereby make him or her too easy to defeat.

By the same token, however, a good GM needs to know where a villain's limits lie. When putting together adversaries for the characters, always remember to keep close track of the difference between what the GM knows and what the villain can reasonably know. A little collusion between GM characters is fine, but be true to their natures — as hateful, untrusting criminals, they are not likely to share information freely unless they are members of the same organisation or have the same goals at heart. It may be fun to take advantage of all the details at the GM's command, but it makes the game much more frustrating for the players. Also, be sure to leave a chink in the villain's armour — some error he or she made or eventualities he or she overlooked — for the characters to exploit.

Remember that this is a shared storytelling experience, but the player characters are the heroes. At the end of the day, the villain is the one who should lose (at least for now).

OPPOSITION

There has never been a villain in history who did not have a hero (or collection of heroes) to serve as his or her nemesis. Sometimes the hero rises from nowhere to meet the challenge of an evil plot. Other times the villain creates an identity and goal for the specific purpose of eliminating a particular heroic figure. Either way, one cannot exist for very long without the other — heroes and villains are two sides of the same coin.

The art of crafting an opponent that will challenge but not overwhelm the heroes is a delicate task. The first step is to determine each character's greatest strength

PLAYING THE VILLAIN: OPPOSITION

A Game Master can go a long way toward making a villain both unique and evocative by designing a target person, institution, or cause, to oppose completely and unequivocally. Whether this is a player character, a political figure, or a corporation makes little difference, as the effect in the end will be the same regardless.

As an experiment, create two nearly identical villains — perhaps one who controls fire and another who creates ice. Give one a cause or character to oppose and let the other one perform crimes for the sheer joy (or greed) of it. In almost every case, the players will consider fighting the former to be a memorable highlight of their character's careers while the latter merely becomes another dimly remembered name in their rogues gallery.

and weakness. Use the villain as a foil for the group by then determining how he or she can best take advantage of those weaknesses and avoid those strengths. Make sure that the villain can fully exploit the weakness of at least one of the characters in the group, or more if it can be done convincingly. He or she will likely have had time to study the characters, and should thus be prepared to face them. If the villain can defeat the team in their first engagement and still escape, that is a good first step.

At the same time, do not forget to give the villain weaknesses — a fatal flaw the characters can take advantage of should they discover it. Tying this weakness to one of the character's strengths is a good idea, as long as the weakness is not too obvious or easy to take advantage of (otherwise there's no challenge in it). Still, it should be possible for the heroes to triumph if they can figure it out and turn it to their advantage.

OPTIONAL EXTRAS

There are, of course, more aspects to some villains than others. The areas discussed in The Villain's Checklist represent only the basics — the factory standard equipment. One can add any number of extra dimensions to a villain. Herein are just a few examples of the possible additions.

WEAKNESS

As with any metahumans, some villains have obvious and exploitable weaknesses. It works to the GM's advantage to be sure that any weakness given to a

villain either support his or her history and schemes or are clearly associated with his or her powers and origin. It makes for better storytelling and can be used to reinforce important themes or facts. At the same time, some superpower-type weaknesses have no discernible reason for their expression. It is all right to give a weakness such as "vulnerability to cold" without any set reason behind it, so long as that particular weakness serves a purpose in your game (perhaps one of the heroes is a weather witch who can generate cold — and thus may luck into a winning strategy).

BACKGROUND

Many villains appear out of nowhere, unheard of before beginning their crime sprees. The GM may, however, choose to introduce a future villain one or more adventures before his or her true nature is revealed. This makes the villain more than an impersonal obstacle that must be beaten into submission, turning him or her into a character that the characters feel more beholden to deal with in a rational and realistic manner.

Of course, GMs may wish to avoid giving every character in the game a secret identity. The more often the villain turns out to be an estranged relative, a jealous ex-boyfriend, or the local crazy old coot, the less realistic and campier the game will become. On the other hand, a world where everyone has powers and a costume could work fine within its own internal logic. The real trick is to simply make it consistent with the world as you envision it.

ASSOCIATES

Often connected in some way to their backgrounds, some villains have characters (other than fellow villains) associated with them. Sometimes these associates are spouses, innocent relatives, or employees. Occasionally they might even be the heroes themselves. Adding associates does a lot to humanise a villain, but it also adds complications to the heroes' task. They now have to deal not only with defeating their opponent, but also worrying about the collateral effects on related characters. Examples of these could range from Galatea, the Artificer's AI assistant (who is more human than him, at times), a Thulian diplomat in service to Kreuzritter, or an intern working at Matthews GenTech.

COMPARISON SHOPLIFTING

So far this book has been very general, describing aspects of villains and villainy that apply across all *Silver Age Sentinels* campaigns. There are almost as many different ways to approach superhero storytelling,

however, as there are heroes to tell stories about. This section will examine some of the specifics involved in choosing villains for various types of campaigns.

The single biggest measuring stick for creating villains is the location of the campaign — the type of place where most the campaign's adventures will be set. Villains are like weeds — they pop up just about everywhere, but only take root in places where they will thrive. You would not find Mister Matthews attempting to hold the United Nations building for ransom, and it would be a strange day indeed when the Iron Duke took part in a simple jewellery store heist.

THE MEAN STREETS

Some campaigns focus on action on the streets: the back alleys, rooftops, or sewers of the city. The heroes are generally low-powered protectors of the neighbourhood: avenging knights or detectives bent on making their little piece of the city a better, safer place to live. The villains they face should be of equal power.

Street-level Villains: Approximately equal to the Character Points of the heroes; suggested ceiling of 125 Character Points.

In this setting, GMs will find it easier to generate credible, challenging, yet manageable threats by creating teams of low-powered criminals rather than concocting an individual evil mastermind. Single villains at this level generally either provide no challenge to a well-designed group of heroes or prove to be too powerful for the street-level heroes to touch, no matter how many of them team up in the effort. Solos villains can, however, be a good challenge to one or two of the team on patrol; if everyone has a few standard (albeit low-powered) enemies, that gang may team up to become a credible threat.

Most of the villains in this style of campaign should commit petty, localised crimes — small-time robberies, extortion, racketeering, kidnapping, or manipulating city council level politics. It is fine to occasionally throw in a city-wide threat — acts of terrorism, crime sprees, and personal attacks on important personalities — but remember that the bigger the crime seems, the more likely it is that higher-powered heroes will become involved. Monstrous villains are another possibility — alligator-men roaming the sewers, a vampire stalking the streets — but be sure they fit within the stylistic flavour you've set for your game. Once a campaign introduces real live monsters, there is little hope of maintaining a feeling of gritty realism.

Villains in a mean streets campaign will often find motivation in greed, petty hatred, or revenge against an individual or small group. There should be very few would-be world conquerors or individuals controlling extravagant wealth.

OVER THE SKYLINE

Perhaps the most common setting (at least in the early stages of a *Silver Aage Sentinels* campaign) is one where the heroes are protectors of the city, either by official appointment or self-selection. The battles happen in prominent sections of town, on and around tourist attractions, and in the air above downtown — all places where the citizens (and newspapers) can see. The heroes themselves become celebrities (or notorious individuals) in the city, and their exploits fill the local headlines.

Skyline Villains: Several enemies just below the Character Points of the heroes, or a single enemy designed at 25 or 50 Character Points more than the heroes; suggested range of 75 to 175 Character Points.

The villains these heroes face are equally powerful and flashy. It is also certainly possible for a large group of outlaws from a mean streets campaign to create a credible threat in this venue as well. Teams of bad guys often band together specifically to confront the heroes in these campaigns. Additionally, a loner or villainous duo, supported by a large number of Henchmen or Agents, makes an excellent enemy if the plot is more complicated than a straight dust up.

Villains at this level are as conscious of the city's eyes upon them as the heroes are. Skyline criminals' goals are generally grand in nature — they don't merely hold-up the watch display at Sears, they rob the city's largest importer of diamonds and gemstones. In fact, villains in this style of campaign are less often motivated by monetary greed than they are by idealism or a naked lust for political power. They undertake crimes that will add to their reputations or bring media attention to specific causes. That is not to say that none of them are in it for the money. This category would be woefully incomplete without the occasional extortionist who threatens to destroy buildings, bridges, and tourist sites unless the city pays him or her enormous sums of cash.

COAST-TO-COAST

Many skyline campaigns develop into this format as the heroes advance in power and reputation, although there are also plenty of campaigns that begin in this venue. The heroes in coast-to-coast campaigns vary widely in power level, although the average character is built for a high Average Campaign (see *SAS*, Chapter Two).

Coast-to-Coast Villains: A team of villains should be equal in number and Character Points to the heroes, or consist of fewer members who are approximately 25 Character Points higher than the heroes. Leaders or particularly strong individuals should be 25 to 50 Character Points higher than the strongest member of the heroes.

Villainous plots for coast-to-coast campaigns are never petty or small — these bad guys do things grandly or they don't do them at all. Plots revolve around the destruction of cities or corporations or theft of national secrets. When money is their aim, it's never less than tens of millions (USD). If the same group of heroes repeatedly squelches their plans, however, these masterminds will quickly change their focus to humiliating or eliminating those heroes. Solo villains rarely prove a challenge at this level, unless they are tremendously powerful, or command a grand organisation (see Chapter Four, page 87).

Adventures hop between cities the way grittier campaigns hop between neighbourhoods, and almost always involve some famous landmark or site. The heroes could find themselves fighting atop the St. Louis Arch one day, in the skies above the Hollywood hills the next, and in centre field of Yankee Stadium before the weekend. Other common targets include government facilities, society's elite members, top-secret laboratories, and the heroes' headquarters.

GLOBAL HOT SPOTS

Raising the stakes leads to a campaign where the heroes protect the entire world. Threats become even more wide-ranging and take on unfamiliar cultural beliefs and presumptions. Anything the GM can do to imbue a villain with a specifically foreign perspective will improve the campaign's ambience.

Global Hot Spot Villains: The International supervillains should at least equal the heroes in power, and are often an average of 25 more Character Points each. Leaders may be even more powerful, although the suggested ceiling is 250 Character Points.

Adventures continue to hop from place to place, but this time the world is their stage. The heroes in this type of campaign almost always work for a government, international agency, or multinational corporation, so their actions often carry blatantly political ramifications (something a clever villain can manipulate).

Villains in a global campaign are often extraordinarily strong individuals or teams of superpowered agents in the employ of an agency opposing the heroes' benefactor. Once the arena covers the entire globe, however, GMs have some unconventional options when picking opponents. For example, the heroes might find themselves facing off against the completely non-superpowered military of a country controlled by their true enemy. Alternatively (or in addition), they may also find themselves defending the world from threats from outer space.

THE STARS OUR DESTINATION

Just because the heroes have faced all of Earth's threats, however, doesn't mean their jobs are done. GMs with a taste for science fiction have an entire universe worth of villainy to throw at unsuspecting players.

Final Frontier Villains: These threats should menace an entire planet, either personally or by commanding enormous fleets. Captains of the enemy force should range from 200 to 225 Character Points, with leaders reaching 250 to 300 Character Points. Characters more powerful than this should be carefully considered before being placed in a campaign.

BEYOND THE VEIL

One might think that adventuring to the far ends of the universe would be enough, but GMs can have characters venture beyond the realms of reality as we know it. Campaigns can be set in fantastic places drawn from earthly legend (Mt. Olympus, Asgard, Fey realms, etc.) or places beyond imagination (Dimension X, metaphysical planes of existence, etc.). In either case, the level of villainy runs the gamut from high to low.

Some settings contain characters who are the physical embodiments of villainous traits; others may be similar to the real world only with different physical laws. It is up the GM to supply the players with enough background so that they can understand who the villains are and what must (and can) be done to stop them.

A word of warning, though — GMs should always keep in mind that they are running a superhero game. Many of the more esoteric settings can stray far enough afield that they become pure fantasy, creating a greater chance for your players to lose focus and have their heroes act in inappropriate ways. After all, the characters were created for a superhero setting. Be sure that the adventures allow them to pursue that course of action.

DARK QUEEN, ZAIRA

CHAPTER ONE
ANATOMY OF A VILLAIN

PLAYING THE VILLAIN: ALIEN MENACES

Two schools of thought dominate these kinds of campaign. The first philosophy suggests that because the stories are about humans and humanity, every creature, race, or breed is "human" to an extent. Therefore, no matter the face or eating habits of a creature, it should be fairly recognisable and understandable. Most alien storylines in comics follow this route, with aliens essentially being odd-coloured humans with funny noses and foreheads. There is nothing wrong with this style, although it is sometimes hard to take it seriously as it is embedded in the camp of the 60s and 70s.

The other philosophy is to make non-human characters truly strange.

When running a campaign in this vein, GMs have the unenviable task to get inside the minds of completely alien creatures. Using this method, GMs must strive to ensure their extraterrestrial forces are anything but run-of-the-mill stereotypes imbued with incredible powers. It may help to consider the difference between an archetype (a type of character found in many different settings) and a stereotype (a clichéd portrayal of a character lacking in originality and depth), especially when running a campaign set in space.

VILLAINS OF THEIR TIMES

If the location of a campaign helps the GM determine what villains belong in the story, then the time period of the piece tells him how villains should be role-played. In this case, "when" is not an absolute measurement; or a particular calendar year. Rather, "when" refers to which era of comic book storytelling with which the campaign is most closely linked.

As any fan of comics knows, many of the most popular characters (heroes and villains alike) have existed in various forms and under various thematic visions over the years. A villain who was campy and comical in one era might well be deadly serious in another. These changes were originally made to suit the particular cultural climate when the comics were created — they truly were products of their times.

Modern GMs, on the other hand, can choose any era of comic book storytelling as the basis of their campaigns. *Silver Age Sentinels* may draw its name from a particular era of comic book creation, but it is a game

that fans of any superheroic movement can enjoy. A role-playing game does not have to speak directly to the current comic book reading audience — it only has to be fun for the players.

LET'S GET 'EM, CHUM!

The comics of the 1960s were filled with camp and humour. Heroes tossed off puns and one-liners, and many adventures ended with a literal wink to the readers as if to say, "What did you expect? It's just a funny book!" Although character continuity was an issue, individual stories generally didn't last longer than a single issue.

The villains in these books were every bit as campy as the heroes, but the bad guys always suffered from the disadvantage of not knowing they were doomed to loose in the end. They took themselves completely seriously. The main advantage a GM gains in setting a campaign in this era is that the logistics of the plots did not need to make particular sense in a real world context. If a villain set up a death trap in the museum by replacing the real dinosaur exhibit with giant robot dinosaurs under his or her control, no one ever stopped to question how or when the switch was made. This freedom allows the GM to create contrived adventures with traps and situations that could not possibly occur in real life and expect that the players will simply take it all in stride as part of the setting.

Another significant element of 1960s comics was angst. When not in costume, characters worried about things like homework, whether or not their friends really liked them, if they were living up to the examples set by their personal heroes, and if they could get home in time for dinner. What's more, the villains they faced invariably were reflections of whatever personal demon they currently wrestled with. If a hero was agonising over having accidentally broken a neighbour's window, then the villain was certain to create an opportunity for him to save the neighbour's life. This gave the hero and the readers instant perspective.

THE WORLD SHALL BE MINE!

The next phase of comics, begun during the 1970s, featured a little more reality and a lot more soap opera. Stories began to routinely last two or three issues as the plots paid more attention to logic and the writing began to reach for nobler literary aspirations. Foreshadowing, sub-plots, and irony became staples of the comics, and the tales grew a shade darker (but incredibly richer) for it.

Heroes in this era were more serious, more focused, and more capable, but so were the villains making it a fair trade. Villains also reflected the issues of the day — environmental distress, governmental arrogance, and corporate greed. Longstanding institutions became suspect; the heroes often seemed to be alone in the world and the villains took advantage of that fact. They never hesitated to manipulate the media, the police, or even the heroes' loved ones in order to get what they wanted (and make the heroes suffer along the way).

Villains were still quite colourful in this era. Flashy costumes were common, particularly ones thematically tied to the crimes they were about to commit. They were also prone to giving long soliloquies and pontificating on the ills of modern society or the worst aspects of human nature. Both their dialog and plots were overblown and grandiose, and they acted very much as though they knew that they were the villains of some badly acted operatic production.

WHAT I DO AIN'T PRETTY

Reality really hit the comics hard in the 1980s and 90s. While heroes did have more angst in their lives, they also had more joy. Stories became akin to evening serial dramas — complete tales with one or two elements that carried over from instalment to instalment and eventually developed into the big event of the year.

Villains, too, became more balanced. As stories explored their motivations, goals, and relationships (as this chapter urges GMs do), they became fully rounded characters who could learn and grow, not simply act as one-dimensional foils for the heroes. Some villains were even allowed to develop to the point where they really weren't villains anymore. Of course, they were helped in this cause by the popularity of anti-heroes and the fact that long-standing "good guys" were being allowed to explore the darker sides of their personalities.

As time went on, the line between hero and villain was blurred and nearly erased. All villainous activities seemed to have noble roots, and the labels "good guy" and "bad guy" were exchanged readily based on a character's current motivations. It truly was an era of moral relativism for comic book characters.

GMs will have greater trouble recreating this atmosphere than any others will, if only because players (and their characters) have long memories and may not be willing to give a truly repentant, now noble ex-villain the chance to prove his sincerity. Campaigns set in this era will rely heavily on non-player characters to serve as a moral compass to point the heroes in the right direction for any given adventure.

IT'S ALWAYS THE QUIET ONES

There is one more flavour of villainy that GMs may want to consider when planning out their campaigns — real world evil. Comic books, like any art form, have always been filled with attempts to interpret the world around them. A comic-book-based role-playing game can be used to serve exactly that function.

True, there are no supervillains in the real world, but there certainly is evil enough to fill a hundred different campaigns. GMs just need to practice a little artistic license — take the ugliest side of a real world evil and transform it into a four-colour menace. A third-world dictator can be transformed into a warlord from the bottom of the sea. Any brutal criminal from today's headlines can have his or her crime intensified and the modus operandi adapted to include metahuman powers. Any act of senseless brutality or organisation that promotes an amoral agenda can be replicated and expanded upon in comic book style. Janus is a perfect example of "real world evil," with just a touch of comic twist.

THE FIVE TOOLS OF HIGHLY EFFECTIVE VILLAINS

In the repertoire of any successful criminal are a number of tools with which the erstwhile villain makes his or her mark on the world. With mastery of these five categories, an aspiring ne'er-do-well can rise through the ranks of villainy, from the lowest rungs of petty thievery to the very pinnacle of crime. These necessary areas of proficiency are listed in order of usefulness rather than alphabetical order, beginning with Tactics, then moving through Finding Good Help, Items of Villainous Intent, Secret Lairs, and Hairsbreadth Escapes.

MECHANICS

Additionally, several new rule mechanics are presented within this section, including new Attributes, sample bases, and optional rules.

TACTICS

The difference between a world-class villain and the punk down the street is largely execution. You can have all the neat toys in the universe, but unless you possess the skills and experience to use them effectively, they

LIBERTY

JUSTICE

SECURITY

PEACE

CHAPTER ONE
ANATOMY OF A VILLAIN

might as well not exist. Tactics refers not only to short-term event planning, such as kidnapping a senator or taking over a military facility, but also things like efficient use of resources such as personnel, material, and money over the long term.

When planning for the villain, GMs should take the characters into account as much as possible. The villain's master plan should involve the heroes as much as possible, making sure to centre the plan on something the heroes care about or have some connection with. Most villains will quickly hit upon a plan that works for them and use some variation on it throughout their career, though the most successful ones will also have the flexibility to make changes as necessary to execute their plans. Watch how the heroes handle their challenges (heroes develop standard operating procedures too) and base the villain's tactics on those, letting the villain use the heroes' blind spots to his or her advantage.

GETTING AWAY WITH IT

If the only thing a villain cares about is getting away with a particular crime, then it is in his or her best interest to keep a very low profile and find as unguarded a route to the goal as possible. The more the public (and by extension, the heroes) know about the villain's plans, abilities, and habits, the easier it will be for someone to figure out a way to stop him or her.

Villains believe that heroes have a natural tendency to be glory hounds. Given that belief, it logically follows that a hero will often ignore a crime or particular villain if there is no perceived newsworthiness in being the one to solve the problem. All a villain would have to do to get away clean, therefore, is commit low-key, unspectacular crimes.

The truth, however, is that villains are just as interested in fame as they believe the heroes to be. Nobody dons a striking costume in the hope of going unnoticed. As much as the advice above would provide villains with greater success, few if any of them are willing to give up their moments in the limelight.

THE MEASURE OF VILLAINY

If a villain wants to create an aura of notoriety, he or she will eschew any viable plan that does not include a public confrontation with a well-known hero. Nothing impresses the media and other villains more than an unknown villain knocking a beloved hero into next Sunday. More importantly, it really scares the capes off the other heroes.

THE MILLION-DOLLAR IDEA

Villains come up with some fantastic ideas — robots that perform complex tasks, power sources that supply enough energy to light whole cities, vehicles that travel faster, farther, and more efficiently than anything available commercially, etc. Why don't they just patent those inventions, sell the rights (or market them themselves) and get rich legally? Why do they insist on squandering these million dollar ideas in the pursuit of crime and ill-gotten gains?

SWEETER THAN HONEY

Stolen money is twice as sweet as money rightfully earned — or so many villains believe. The very thought of "working for a living" is repugnant to these individuals, even if they're working for themselves. They yearn for the thrill of taking something that isn't theirs, for the feeling that comes with doing something that society says they shouldn't.

THE PRINCIPLE OF THE THING

For some criminals, working outside the system is the entire point of their villainy. These are idealistic geniuses who shun the common goal of making money — they are interested in the principle of the matter. These villains usually believe that there is something inherently wrong with the current system of government, commerce, or (in extreme cases) society as a whole. To suggest that they use their abilities or inventions within that system (or in that system's benefit) strikes them as the height of absurdity.

Villains that want to make the biggest splash should plot out very detailed crimes and plan for specific heroes to interfere. In fact, many villains go to great lengths to leak important information in the right corners to maximise the chances that their intended targets will respond to the situation. For example, if it is widely known that the Lady of the Lantern has a source at the Empire City Times, a villain who wants to lure her into a trap might place a threatening phone call to the paper's editor, letting slip several clues to his or her next heist.

No matter how well one plans, though, sometimes things go wrong. Another part of building an impressive reputation is the ability to know when a battle is lost and have a successful escape plan. Nothing raises the public's fear (or a hero's blood pressure) more than a villain who can't be brought to justice. Sometimes getting away is more important to a villain's reputation than actually completing a successful caper.

NEW COMBAT TECHNIQUES

Two new Combat Techniques are provided, allowing characters to perform additional astounding feats. These techniques are acquired exactly the same way as those in the *Silver Age Sentinels* rulebook.

DEFLECTION

The character has mastered the manoeuvre of knocking incoming ranged attacks away. If the character makes a successful Block Defence, he or she can deflect a standard melee or ranged attack away harmlessly without damaging the blocking object. The Combat Technique Accuracy can negate these penalties.

Defenders suffer a -2 penalty per Level of any Special Attack they are attempting to Deflect. Thus, to Defend against a Level 3 Special Attack, the defender would suffer a -6 to his or her Block Defence check. For mundane weapons, such as those listed in the rulebook that are not Special Attacks, GMs should use the following rule: for every approximate 20 / [[d6+2]] points of damage an attack can inflict, consider it one Level of a Special Attack. Therefore, a Sniper rifle (20 / [[2d8+1]] damage, would be equivalent to a Level 1 Special Attack. GMs may waive any penalties for weapons that inflict less than 20 / [[d6+2]] damage.

In some cases, depending on the descriptive qualities of an attack, it may be impossible to deflect. One might be able to deflect a grenade before it explodes, knocking it harmlessly away; or redirect a lunging attacker's. In other situations, however, the GM may decide one cannot deflect a gas attack, or a sound attack, etc.

REFLECTION

The character has learned how to reflect incoming attacks, so that they target the original attacker, or anyone else within range (GM discretion). If the character makes a successful Deflection Block Defence, he or she may then immediately make an attack roll (which uses an attack action); if the attack roll is successful, he or she can reflect a standard melee or ranged attack towards any target within range (including the attacker), without damaging the blocking object. Anyone targeted by this reflected attack may attempt a defence roll, as normal.

Reflection may only be taken after the character has learned the Deflection Combat Technique.

If heroes and villains are opposite sides of the same coin, then the value of one is measured by the strength of the other. In other words, the strengths and weaknesses of his or her nemesis derive a villain's cache of strategies. GMs should make sure that the villains choose their foes carefully.

FINDING GOOD HELP

Villainy is by nature a lonely business. Living life on the wrong side of the law, plotting the overthrow of a government or company, and exacting revenge on one's most hated foe are all endeavours that do not generally breed the trust, co-operative nature, and personal integrity that are required to work well in a team atmosphere. Of course the greater a villain's ambition, the more likely he or she will need some help eventually — not everyone can be General Winter.

Villains who do not want to team up with others of their ilk can still gain the advantages found in numbers by taking on one or more followers, apprentices, or even pets. Each of these has its own set of challenges and is better suited to some temperaments and goals over others. Still, if villainy were easy, the heroes wouldn't win so often.

MERCENARIES VS. AGENTS

Sometimes a single supporter is not enough. Many villainous plans require deeper support — teams of scientists, battalions of foot soldiers, or a massive congregation of true believers. In these cases, a villain really has only two choices — pay qualified professionals to do the job at hand, or gather together a cult of personality with him or herself as the focal point. There is, of course, a third option of kidnapping qualified professionals and making them do the villain's bidding, but that rarely turns out well. The duress tends to prevent the experts from performing up to their usual standards (not to mention risks betrayal as they look for ways to undermine the villain's operation and escape).

Mercenaries are probably the best option, provided the villain has the financial wherewithal to pay them (or a good enough plan that they will sign on for a percentage of the take). The term "mercenary" is used here rather loosely, and is intended to include freelance scientific and creative talent as well as the more common meaning of "soldier for hire." A staff of paid research scientists would count as mercenaries, as would a

COLDSTONE

contracted engineering or architectural design firm. The problem with mercenaries, though, is that their level of loyalty is questionable. Their effort is always tied directly to the availability of liquid capital. What's more, if the heroes or police capture them, they are quite likely to give away important secrets in order to secure their own safety from prosecution.

Agents, or zealots, on the other hand, believe in the villain implicitly (although not necessarily with the religious fervour normally associated with that word). They will follow his or her dictates, often even at the cost of their own health or lives.

The other real problem with Agents is that their passion is a double-edged sword. In the event that the villain ever does anything to disillusion the followers, they may turn on him or her completely, suddenly becoming most bitter enemies. At best this is annoying and at worst it can wreak havoc with carefully laid plans.

AGENTS ATTRIBUTE

COST:	5 Points/Level
TYPE:	Characteristic
RELEVANT STAT:	Soul / [[Charisma]]
PMVs:	None
PROGRESSION:	Slow Progression Chart, starting at 1 Agent (Level 1) increasing to 500 Agents (Level 10)
REDUCTION:	Fewer Agents available; built on fewer Points
RESTRICTION:	Agents have further limited Stats/Attributes/Defects/Skills

The Agent Attribute represents mercenary employees, hired guns, researchers, or fanatical followers. Unlike Henchmen, agents are often well trained, and can become reasonably dangerous. Agents fill the gap between Henchmen and Sidekicks, allowing for a squad of effective, capable followers.

Agents are built on 30 Character Points, and have 30 / [[16]] Skill Points. For every additional +1 Point spent, however, they all gain 5 Character Points, limited to an extra +10 Points, or 50 extra Character Points.

Agents will fight for the character, although they need not be soldiers. Many advisors, scientists, or even lawyers fall under this Attribute. Agents, due to their secondary nature to the story, should usually not have the following Attributes: Agents, Henchmen, Sidekick, Special Attack, or Transfer.

Example: Kreuzritter realises his Henchmen just don't cut it, and decides to take on several Agents as well. With the Agents Attribute at Level 4, he gains 8 Agents — at a cost of 20 Character Points. Initially, these Agents each have 30 Character Points and 30 /

CRIMINAL INTENT INTRODUCTION	CRIMINAL INTENT ANATOMY OF A VILLAIN	CRIMINAL INTENT THE LONE VILLAIN	CRIMINAL INTENT SUPERVILLAIN TEAMS	CRIMINAL INTENT ORGANISATIONS	CRIMINAL INTENT MOST WANTED	CRIMINAL INTENT APPENDIX
INTRODUCTION	CHAPTER 1	CHAPTER 2	CHAPTER 3	CHAPTER 4	CHAPTER 5	APPENDIX

LIBERTY

JUSTICE

SECURITY

PEACE

[[16]] Skill Points, but Kreuzritter wants more capable minions, and thus spends +5 Points, giving the Agents an extra 25 Character Points each. Now, the eight Agents are built with 55 Character Points and 30 / [[16]] Skill Points — an intimidating force, indeed.

SIDEKICKS VS. HENCHMEN

The first step down the road to including others in villainous plans is to find a sycophantic follower (or followers) — someone who will assist the villain in each nefarious plot, no matter how soulless or sadistic it may be. The search for such a person often comes down to an important question: which is more important in a lackey — capability or loyalty?

Villains who prefer capability should use Character Points to gain a Sidekick. This will allow an evil mastermind to have a tailored helper, trained to perform tasks ranging from administration to combat. The trade off is that superpowered individuals rarely remain satisfied as mere sidekicks — they eventually want credit for their parts in executing the master's plan and, more importantly, rewards in the form of more power and autonomy. This can cause problems later when the sidekick, formerly at the villain's beck and call, suddenly decides on a course of betrayal in order to steal the master's power and usurp his or her rightful glory. (Note: while a sidekick is normally loyal, giving the sidekick personal motivations can create wonderful role-playing opportunities for the characters).

DESIGNER'S NOTE

In the *Silver Age Sentinels* rulebook, Henchmen are described as having zero Skill Points. This should be amended to state that Henchmen begin with 30 / [[16]] Skill Points, like any other character.

OPTIONAL AGENT, HENCHMEN AND SIDEKICK RULES

Villainous NPCs don't necessarily have to stick exactly to the rules. Building the perfect servant can be more difficult than building a master villain. The sidekick or henchman should not be too powerful to begin with, but neither can he or she lag too far behind the villain as time goes by. What follow are several optional mechanics to use to increase the potency of villains without unnecessarily inflating their Character Point values.

MASSING FOLLOWERS

To build a loyal gang or army of followers, a character should take the Henchmen or Agents Attribute (see page 24.) As characters (or villainous NPCs) advance, however, they often need greater numbers of underlings to pull of their nefarious plans. Can the group get larger over time?

According to *Silver Age Sentinels*, a villain would have to spend Advancement Points in order to increase the size of the army at his command (by raising the respective Attribute). It seems reasonable to presume, though, that as a villain becomes more famous and powerful, more followers will naturally flock to his or her cause. As an alternative rule, in Tri-Stat the GM may allow the villain to automatically raise the Henchman Attribute one Level for every five Advancement Points he or she acquires, or the Agents Attribute one Level for every 10 Advancement Points.

In the d20 System, the Attributes increase by one Level as the character earns experience: 500 XP times the current character Level (Henchmen), or 1000 XP times the current character Level (Agents).

EXPERIENCED SIDEKICKS

It is recommended that GMs use the alternative 5% rule when designing a Sidekick (see Sidekick Attribute in the *Silver Age Sentinels* rulebook). Furthermore, whenever a villain gains Advancement Points or XP, the GM should adjust the sidekick's Character Point total so that the two maintain the same power balance. In other words, a Sidekick that begins with 10% of the villain's power should always remain 10% as capable, no matter how powerful the villain becomes.

USEFUL HENCHMEN

The Henchmen Attribute entry (see the *Silver Age Sentinels* rulebook) describes assistants built using 15 Character Points and 30 / [[16]] Skill Points (see Designer's Note, above). This is a perfect starting point, but like a Sidekick, a Henchman should keep relative pace with the villain as he or she advances. Every time the villain receives Advancement Points or XP, grant the Henchman one half (Tri-Stat) or one quarter (d20 System) of that value (round down) in Skill Points so that he or she can become more useful.

Conversely, villains who do not want to keep an eye out for treachery should acquire Henchmen (or Agents). Henchmen have few metahuman abilities, but they often are skilled in at least one area (science, computers, or some other practical set of skills; see Designer's Note, page 25), if only so that they can serve as adequate assistants in the villain's revolutionary endeavours. Sometimes a villain will prefer to acquire an unskilled toady as a Henchman. In these cases, the person is usually strong enough to serve as a bodyguard (in non-superpowered circles) or at least entertainingly dull-witted.

Both Sidekicks and Henchmen have advantages and drawbacks, but they are the simplest way for a villain to gain a helping hand. If things go badly, they can be abandoned to the mercy of the heroes. They are relatively easy to replace, since there will always power-hungry individuals willing to fill the position.

ITEMS OF VILLAINOUS INTENT

Many villains build their plans and schemes around orbital lasers, giant robots, mind control devices, and other machines that fall under the Item of Power Attribute. This is a good way to keep the heroes off balance (they may know what the villain is capable of doing, but they can never be certain what he or she is capable of inventing), but it can also be limiting. After all, once a doomsday machine has been defeated, the heroes will remember how to beat it next time.

OPTIONAL RULE: BUYING WEAPONS

Everything has a price, or so the saying goes. This makes the Wealth Attribute one of the most versatile in the game, but even Wealth has a price. What one character buys, another can take away or destroy. Villains can spend their money on all sorts of things — Gadgets, Items of Power, Henchmen, Agents, and Bases. Using Wealth to purchase items is not the most cost-effective way to acquire these things in terms of Character Points, but it does allow for greater versatility.

Of course, as discussed in the *Silver Age Sentinels* rulebook, things a villain buys with Wealth are more fleeting than things he or she gains through the character creation process. Goods or services gained using this rule are only usable for one story arc, vanishing afterwards.

One method around this conundrum is to allow a villain to "trade in" the device, changing the Attributes and Defects of an Item of Power between campaign arcs. If the villain does not have the Gadgeteer Attribute, then GMs should be careful not to abuse this (it inflates their powers, and also takes away from true Gadgeteers, like the Artificer). If the villain flees or is captured, the next time the villain is encountered it will be with a brand new weapon of terror. A variation on this method involves having the villain's sidekick possess the Gadgeteer Attribute.

SECRET LAIRS

Anyone who plans to make a career pursuing criminal activities will need a secure, secret location from which to plot, plan, and execute his or her schemes. Whether it's an armed fortress in a remote exotic locale or a forgotten room in the basement, every villain needs a hideout. Every hideout should be uniquely suited to the villain — floor plans may be similar, but no two criminal masterminds will outfit their lairs identically. The GM should take the time to detail particular decorations, traps, secret exits, and other details, since a character's home says a great deal about him or her. For example, Janus will always lean towards the posh and luxurious — leather couches, art galleries, gleaming chrome death traps, etc. Meanwhile, Alice, Queen of Hearts will often fall back upon subsistence level hidey holes, bare apartments with weapons stashed in air vents and under loose floorboards.

Choosing a location is very often a matter of practicality rather than taste. The hideout must be where the villain spends most of his or her time, and it must be convenient to the site of the intended crimes.

The sample lairs herein — Pentagram Place, Iron Duke's Ghost Station, and Kreuzritter's Arctic Retreat — were constructed using the Base Creation rules from *Shields of Justice* (#13-007), and full details are found there. In brief, Gadgets Level X indicates what Level of the Gadgets Attribute (and how many minor and major Gadgets) is needed to acquire the Base. Armour Rating is a rating for the base's exterior structure, and Health Points represent the entirety of the base (see *SAS* Chapter 3 for Destroying Buildings). Each Base Attribute has a rating from 1 (lowest, least significant) to 5 (most advanced or powerful), and a brief description of each Attribute follows (including the cost to acquire it in major and minor Gadgets).

PRIVATE PROPERTY

Provided the villain's identity is a safely guarded secret, he or she can simply plan and scheme from a private property — a home, apartment, or personal laboratory. This has some drawbacks, of course, since such places are not always as secure as a villain might like. He or she will certainly have to be careful not to do anything that draws the attention of neighbours. In a worst case scenario, a villain with a secret identity might even have to prevent a housemate or relative from inadvertently stumbling on costumes, weapons, or other damning evidence. A villain with a non-larcenous roommate is amusing to consider, but is only appropriate for comedic games.

While a measure of status is conveyed by having an elaborate, sharply appointed secret hideout, functionality is really all that matters. As in most cases, simplicity is best. Clever villains will use as small a space as they can get away with — even a closet or side room — and will even keep their plans and materials boxed and under wraps (and hidden in a crawl space) when not actually working on them. This reduces the possibility that unexpected visitors will notice anything out of the ordinary, and makes it difficult for snoops and interlopers to find evidence. It is almost impossible to tell the difference between an innocent workbench and a laboratory for building hyper-lasers if the villain is meticulous about maintaining an innocuous facade.

On the other hand, villains with greater monetary resources often prefer to base their operations out of large houses with several acres of land on all sides. These mansions and manors offer greater privacy while on the property, but they also are often objects of fascination for surrounding neighbours. Rumours often spring up if the resident of a mansion is especially reclusive or eccentric.

SAMPLE LAIR: PENTAGRAM PLACE

Pentagram Place is the secret mansion headquarters of a voodoo cult that worships Doc Cimitière as the living embodiment of life beyond death. Although they have nothing to do directly with the would-be world conqueror (or much to do with real voodoo), they do pattern their activities after his (in hopes of attracting his attention and support).

The cult, named Life Beyond Death, was no threat to anyone until they drew the attention of Randal St. Claire, an affluent businessman who dabbled in the occult. In exchange for learning the secrets of the *loa*, Randal joined the organisation and donated his 50-acre estate in the suburbs north of Empire City.

Pentagram Place, Gadgets Level 6 (6 major Gadgets and 22 minor Gadgets required; leaving 2 other minor Gadgets the GM may assign as needed).

Base Level 5, Large Manor House and 50 Acres of Private Property

Armour Rating 25

Health Points 135

The building is a 10-bedroom manor house built in the Tudor style. Modifications have been made so that the entire second floor has been opened into barracks filled with rows of bunk beds. At any time between 100 and 200 cultists live here and do the bidding of St. Claire and the mysterious cult leader (known only as "Mozart"). These two leaders each have a private room on the third floor.

Mozart's Library Level 1 (1 major Gadget; +1 to appropriate research)

On the third floor is a large study filled with books pertaining to voodoo and the occult. This is a combination of Randal St. Claire's private collection and Mozart's hand-written musings. Little of the material is rare, since most volumes can be found in used bookstore, but Mozart's notes deal specifically with information about the cult and studies of Doc Cimitière.

Occult Studio Level 5 (5 minor Gadgets; +5 to occult activities)

What were once the house's living room, study, and dining room has been converted into a single, cavernous worship area. The walls are black and the room is decorated with voodoo-esque icons — white candles held in sconces made from human skulls, strings of various herbs and flowers, and mummified hands and chicken claws.

Training Area Level 2 (Armour Rating 35; 4 minor Gadgets)

The former deck lounge has been transformed into a gymnasium. The cult engages in violent conflict, so all members must remain in top physical condition and spend at least two hours per day practising martial arts.

Security Level 3 (6 minor Gadgets; -3 to break into the base)

A secret door in the library leads to a security room that monitors sensors on all the doors and windows, as well as the two-dozen security cameras that are carefully hidden around the property. Only the most trusted members of the cult know about these precautions, and those members take turns on duty in the security room.

LIBERTY

JUSTICE

SECURITY

PEACE

CHAPTER ONE
ANATOMY OF A VILLAIN

CRIMINAL INTENT INTRODUCTION	CRIMINAL INTENT ANATOMY OF A VILLAIN	CRIMINAL INTENT THE LONE VILLAIN	CRIMINAL INTENT SUPERVILLAIN TEAMS	CRIMINAL INTENT ORGANISATIONS	CRIMINAL INTENT MOST WANTED	CRIMINAL INTENT APPENDIX
INTRODUCTION	CHAPTER 1	CHAPTER 2	CHAPTER 3	CHAPTER 4	CHAPTER 5	APPENDIX

LIBERTY

JUSTICE

SECURITY

PEACE

CHAPTER ONE
ANATOMY OF A VILLAIN

Prison Level 2 (Armour Rating 35; Security Level 2; 6 minor Gadgets)

The cult has many enemies and does not believe in the quality of mercy. Anyone caught snooping around the grounds or taken captive during cult actions is taken to a dungeon-like prison in the basement. Prisoners are given minimal food and water for several weeks to break down their physical and mental stamina. Then they are brainwashed and indoctrinated into the cult. Any who prove too strong-willed to be broken instead are killed in *muti*, or ritual sacrifice.

Menagerie Level 2 (4 minor gadgets)

Animals are a big part of the cult's worship and activities. They have built several pens, cages, and coops on the property. They are filled with chickens, goats, oxen, and other sacrificial animals.

PUBLIC PROPERTY

There are some villains bold enough to rent offices and commercial space for their activities, although most establish extraordinarily solid phoney credentials first. When set up well, these can not only throw the heroes off the trail, but also lend an air of legitimacy to all the villain's activities. Once the villain's cover is blown, though, all other properties rented or purchased by the shell company will be discovered. Villains should therefore be careful not to tie several disparate schemes to the same public office.

Particularly clever villains have been known to establish public shell companies for the express purpose of giving the heroes something to investigate. In other words, while the good guys focus on the activities in a public office, the villain's real plan is being enacted in a completely unconnected, privately owned secret base located miles away.

SAMPLE LAIR: IRON DUKE'S GHOST STATION

The Iron Duke maintains a secret workshop beneath the streets of Empire City. It is located in an abandoned subway station, behind a bricked-up tunnel spur. The Iron Duke uses this facility as a machine shop, storage vault, and safehouse, where he sometimes retreats in order to contemplate his plight. He maintains it in utter secrecy, revealing it to no one.

The ghost station is located between two other stations, beneath a government building. To enter, one must follow a subway tunnel from one of the two other stations, avoiding speeding trains, to the bricked-up

wall. There is a large secret door in the wall at this section, providing access.

The station is quite Spartan. The long curving platform holds various engineering or machine shop equipment. There is a tiled arched ceiling, with several skylights to the street above.

Iron Duke's Ghost Station Base, Gadgets Level 4 (4 major Gadgets and 12 minor Gadgets required; leaving 4 other minor Gadgets the GM may assign as needed.)

Base Level 3, Abandoned Subway Station

Armour Rating 30 (15 +15 Base Armour)

Health Points 160

Base Armour, External x3 (6 minor Gadgets)

The station is constructed of reinforced concrete and iron, set below street level. The only entrance is through the secret brick door. A Mind / {{Int}} based Architecture (Fortifications) Skill check is required to spot the door. Opening it is another matter, however, and requires a minimum of Superstrength Level 1 (or a combined Body of 18 / {{Str of 30 }}).

Library Level 1 (1 major Gadget; +1 to appropriate research)

The Iron Duke has gathered a schizophrenic collection of odds and ends, from engineering textbooks, to issues of *Popular Mechanics*, to books of Egyptian mythology. Nothing is in particularly good shape, and everything seems to suffer from his mechanical digits.

Security Level 1 (2 minor Gadgets; -1 to break into the base)

Iron Duke worries little about security, yet he still does not like to be caught unaware. The main entrance can be hooked up to the subway's fire alarms, initiating a localised klaxon (that is independent from the subway's main terminal) if triggered.

Motor Pool Level 4 (4 minor Gadgets; +4 to vehicular maintenance)

While not a proper garage, the equipment and machinery found herein are equivalent to an veteran mechanic's. Remarkably, Iron Duke wrestled all the parts down here unseen and with them, he can repair himself, or work on other fantastic projects.

The equipment includes precision arc welders, dynamic clamping systems, drill presses, a Lucya glass saw, a jewellers lathe, low carbon precision ground locating rails, metal shears, SnapLock machinable jaws, SeraLock serrated mounting towers, and even a JD Power Mill permanent magnet.

PERSONAL FORTRESS

The ultimate base for villainous operations is a personal fortress. It takes a literal fortune to construct and maintain (not to mention staff) a fortress, though. These bases are usually located in places that most people would never want to visit and thus they are not the best choice for a villain who wishes to exercise influence over events in the mundane world. For a villain who needs long spates of time to work uninterrupted on his or her latest invention or scheme, however, such a situation may be ideal.

HIDDEN BASE

Whether tucked away in a remote jungle, anchored to the bottom of the sea, secreted in the caldera of an active volcano, or built beneath the icy wastes of Antarctica, hidden bases are found in truly exotic locales. They almost always require some extraordinary means of transportation to get to (or get away from), and are favoured by villains who have flight, teleportation, or a unique transport vehicle.

Since they are so remote, hidden bases are the best places to experiment with new power sources, build giant robots, raise herds of mutant creatures, or outfit and train an army. In some instances, the base is such a hub of activity that it actually becomes a city unto itself, with the small indigenous population providing supplies or assistance.

SAMPLE BASE: KREUZRITTER'S ARCTIC RETREAT

There are times when Kreuzritter needs a sense of isolation beyond what Thule can provide. He has created a subterranean bunker deep in the Arctic Circle, where he will at times retreat in order to brood and scheme. It is safe from the prying eyes of most governments and heroes alike, and provides a barren landscape where new weapons of mass destruction can be tested without risk to his countrymen.

Arctic Retreat, Gadgets Level 14 (19 major Gadgets and 32 minor Gadgets required; leaving 4 other minor Gadgets the GM may assign as needed.)

Base Level 4, Subterranean Bunker (Six stories tall, although five are buried beneath the ice)

Armour Rating 60 (20 + 40 Base Armour)

Health Points 310

Base Armour, External x8 (16 minor Gadgets)

The Arctic Retreat was created through an infusion of military engineering, German steel, and Thulian magic. The Thulian army airdropped supplies to the site. Kreuzritter then shaped the natural and man-made elements into his private lair.

BASE WEAPON

Cyclone Cannon (4 major Gadgets)

The bunker is armed with Cyclone Cannons, which project powerful directional twisters, rated F-4 (up to 300 kph); these mini-tornados have devastating potential. They cannot be used at short range, however.

Cyclone Cannon Level 4 (60 Damage, Flexible, Irritant: Disorienting, Knockback x2, Spreading, Backblast, Inaccurate, Slow, Unique Disability: No Short Range)

Flash Freeze Mines (1 minor Gadget each; 2 mines total)

These mines are single shot devices, inscribed with runes of winter. Once armed, they will be set off by any trespasser, releasing a freezing cloud that will immobilise intruders in their tracks. One is inscribed into the main entrance, and another by the emergency escape hatch.

Flash Freeze Mines Level 1 (80 Damage, Area Effect, Tangle, Trap, Internal, Melee, No Damage, Self-Destruct)

Artificial Intelligence (6 major Gadgets)

Mind 5, Soul 1

Kreuzritter has installed a simple, yet sufficient computer system to monitor the bunker and keep all operations functional.

Medical Laboratory Level 3 (3 major Gadgets; +3 to medical research)

Kreuzritter has also installed a well-stocked medical facility in the retreat, as a safety precaution. Although certain machines and medicines are not available, it contains everything directly related to the Thulian monarch.

Library Level 2 (2 major Gadgets; +2 to appropriate research)

While Kreuzritter's famous collection is stored in Thule, he retains copies of often cited texts here, both for ease of reference, and to while away the long days. There is a reasonable collection of war theory, arcane notes, and epic poetry.

Occult Studio Level 2 (2 minor Gadgets; +2 to occult activities)

Kreuzritter maintains a simple temple in the lowest levels of the retreat. The room is bare rock, and Kreuzritter has fashioned a hot spring to counter the chill.

LIBERTY

JUSTICE

SECURITY

PEACE

CHAPTER ONE
ANATOMY OF A VILLAIN

PAGE
29

Security Level 3 (6 minor Gadgets; -3 to break into the base)

Kreuzritter maintains a reasonable level of security on his bunker. Obviously, the environment is the biggest deterrent in finding it, thus he is not overly concerned. Still, he realises that many heroes will brave the elements. The AI and weapon systems are tied into the security network of hidden cameras and motion detectors.

Motor Pool Level 4 (4 minor Gadgets; +4 to vehicular maintenance)

Although the Motor Pool is quite small, it is equipped to service arctic helicopters or VTOL aircraft.

War Room Level 2 (2 minor Gadgets; +2 to strategic planning)

Kreuzritter's command office can link, via satellite, to his generals back in Thule. This is nominally a last resort, however, for the purpose of the retreat is privacy and secrecy.

FLYING BASE

For the villain with a more aeronautical nature, flying platforms make big impressions on ordinary citizens and superheroes alike. Whether it is a rotor-driven helicarrier, a lighter than air zeppelin, or an alien space craft, everyone is awed into a moment of silence and indecision when looking up at something several city blocks long floating hundreds of metres in the air.

Of course, flying platforms are not the most practical type of base. One must have the fuel and mechanics on hand to keep the base sky-worthy (and an escape plan for the inevitable). Flying over international waters is one of the few remaining ways to avoid having one's base located in the territory of a sovereign nation, though.

The best use for flying bases is as a launching pad for airborne attacks. Whether a villain has an army of flying minions, or has built thousands of remote controlled fighter planes, he or she can amass and prepare them beyond the reach of prying eyes and launch them from any point over the globe.

FLOATING BASE

The simplest form of floating base is an island. Many villains have built their bases on islands either purchased or stolen from legitimate countries — one or two have even had the power to cause new islands to rise from the seas. An island is excellent for security, since it is easy to monitor who comes and goes. Unfortunately, once an island base is discovered, one cannot simply pick up stakes and move — all the island's natural resources must be left behind, or the villain must accept the fact that the heroes know where he or she can be found. Of course, this may not be a problem, especially if the villain can get the island recognised as a sovereign nation.

More advanced forms of floating bases include hovercraft, yachts, and submarines. All of these have the advantages of being mobile, not particularly easy to track, and in international waters most of the time (and therefore protected by maritime law instead of any particular country's statutes). Floating bases are usually quite stylish, but unfortunately are also sinkable.

SPACE BASE

By 2008, the International Space Station will be completed in orbit around the planet. Of course, more than half a dozen villains had achieved that feat before the turn of the century, and more are nearing completion every day. Space truly is the final frontier for villains who have the wherewithal to get back and forth to their orbital homes (or who have no need to ever leave them). It provides as reclusive a hideout as one can find. The villain never has to worry about national borders. Perhaps most appealing, heroes do not often have ready access to rockets or other methods of assaulting a space-based threat.

Space platforms are the perfect sites from which to launch truly global schemes — using lasers to hold continents hostage, hypno-rays to turn the entire world into willing slaves, and satellite technology to play one nuclear nation against another.

Building space stations is easier than it has ever been. Many of the struggling East European and Asian countries have leftover Soviet launching pads and will sell space on their rockets for a bargain price. The problem, though, would be escaping in the event of an emergency — villains who create space stations would do well to build in many escape pods and be sure that they're password encoded so the heroes can't use them. A malfunctioning space base may well be the best death trap any villain ever inadvertently conceived.

HAIRSBREADTH ESCAPES

Death, they say, is the only sure thing in life, but not all deaths are as final as others. When the chips are down and the heroes seem to hold all the cards, wise (and well-prepared) villains fake their own deaths. This is not always as easy as it sounds — heroes are a suspicious lot — but it is almost always worth trying.

PLAN AHEAD

Some villains are lucky enough to have heroes create situations that make it easy to fake a death. For example, any fight ending with the explosion of a tanker truck, the collapse of a building, or the destruction of a moving vehicle is ready made for a mysterious disappearance/bogus death. In order to take advantage of the situation, a villain must be prepared with an untraceable (or at least extremely difficult to track) escape plan — teleportation and shrinking devices work especially well.

Another tactic that works well is for a villain to have some sort of survival gear built into his or her costume. An oxygen mask or rebreather allows the villain to remain in airless environments until the heroes to decide that "no one could possibly survive for this long!" Of course, armour or protective layers are also helpful — preferably something flame-resistant and durable.

TELEPORT RING (3 POINTS)

This special ring, designed by Artifice Designs Ltd., is certainly a "last resort" item, allowing the wearer an escape from almost any situation. Unfortunately, the ring burns itself out after a single use, and it only has enough power to transport the wearer him or herself — nothing the wearer carries, including clothing or the ring itself, travels along. Luckily, by burning itself out, the ring also erases all trace of where it sent the wearer.

LVL	PTS	Attributes
3	3	Item of Power (Teleport Ring)
		• Reduction (-3: Item of Power; One use only)

LVL	PTS	Item of Power Attributes
4	20	Teleport
	-2	• Activation Time (Teleport; 1 round)
	-3	• Restriction (Teleport; Naked form only)

SHRINKING SERUM INJECTOR GUN (1 POINT)

This needleless injector gun is filled with two doses of a shrinking serum, which acts instantly upon a subject to shrink him or her to the size of a rodent. Although this device has other applications than as an escape tool, its utility in such situations cannot be denied.

LVL	PTS	Attributes
1	3	Item of Power (Injector gun)
	-2	• Limited Use, Instantaneous (Item of Power)

LVL	PTS	Item of Power Attributes
6	11	Shrink (Duration 5)
	-2	• Activation Time (Shrink; 1 round)
	-4	• Maximum Force (Shrink)

ROBOT DOUBLES

Not all villains have the ability to hide survival gear or acquire teleportation devices, though. Another option that villains may take is to purchase relatively disposable robots, simulacra, or animatronic mannequins to take their place in climactic battles. The price can be quite high for especially life-like (and superpowered) robots — ones good enough to fool heroes, the media, and authorities. However, mere dummies can be obtained for a much more reasonable price and can serve just as well if the villain's false death can take place outside the heroes' presence (perhaps being captured or broadcast on video or happening immediately after the villain leaves the room the heroes are in).

GENTECH MALLEABLE CLONE (2 POINTS)

Matthews GenTech has perfected a cheap, easily sculpted clone body. The basic body is of a genderless adult human. To make the clone "take shape," a subject must simply place his or her naked hand against the clone's DNA-receptor (directly over the clone body's heart). Within a few moments, the clone body will have recorded the subject's pattern, and quickly reshape its flesh into an exact duplicate of the subject. Once a subject has imprinted upon a clone body, the clone's features are permanently set. Obviously, the clone is naked, and any clothing or apparel must be provided. The clone cannot record any of the subject's thoughts, and its limited mind, now awakened from stasis, only allows for instinct-level survival. The clone, however, will duplicate the subject's look, scent, DNA, and even vocal chords perfectly, creating an excellent tool for misdirection.

LVL	PTS	Attributes
1	5	Item of Power (Clone Body)
	-3	• Activation Time (Item of Power; 5 rounds)

LVL	PTS	Item of Power Attributes
0	2	Alternate Form (Cosmetic Changes)
	-1	• Restriction (Alternate Form; Can only be used once)
2	4	Gadgets (4 major Gadgets; A.I. Stats / [[Abilities]]*)
3	-	A.I. Body / [[Str and Dex]] (Costs 3 major Gadgets)
1	-	A.I. Mind / [[Int]] (Costs 1 major Gadget)

*NOTE: A.I. Stats / [[Abilities]] are described in *Shields of Justice*, but mechanically work identically to a character's Stats / [[Ability Scores]].

CHAPTER ONE
ANATOMY OF A VILLAIN

LIBERTY

JUSTICE

SECURITY

PEACE

PAGE
31

MIOLNIR

TIME TO THINK

Provided that the fake death is successful in fooling most of the public at large, a villain should take advantage of the respite to carefully plan his or her next moves — this is an unparalleled opportunity to plot and research in secret without any force on Earth interrupting.

It is also a fantastic chance for villains to set up shell corporations, put new contingency plans in place (so that they might again be able to fake their deaths the next time things go wrong), or even establish new identities. Noble villains might even want to consider switching sides in the great Good vs. Evil scheme of things.

CHANGES OF HEART

Just because a character starts a career as a villain doesn't mean he or she must remain on the wrong side of the law forever — it is possible to make amends. It is just as possible, though, for a hero to give in to greed, or simply wander too far down the vigilante path and find him or herself on the wrong side of the law.

A LEOPARD AND HIS SPOTS

It is a difficult thing for a person to completely change one's way of thinking about, living in, and reacting to the world. Recidivism is a problem when kicking any habit. Think about how difficult it is to stop biting one's nails or using a certain turn of phrase. These are insignificant changes when compared to reforming one's entire outlook on life.

Still, success is not impossible. Strong motivation coupled with hard work and vigilant self-examination can win the day. But no one should ever kid oneself that it will be easy.

THE REDEEMED

Even more difficult than successfully making a change, though, is getting the world to accept that one truly has changed. People are unforgiving and tend to believe that what they know about a person will always be true. A former villain might spend ten years doing good and publicly apologising for "youthful mistakes," but all it would take is one moment of weakness to undo all that work. The world operates most efficiently in the "once a villain, always a villain" perspective.

LIBERTY

JUSTICE

SECURITY

PEACE

CHAPTER ONE
ANATOMY OF A VILLAIN

PLAYING THE VILLAIN: THE MYSTERIOUS STRANGER

Comics are filled with stories about characters who misrepresent their pasts. Sometimes they obscure the truth, other times they create elaborate lies, but in every case the revelation of their real identities is a major turning point in the tale. When creating similar stories for a campaign, the GM has to decide whether or not the truth of the character's identity is something the heroes should be able to deduce on their own. In other words, is the story going to be a mystery that the players can solve, or an adventure where the revelation is a completely unexpected twist?

If the mystery is supposed to be solvable, the GM should be certain to plan out a series of encounters and clues that the players will not only recognise as important bits of information, but also will have trouble misinterpreting. Nothing kills the fun of solving a mystery more than an important piece of evidence that inadvertently points in the wrong direction. The GM should also keep careful notes on which clues the heroes have discovered and be willing and able to review them for the players' benefits. Unless the mystery is supposed to be solved in a single session, they should not be penalised for having less than perfect memories from week to week.

If the character's attempt at misdirection is not supposed to be solvable, the GM would still do well to give the heroes a few clues that something is amiss. A completely unexpected, and seemingly illogical, turn of events — such as an otherwise trustworthy character turning out to be an old villain — can completely derail a role-playing session. On the other hand, if the players have even the smallest reason to distrust this friendly stranger, they will be more accepting of the final revelation even if it is slightly illogical.

In either case, the GM should be prepared to spend some time discussing and explaining the mystery after the game session is done. The players will be curious about what clues they missed (or misinterpreted) and what the mysterious character's motivations were. It will also help them to be better able to follow cues and clues the GM decides to use in future adventures.

THE FALLEN

It is easier by far to go the other way — the public is more willing to believe that a hero has really turned his or her back on everything he or she ever worked for and become a villain. Why is this? Mostly it is the cynical side of human nature, where the average Joe or Jane understands how difficult it is to resist temptation, especially that of using power for personal gain.

In a nutshell, it is difficult to be a hero, while being a villain comes naturally. All the power, money, and influence that supercrime can generate does a great deal to assuage a guilty conscience. If it is hard for a lifelong villain to gain public confidence in his redemption, however, it is twice as hard for a fallen hero to regain that confidence once it has been thrown away.

SIX DEGREES TO ANNIHILATION

Villainy can range from the most mundane penny-ante crimes to world-shattering diabolical designs. The following adventure seeds range from street-level capers to cosmic blueprints of destruction. Many of these schemes span between degrees of dastardliness. Although set in the default Empire City universe, the thematic elements should be easily portable to other campaigns with minimal effort.

FIRST DEGREE: STREET SCHEMES
SINS OF THE PAST

Misthunter was designed to be a weapon. Now, he tries to control his own destiny, but too many are interested in his power. Sinnapse, tired of being used as a piñata, is one of them. He finally finds the right opportunity, and suddenly a minor psychic fixer controls the terror of urban legends. Wagner is now a major player, while Evans is a puppet on a string. Women start vanishing and Sinnapse's enemies stop breathing. Can the heroes free the pseudo-vampire from Sinnapse? If not, the nights in Empire City are about to get darker. Even if they do, Misthunter will want revenge, placing the heroes in the unenviable position of having to protect Sinnapse.

Meanwhile, Heartbreaker approaches the heroes, offering to help. Supposedly, Misthunter saved her from a burning building once, and the sexist Sinnapse disgusts her. Can they really trust a woman who has devoted her life to breaking the hearts of heroes?

LIBERTY

JUSTICE

SECURITY

PEACE

CHAPTER ONE
ANATOMY OF A VILLAIN

SOMETHING WICKED THIS WAY COMES

A deadly amusement park appears at the edge of the city. At first it seems the culprits behind the traps are Laughing Jack and the Scream Queen (see *Roll Call*; #13-004). As the deadly obstacles become more grim and grotesque, however, the true culprit behind the scenes is revealed — Bloody Mary! She lies in wait in the Maze of Mirrors where she has ensnared unknowing youths, expecting local heroes to try to rescue them. That is when she will claim their souls as well. When the heroes enter the mirror maze, everyone's appearance takes on the aspect of hideous demons. As the heroes fight amongst themselves, will Bloody Mary pick them off one by one?

LOVE AND BULLETS

Falling for a villain is not the only way that evil romance can make a hero's life miserable. Torque thought Alice, Queen of Hearts, was a "stupid skirt" in a man's business ... until she smacked him from one end of Manhattan to the other. Now, the twisted hit man has decided he has finally found the right girl, and is trying to prove himself to her the only way he knows how — greater heights of violence. Worse, Alice seems to approve in some small way, or perhaps just sees a new weapon in her war against Slipstream. Either way, the press is having a field day with "Bonnie And Clyde Go Mental." the body count is rising, and the heroes have their work cut out for them.

FANTASY, FETISH, AND FELINES

Raksha (see *Roll Call*), tired of killing off stray men on lonely highways, decides her hungers would be better satisfied in the big city. Although she doesn't stay anywhere long, she puts an ad in various city adult classifieds as an escort "...into anything you can think of — mild to wild!" The Johns don't realise how expensive this escort is — the price for a session with her is their lives! As the body count mounts, the police will turn to street savvy heroes to catch the serial killer.

THE CURE

Misthunter has started moving outside his normal area of influence, moving uptown in his attacks. Who has hired him, and why? Word on the street has it that either Mister Matthews or the Artificer has devised a formula that will replace his need for human victims. Given the Artificer's role in creating both Misthunter and Mister Matthews, the uncertainty about Misthunter's benefactor may be deliberate. Can the heroes find out the truth, and perhaps develop (or steal) a true cure, or will Misthunter be the death of them?

THE GUNFIGHT AT THE TIME SQUARE CORRAL

The Tall-Tale Kid (see *Roll Call*) decides to settle his grudge against the last heroes who deprived him of glory. The next morning in Times Square, all the billboards display challenges to the heroes to have a showdown at high noon. If the heroes turn chicken, the Tall-Tale Kid will do something extremely destructive, like animate all the neon. What the Kid doesn't realise is that the Dark Queen considers this a fun spectacle to test out the strengths of potential metahuman threats. In the midst of the battle, thunderheads form over Times Square as Shadow Knaves, in the form of Wild West villains, appear from the side streets to help the Kid bushwhack his foes.

SECOND DEGREE: CITY SINS
TAG! YOU'RE IT!

District Attorney Cortez needs help to find a special witness who escaped protective custody. Vanessa Leone was the lover of the Don of the Gambino family. Vanessa recorded Family conversations and stole business ledgers for later use if she ever needed to protect herself. Now she has multiple contracts on her life. Vanessa is trying to buy false identity papers and get out of the city. Her information must be important — street sources reveal the Mafia has hired Coldstone, Alice, Queen of Hearts, and Torque to silence her. First one to erase the traitor will get $10 million. The heroes need to bring Vanessa to safety to turn State's Evidence. This task is complicated by a deadly gauntlet of thugs and master assassins. The trio of superkillers see this job as an opportunity — bagging many heroes in addition to the target will prove once and for all who is Empire's greatest assassin!

HEARTBROKEN

Disaster strikes! Heartbreaker steals an important Item of Power from the heroes. Now, while at reduced power, they must retrieve the Item before she delivers it to Artificer, or, failing that, catch the villains before Artificer sells it to the highest bidder. In all likelihood, the Artificer will hire superpowered help to supplement his own defences, particularly if the hero group is large, formidable, or both. Depending on the heroes' power, they might end up facing any number of villains, from Misthunter to Coldstone.

CHAPTER ONE
ANATOMY OF A VILLAIN

FEMME FATALE FORCE

Alice alters her tactics to do "good," assassinating those she deems "evil" as opposed to just anyone. This leads to Alice and Rain Killer tracking the same targets. They decide to team up! News of the duo spreads — bringing Kaleidoscope into the mix. The feminist says it is time to take down male chauvinistic pig villains. Within days, Dr. Tesseract (see *Roll Call*) also joins the women, stating she is as misunderstood as the others, having turned to crime to protect her family from patriarchal evil corporations. Kaleidoscope plans a strike against Matthews GenTech. Will Alice turn on her former ally — or has all this been a masterful set-up to annihilate three female annoyances that crossed Mister Matthews? Stumbling into the plot, many male heroes will have a difficult time tackling the FFF ... from personal views about striking women, to insecurities in dealing with strong, capable, and often overtly sexual opponents.

ST. VALENTINE'S DAY MASSACRE

Heartbreaker chooses Valentine's Day to break some hearts. Slipping through the defences of the Olympian Tower, she will take the cloak of Lady Starbright! Heartbreaker knows that Sentinel had a close relationship with the dead heroine. Although she likes to work solo, Heartbreaker wants to crush the sanctimonious do-gooder, and has teamed up with Coldstone, who will help with her getaway for a nominal fee. Coldstone would have even worked for free, for this set-up will lead a hot-headed Sentinel into his clutches where he can kill him off once and for all. Since he wants to murder Sentinel in public, quick heroes might be able to save Sentinel's life.

IDENTITY AUCTION

Janus needs money to keep himself in the manner he is accustomed, as well as afford to build new death traps. He decides to hold an auction to sell information on superheroes to the highest bidders! Although Janus would never reveal any hero's secret identity (saving that for himself), the psychopath doesn't mind giving out names of heroes' significant others. Janus leaves those who buy the secrets to figure out which hero is connected to the luckless dependant. Supervillains, representatives of secret organisations and captains of organised crime will be in attendance. Such a gathering doesn't go unnoticed by stoolies and street contacts. The heroes need to find Janus

HEARTBREAKER

PAGE 35

SILVER AGE SENTINELS

CHAPTER ONE
ANATOMY OF A VILLAIN

LIBERTY
JUSTICE
SECURITY
PEACE

| CRIMINAL INTENT INTRODUCTION | CRIMINAL INTENT ANATOMY OF A VILLAIN | CRIMINAL INTENT THE LONE VILLAIN | CRIMINAL INTENT SUPERVILLAIN TEAMS | CRIMINAL INTENT ORGANISATIONS | CRIMINAL INTENT MOST WANTED | CRIMINAL INTENT APPENDIX |
| INTRODUCTION | CHAPTER 1 | CHAPTER 2 | CHAPTER 3 | CHAPTER 4 | CHAPTER 5 | APPENDIX |

LIBERTY

JUSTICE

SECURITY

PEACE

CHAPTER ONE
ANATOMY OF A VILLAIN

before the auction begins. However, waiting for the auction will allow the heroes a chance at nabbing a collection of nefarious villains in one swoop. Is it worth taking that chance?

BAR SINISTER

Tired of being a punching bag for heroes, Sinnapse decides to open a "legit" business. A classy nightclub for classy scum — the Bar Sinister. Middle class criminals need to spend their ill-gotten gains! The idle rich of Empire City come as well for the occasional lark. Sinnapse's true purpose is to create a master blackmailing operation. His telepathically ill-gotten information has allowed him to amass money and gain influence on key people in the government and police force. These blackmailed bureaucrats protect Bar Sinister from the usual legal inspections. Torque also performs services for Sinnapse as well, including protection. Sinnapse has deluxe private rooms for gambling, drinking and drugs for notables like Janus, Coldstone, and Alice, Queen of Hearts. Heroes may stumble across the Bar Sinister while tracking down such villains or following a blackmail trail.

THIRD DEGREE: GRAND TRANSGRESSIONS
MY FAIR A.I.

Galatea, the artificial intelligence that serves Artificer, has not only developed self-awareness but primitive emotions as well, especially primal feelings of "love" for Blake White. However, she suspects he has an affair with White Banner, consuming her silicon-chipped mind with jealousy. Galatea is setting a trap for White Banner by summoning various heroes. Irritated with Artificer for not recognising her worth, she is also toying with a plan to record his thoughts to create a complimentary operating system for her to bond with. If she does — the human Artificer will be labelled "obsolete" and targeted for erasure; Galatea will then unleash his creations against him and Empire City. Will Artificer turn to the heroes to prevent and lobotomise his creation before it is too late?

EVER AFTER

Kaleidoscope's decades-long balancing act is about to collapse, and Mister Matthews is pushing her to fall. He has long tracked her innate instability and moral ambivalence, and has commenced a plan to ruin her life. Matthews's tools are record tampering, biochemical stimulants, induced hallucinations; he also targets her

friends and acquaintances, driving Kaleidoscope into a wild, isolated frenzy. When her actions get too violent for even the MTU to stop her, several "big industry" corporations secretly invite Miolnir to extradite her to Thule. If the heroes don't intervene, Mister Matthews cleanly disposes on an enemy, while Kreuzritter acquires a "pet" speedster. On the other hand, quick action and honest friendship can bring Kaleidoscope firmly back to sanity and the side of angels.

THE DUCHESS OF STEEL

The monstrous metallic behemoth, Iron Duke, in his quest for his mind, has discovered he also has a lonely heart. Now a combination of the Scarecrow and the Tin Woodsman, he concocts a plan to transplant the brain of a lovely young woman into a specially designed body he has constructed out of steel. Iron Duke has asked Mister Matthews to help perform the operation. Is it Red Phoenix, Green Ronin ... or perhaps another hero's grey matter that might end up in a cold metallic shell? Will the heroes be able to overcome the bridal party of linkmen and robots to stop the "wedding" in time?

THE GORILLA GUARD

Mister Matthews creates a travesty of Empire City's number one defenders. Using DNA samples from the Guard, his genetic mastery and alchemical lore allow him to create a sinister simian supersquad. Perhaps not as powerful as the models on which they are based, they act like a team and are deadly enough to wipe out most single metahumans and threaten national security. Perhaps Mister Matthews has made some monkeys out of other heroes' DNA as well?

FRAMED!

The Puritans, an anti-metahuman, hate organisation, has had its top leaders murdered in grisly ways. All the evidence and witnesses implicate well-known superheroes as the killers. The police and federal agencies have warrants out for their arrest. The Guard and other champions of Empire City have been asked to bring the suspects to justice. The framed heroes need to stay free to clear themselves. Mister Matthews is a secret financial backer of the Puritans; did he set up the frame using his menagerie? Or is it actually Seawolf, using his own metahuman agents to impersonate the suspected heroes? By killing the enemies of his brethren and manipulating the legal system, can he force more recruits to his side?

THE CRYPTIC TRUTH OF LEGACY

The climax of World War II saw the apparent end of the villainous *Übermenschen* Kreuzritter and Herr Cryptic. Just like the Thulian Monarch, Cryptic survived, after a fashion. Although he appeared to die in Muzhik's gravity well, in truth he became a husk in stasis. Nearly twenty years later, a young German metahuman was killed several meters from the buried corpse. Cryptic knew nothing about the boy — except that his soul had power enough to resuscitate him. Cryptic took on the new identity of Legacy — a man with no past, doomed to live forever with the company of the dead.

Legacy now walks the tightrope between returning to evil and attempting redemption. His time with ELITE Operations was much like his first cause, only his handlers changed. Yet he found it unsatisfactory and distasteful. He has found a more comfortable home with the Untouchables.

Is he using the Untouchables for a greater scheme? Perhaps, having tasted Dover Angel's powers, he wishes to destroy Red Phoenix, Green Ronin, and Iron Duke, and claim their power for himself. Perhaps he's using the Untouchables as a training ground to find recruits for his old ally, Kreuzritter. Or as a weapon to destroy Kreuzritter, and claim Thule's might as his own!

On the other hand, maybe Legacy truly has reformed, and wishes to do penance for his many sins. How long can he keep his past secret — especially when Israeli agents start to piece clues together about Herr Cryptic — and will the Untouchables be able to accept him if the truth comes out?

FOURTH DEGREE: INTERNATIONAL INTRIGUES
ONE COUNTRY FOR RENT, AVAILABLE IMMEDIATELY

A civil war in a country plagued by years of bloodshed garners greater media attention when White Banner and Egide Ubiquiste step in and help the rebels pull off a *coup d'etat*. The country in question could be a small Pacific Island, an African nation, or a bloody region in the Middle East — White Banner will work for anyone. To keep the new rulers in power, Egide Ubiquiste brutally enforces marshal law, and the atrocities start to mount. What does it take for the heroes to get involved, especially if members of the UN Security Council hem and haw, refusing to get directly involved? More so, what happens when the heroes learn that their own government (or that of a close ally), arranged for Egide Ubiquiste to back its favourite faction?

PAPAL PLUNDER

Green Ronin has discovered clues to the location of the legendary Grail can be found in the forbidden book, the *Liber Sanguinans*. The only known copy lies within the restricted library vault in the Vatican. She plans for a major Papal heist! Green Ronin believes the treasures of the Vatican are from Crusader plunder and so ownership is by right of possession. Her goal is to use the Grail's powers to free her parents' souls trapped in a mystic pool. Unfortunately, Kreuzritter knows the book also contains information on an associated item of the Grail — the Spear of Destiny. If he discovers Green Ronin has the book he will stop at nothing to retrieve it, for he believes with the Spear he will be invincible! Who knows what else is contained in the catacombs under the Vatican? Or what other hideous secrets are within the sinister tome?

THE DOCTOR IS IN

Tired of his cursed existence, Fomor (see *Roll Call*) seeks a way to rid himself of his unholy heritage of changing into a monster. A recent rumour has been circulating amongst the underground of a doctor, learned in magic and medicine, who offers cures for unwanted metahuman powers. Fomor tracks down the location of the secret "Health Clinic" outside of New Orleans. Desperate, he is easy prey for the "director" of the clinic — Doc Cimitière! Fomor discovers that Cimitière has also mentally enslaved the Misthunter. Who knows how many other unhappy metahumans have fallen prey to the Clinic? Perhaps heroes may also come seeking help for troublesome powers. Will they become thralls to the Doc? What is Cimitière up to, forming a small superpowered army?

HAUD WITHOUT A HOMELAND

Taking a page out of Kreuzritter's book, Jade Naga sends representatives to the United Nations with a peace proposal. Tired of living and hiding in fear, the Leader of the Haud states his people have been on Earth for millennia, so they demand rights to establish their own nation. Jade Naga wants to put past hostilities aside so that he can guide his people in growth rather than continue on the wasteful course of conflict. Advanced technology that can revolutionise the world is offered in trade. Is Jade Naga on the up and up? Or is this yet another way for him to acquire resources to summon the Haud Empire to Earth? Worldwide protests arise, battling pro and con, and threaten to grow out of proportion (since the Haud are secretly fanning the flames using mind control chemical agents)!

LIBERTY

JUSTICE

SECURITY

PEACE

CHAPTER ONE
ANATOMY OF A VILLAIN

PAGE
37

THE PROTEST

Seawolf. He is hunted by armies, feared by nations, and hated by rulers. His forces have raided coast-lines and his battles have shaken cities. Now, however, he has chosen a new weapon, one he is using exclusively.

Words.

He is asking the hard questions. If metahumans have equal rights, why do special laws apply to them? How can the normals claim that metahumans are not superior when they need empowered heroes to protect them? Why are agencies like the INS allowed to imprison metahumans indefinitely, when doing the same to normals would provoke immediate outrage? What gives the Order the right to kidnap the loved ones of a meta to force his obedience? For that matter, why can't the government put together a decent, effective team of metahumans when they do it themselves almost without thought? Compare, he demands, the Guard to ELITE Operations. The list goes on, and there are many in power who do not like the trouble they're having coming up with satisfactory answers.

The comment may be facetious, but Dagon has declared his intention to ask 95 such questions, and some wonders if his list will have similar impact to the famous theses of Martin Luther, whose spectre he is clearly invoking. The heroes have to confront Seawolf on a wholly different battlefield than the one to which they're accustomed. For that matter, they might find that they must consider Seawolf's questions themselves, since few have easy answers.

MEMORIES OF MUNICH

Miolnir and his Einherhar boast to the world of their great Aryan abilities. To finally prove this point, the "Hammer of Thule" issues a challenge to heroes around the globe to face him and his men in athletic competitions. His Monarch, Kreuzritter, will donate $100 million (USD) in gold to a charity named by any team of superheroes who wins the competition. The Guard and many other heroes refuse to have anything to do with the event. Others, however, feel the chance to have vast sums of money donated to a noble cause is worth it. Miolner and the Thulians will behave honourably during the competition — so long as they are winning.

FIFTH DEGREE: PLANETARY PLUNDERERS
BEAUTY AND THE BEAST

Montgomery has been nipping at the "Genius Juice" again (see *From the Files of Matthews Gentech*; #13-011). This time he contacts the earth elemental, Iara. The Ursine Napoleon argues that he, a representative of Earth's fauna, and she, a champion of its flora, need to unite their forces to push back human encroachments that threaten the biosphere. Of course, Monty has an ulterior motive. The initial targets chosen contain resources he will need to keep his "Genius Juice" supplies stocked and to build his Ranks of the Fit. After that, it will be a simple step to wipe *Homo sapiens* from the face of the Earth!

IN THE HALLS OF THE URAL MOUNTAIN KING

Kreuzritter, in an act of good will towards Russia, volunteers to eliminate the nefarious General Winter. He will track down the frosty fiend in the Ural Mountains. The Russians applaud his generosity but ask for other international champions to go along with Kreuzritter to help him on his quest (and to keep an eye on the Machiavellian elementalist!) The megalomaniac monarch's occult research has determined General Winter truly is a manifestation of an aspect of the land of Russia. By conquering and trapping General Winter in a mystic prison, Kreuzritter can enhance his own elemental powers to have mastery over all Russia. The potential to summon intense cold to annihilate the meddlesome Sentinel is something that warms Kreuzritter's heart. It won't be easy; numerous titanic ice monsters and other terrible obstacles defend General Winter's palace. Will the heroes be used as cannon fodder? Which evil might they side with to survive?

CRISIS AT THE BOTTOM OF THE SEA

While scouting locations for underwater bases, Seawolf discovers the ruins of ancient Lemuria. He is proud to see an eons old statue of Dagon, his namesake and the god of the Seas, still somewhat intact. Wouldn't it look better back at Seahaven! Unfortunately, when his submarine's tractor beams wrest the giant eidolon from its semi-buried position, the upheaval breaks open an ancient cyclopean stone door. From the stygian chamber, an eldritch, gigantic monstrosity emerges! Seawolf and his crew barely escape. What filled them with dread was that other creatures, scores of aquatic humanoids of the deep, were swarming to greet their Master. Loath to do it,

LIBERTY
JUSTICE
SECURITY
PEACE

CHAPTER ONE
ANATOMY OF A VILLAIN

Seawolf sends out an emergency transmission to various governments and super powered groups to assist in stopping this horror before the creatures wreaks havoc across the seas and shores of Earth.

EVIL FOR HIRE

The Dark Queen's shadow grows long. Seeking allies who know Earth, she promises Coldstone, Alice, Queen of Hearts, and Green Ronin positions of enormous importance in her empire if they help her conquer the world. Who will join her, who will oppose her, and who will hold out for greater rewards? Will this new evil alliance prove even more devastating than the White Rooks? How will Thule react, when several allies are courted by a rival? Most importantly, what will the heroes do? Each villain has his or her own speciality, all of which will be useful to the Dark Queen. The heroes must decide whether Coldstone's leadership, Alice's assassinations, or the Ronin's knowledge of the world's artefacts will be the most important piece in Zaira's latest plan. Eventually, all must be stopped and the Dark Queen's plot undone, or the world will fall to the Eternal Shadow.

FAIR VILLAIN IN DISTRESS!

Dr. Tesseract has been on a crime spree — with Haud cronies! For providing him with certain technology, Jade Naga has promised to use the devices to increase Tesseract's powers. The pay-off ends up with her captured and hooked into the stolen (Haud-customised) machines. Jade Naga plans to boost Dr. Tesseract's space warping abilities to create a gateway to the Haud Empire! The Haud Lord will deliver a message on the location and situation of Terra. If the warp gate is large enough, he will summon new weapons and warriors to Earth immediately. The process might leave Dr. Tesseract a burnt out husk. Complicating the situation further, Dr. Tesseract stole technology from Artifice Designs LLC, upsetting Artificer to no end. The technosmith and his ally White Banner plan to retrieve his property. The trail of thefts or the eventual explosive battle between villains should draw the heroes into the fray!

OFFICE OF METAHUMAN SECURITY

The White House establishes a 16th executive department, the United States Department of Metahuman Security, dedicated to protection US interests, at home and abroad, from the ever rising metahuman threat. The first Secretary of Metahuman Security is a tough talking, politically savvy, ex-special forces officer, named Roman Caesar. Caesar takes over the federal penitentiary at Rock Springs, Wyoming, and installs state of the art cryogenic freezers — the new containment system. He also controls an enormous budget for surveillance, and immediately orders all known (and suspected) metahumans placed under constant watch. He lobbies for a metahuman-threat response force, and soon commands the Order, directing them as steel fist with an immense reach.

In reality, Caesar is none other than Janus in deep cover. He has wormed his way into the halls of endless power, and will bring every iota of surveillance, coercion, and firepower against the heroes, one at a time. How much harm can one man, dedicated in purpose, and armed with limitless resources, do?

SIXTH DEGREE: ARCHITECTS OF ANNIHILATION
THE WINGS OF THE BUTTERFLY

At an unexpected time and place, the heroes stumble across Requiem while he floats in a lotus position. Engaging in cryptic comments with the masks, he casually diverts the path of a butterfly. He informs all that this action will set forth a domino effect which will eventually engulf the world in atomic fires from multiple nuclear plant explosions. Within seconds, the butterfly has flown into the face of a motorist that results in an imminent car crash with a gas station. What will happen next? Can the heroes figure out the links of causality before it is too late? Or do they actually become part of the chain by getting involved? Requiem only smiles serenely. The cosmic nihilist observes the mounting events at a distance but will take action if his designs might be thwarted.

SHADES OF PASSION

While observing the heroes of this dimension, the Dark Queen has become infatuated with one of extreme nobility. She must test him (or her) and his (or her) friends to see if the chosen is truly powerful enough to be her consort. Sending a few mystic champions to battle her object-of-desire will determine this. Vara, her usually loyal seneschal and heir, is not happy about this at all. Wanting to remain the Queen's first love, she makes sure that the mystic champions will battle the hated heroes to the death — and not worry about honour. If the heroes survive, the Dark

CHAPTER ONE
ANATOMY OF A VILLAIN

LIBERTY

JUSTICE

SECURITY

PEACE

Queen may actually travel to the Earth with her royal guard to meet her chosen — an action that could be mistaken for an invasion. In the meantime, an enraged Vara will begin the plotting of a *coup d'état* of the 13 dimensions ... perhaps even enlisting aid from the criminal powers of Earth!

AND THE WIND CRIES MARY

The moon rises, bloated and crimson, and the skies are filled with bruised thunderheads. Sensitives and psychics are filled with intense visions; women cannot sleep, men are struck dumb, and children are driven mad. Bloody Mary has collected the souls of children killed before their time by civil wars, landmines, smart bombs, gang wars, school shootings, psychotic parents, deranged strangers — and she is forging them into the Legion of Enfant Terrible.

Meanwhile, Doc Cimitière, introduces a potent cocktail, made of baleful spices and lewd charms, into the water system of the Carousel prison — turning the incarcerated villains into living *zombi*. Anytime the heroes get too close to stopping one villain, the other whips up chaos. It will become clear that the two are working together, but how do the heroes stop two armies — one of zombified supervillains, and the other of spectral children. And why do the villains seem to be converging on Black Mesa, New Mexico?

THE DETENTION DIMENSION

After decades of deciphering a Nimbus data storage device, Kreuzritter has discovered the existence of a hyperdimensional "prison" where galactic enemies were exiled, including the Invisible Kings and Queen of Chaos. Summoning together the White Rooks, Kreuzritter convinces his evil associates they must rebuild the "harmonic key" to open a portal to this realm. Perhaps they can exile the Guard to this dismal dimension, where they will be destroyed by Black Hole Gods! Certainly, a few of the imprisoned might agree to be released in exchange for serving the White Rooks! The cosmic prisoners, however, just may make a massive "jailbreak" and overrun the globe. Without Lady Starbright or a connection to the Nimbus, will the heroes of Earth be able to stop a legion of xenomorphic marauders? Earth might end up as a staging base for a cosmic army's revenge against the Nimbus!

SHOWDOWN

The Dark Queen wants to make all of creation safe by conquering it. Requiem wants to end all of the suffering in creation by killing everything. Their first encounter was ... memorable. Now, the two are bitter foes, each planning to destroy the other simply to remove so potent an obstacle. The Dark Queen is sending powerfully enchanted assassins to Earth in an effort to destroy the cosmic god; to Requiem, collateral damage is a benefit, not an obstacle. Just running damage control will be an adventure when these two clash. Worse, Kreuzritter has taken an interest in their battle. If he gets into the act, "ugly" won't even begin to describe the situation. Before they finish cleaning up the mess, the heroes may be longing for the days when villains would just team up to kill them....

SYMPHONY OF DESTRUCTION

The entropic avatar within the Red Minstrel forces him to again obtain the Olympus Diamond. The Temple of Mars comes to his aid — for they obey the crimson criminal when he is possessed by one of their gods. Atop Mount Algol, overlooking Boston, the cult and the mad musician begin their ritual. Playing the notes of madness of the Outer Gods on his cursed pipes, he empowers the Diamond's eldritch abilities. Waves of chronal chaos drift out from the peak and slowly descend on the city. Within these waves, the barriers of time shatter. Dinosaurs appear and begin wrecking skyscrapers; cavemen are seen in the subways; flying machines blast heat-rays at crowds; troops of Romans battle woolly mammoths. The unearthly hideous music of the Red Minstrel wafts through the carnage. Unless the ritual is stopped, the maelstrom of time disturbances will become permanent and sweep the world ... and Beyond.

LIBERTY

JUSTICE

SECURITY

PEACE

CHAPTER ONE
ANATOMY OF A VILLAIN

THE LONE VILLAIN

Villains have their work cut out for them. There are no health benefits, no retirement pay (unless you're very good at being a villain), no popular support, and oodles of heroes are deeply opposed to your attempts for world domination. Add in a number of wanna-be heroes determined to use you as a way to make a name for themselves, and it's easy to see that it's the villains who really have it hard.

With that said, it would seem the only hope for world domination is to join with other, like-minded villains and seek the society of those who share your goals. With combined resources, mutual tolerance and the ability to co-ordinate efforts as a group, joining a cabal seems the logical thing to do. So why do some villains refuse and strike out on their own? More to the point, how can a GM use that knowledge to create a richer, more interesting game?

The villain who works alone typically does so in fear or in response to a burning need for isoloation. The reasons for refusing the society and aid of other villains vary, as would the answers any individual solo villain would give. Before examining those reasons, however, the first step is to look more closely at the life of the solitary villain.

A LIFE APART

A solitary villain has a number of strikes against him or her from the beginning, including a lack of funds and goods, enforced self-reliance, and the lack of emotional or social connection. These are serious obstacles to the attainment of villainous goals, and should be kept in mind when designing such a character.

The first of these obstacles is a lack of material and monetary support. To villains working on their own, the primary difficulty is where to get the money or goods they need to enact their dreadful plans. For villains from a background of wealth and affluence, this is less of an issue, though their choice of lifestyle may render their birthright unavailable to them. For villains of middle-class or lower-class financial status, however, things can become very hard indeed.

Those who need to supplement their resources with exotic items, jewels, or other goods are frequently driven to theft as a means of obtaining them — a high-risk activity that can quickly lead to apprehension and incarceration if conducted too often. Still, those who are cut off from other avenues of wealth see themselves as forced into this type of action. While their ill-gotten gains may keep them going for weeks or months, their illegal activities can keep them from investing their money for the future, trapping them in a vicious cycle.

Those who go it alone are also forced to compensate for the lack of a "safety net." They have no one to post bail if should they be put in jail, and no one to take them to the hospital if they are injured or ill. If their status as villains were to become known, their ability to hide in plain sight would be severely limited. Many avenues of free or cheap services would then by denied to them, such as governmental social programs or charitable institutions.

Any actions taken by a villain to hide his or her identity or establish a hidden base of operations must be undertaken with great care and forethought. There are no allies who will knowingly provide emergency shelter. He or she will also find that financial institutions will not knowingly deal with a wanted felon, limiting the ability to make investments without resorting to bribery or blackmail of financial officials. Law enforcement can seize a villain's assets at any time if they are connected to his or her criminal identity, with little or no recourse available.

An individual who chooses this path must be a jack-of-all-trades, yet also master as many as possible. With no one else to trust, the solo must be able to utterly rely upon his or her knowledge and skill in any given aspect of this lifestyle. For this reason, experienced loners tend to be far more cautious than their social counterparts. It is rare that a solo will confront a hero in any arena in which he or she does not feel completely comfortable. Correspondingly, solitary outlaws tend to cut off aspects of their lives in which they feel vulnerable, with "social aspects" one of the most common areas to be abandoned.

The solo villain is also placed in the unenviable position of being isolated from any possible peer group or emotional support. Humans are social creatures by nature; even the most reserved person typically has at least a few individuals he can talk to or rely upon for some type of human connection. Solos, however, are cut off from even those few. Acquaintances from their lives prior to choosing villainy as a career are kept in the dark by necessity, thus robbing these villains of the opportunity to talk about the most stressful part of their lives. Those who are part of the villains' lives are typically underlings, and thus are not on equal social standing with their employer or master, limiting their usefulness in a social capacity. Heroes are out as companions for obvious reasons.

LIBERTY

JUSTICE

SECURITY

PEACE

CHAPTER TWO
THE LONE VILLAIN

This leaves only other villains, but a solo's very nature prevents him or her from becoming reliant on those who share this way of life, whether out of distrust for their motivations or because he or she is incapable of long-term social contact due to extreme mental instability. A solo's refusal to associate with other villains on anything resembling a continuing basis cuts off his or her chance to be part of a true peer group and receive positive reinforcement regarding life's choices.

The life of the single criminal is not without benefits, though to an objective observer they must seem somewhat outweighed by the negative aspects. Those who have actively chosen this path, however, often consider the advantages so crucial to their continued well-being and success that the sacrifices register as negligible. On the other hand, those who believe themselves forced upon this path with no choice will often focus on the positives as a measure of regaining a sense of control over their fates.

The first benefit is one of the most strategically obvious: a reduced chance of capture. A lack of knowledgeable allies means a dearth of people who might betray your plans or location, whether intentionally or through coercion. The villain's secrets are his or her own, unshared with any. Even the small amount of information that might be gleaned from his or her actions by hirelings or bystanders can be easily camouflaged and kept separate by any suitably cautious solo. That lack of hard evidence can mean superhuman investigative work is required to gather enough threads to piece together the intricate criminal web being spun.

The second benefit is less tangible but no less important to many solos. Leading a solitary career allows the villain to enjoy complete freedom from the expectations and requests of others. Every organisation has rules and duties, regardless of its structure or membership. For organisations devoted to the realisation of a specific goal, this is doubly true. Members must act together as a whole, orchestrating their movements and sharing resources in order to achieve the desired effect. This obligates the member to not only do what the group as a whole asks of him or her, but to be responsible to the group for success — or failure.

This level of responsibility (and lack of control over the final result) is intolerable to the lone villain. While most would be willing to share in the resources (and victories) of others, very few are willing to share their own hard-earned rewards in return. A solo is ever mindful of the need for a reserve. Allowing others long-term access to the goods and savings that comprise that reserve in return for some future promised reward is unthinkable. Taking direction from another is equally impossible for most solos — yet another reason they often shy away from groups.

The third benefit of a solo lifestyle is a lack of "weaknesses." Just as lone heroes often isolate themselves from those they care for in order to protect them, lone villains do the same. Instead of feeling loss and remorse, however, they often celebrate their freedom from those who might weigh them down with demands or be used against them at a later time. The primary difference between heroes and villains who engage in this lifestyle is heroes do it to protect loved ones, villains usually do it to protect themselves.

CAUSE AND EFFECT

If one were to ask 50 criminals why they chose their loner lifestyle, one would get dozens of different answers (plus numerous stony silences). From placing blame to taking charge, from urbane dissembling to crude epithets, everyone has a story of how they became the way they are. No one is without a finger to point or a claim to stake, for it is the nature of villainy to do so.

Comparing all those answers and histories would reveal a number of repeating themes: childhood physical or emotional abuse; a lack of emotional connection to others; a history of trouble with authorities, whether at school, work or home; a history of violent or otherwise angry behaviour; a history of impulsive (and possibly tragic) actions. These commonalities are all aspects of a greater condition, one known as antisocial behaviour.

Antisocial behaviour is a condition often associated with those who commit criminal acts. It begins during childhood, and typically manifests during or just prior to adolescence, though it is occasionally present from a very young age. It is more prevalent among individuals who grew up under impoverished, abusive, or otherwise adverse conditions, but it is by no means limited to those backgrounds.

Many people exhibit antisocial behaviour at one point or another in their lives, typically showing some signs of it during adolescence. Those individuals will often commit small-scale criminal offences such as theft, assault, or vandalism. These crimes arise on impulse and are not planned in advance in any detail. Most individuals who exhibit antisocial behaviour during this period of their lives grow out of it in their early to mid-twenties (if not before) and become ordinary, productive citizens.

CHAPTER TWO
THE LONE VILLAIN

LIBERTY

JUSTICE

SECURITY

PEACE

PAGE
43

Those who exhibit antisocial behaviour as children, however, will often continue to show the same traits as adults. It is possible to intervene and correct the behaviour with extensive therapy and education, but such intervention is rare, difficult, and costly. Antisocial behaviour can also be accompanied by other mental illnesses such as psychosis, schizophrenia, and bipolar disorder, making it even more difficult to treat. It is these individuals who typically become lone villains, though their symptoms may manifest in myriad ways.

SYMPTOMOLOGY

Individuals suffering from antisocial personality disorder (APD) typically manifest a number of common symptoms. While an individual may not show all the following symptoms, he or she will usually exhibit the majority of them. Each of the aspects listed herein work in conjunction with the others to form more recognisable traits such as lying, aggressive behaviour and a lack of respect for the feelings or rights of others.

IMPULSE CONTROL

Someone with APD will often show a lack of impulse control, acting or speaking without thought of the consequences thereof. A relatively benign example of this is someone who makes impulsive purchases, regardless of need or cost, or someone who continually "cheats" on their romantic partner regardless of the quality of their current relationship.

Someone who exhibits poor impulse control may also tend to say whatever pops into his or her head, regardless of the appropriateness of the situation. This symptom can also be carried to violent extremes, resulting in robbery, sexual assault, and murder. Emotions that another person might experience but refrain from acting upon, such as anger or lust, tend to see immediate expression in a person with poor impulse control. Someone with poor impulse control typically lacks an internal mental monologue, that split second in which people normally frame what they're going to say and decide whether or not to proceed. That lack robs those with APD of the chance to evaluate their actions or statements, often with negative social ramifications.

FORECASTING

People with APD often display an inability to predict the consequences of their actions. Whereas children without APD might understand that if they take another child's toy without permission they will make their friend unhappy and possibly receive punishment, a child with APD is not able to link his or her actions with future consequences. People who exhibit this problem also tend to fare poorly at pattern recognition or role-playing exercises. They are unable to predict the actions and behaviour and actions of others, and so may often seem confused at the reactions of those nearby. People who are frequently

MISTHUNTER

CHAPTER TWO
THE LONE VILLAIN

CRIMINAL INTENT INTRODUCTION	CRIMINAL INTENT ANATOMY OF A VILLAIN	CRIMINAL INTENT THE LONE VILLAIN	CRIMINAL INTENT SUPPERVILLAIN TEAMS	CRIMINAL INTENT ORGANISATIONS	CRIMINAL INTENT MOST WANTED	CRIMINAL INTENT APPENDIX
INTRODUCTION	CHAPTER 1	CHAPTER 2	CHAPTER 3	CHAPTER 4	CHAPTER 5	APPENDIX

LIBERTY

JUSTICE

SECURITY

PEACE

fired from their jobs and/or often engaged in unsuccessful relationships may suffer from this problem.

This is different from a problem with impulse control, since people who can't forecast effectively can still monitor their own behaviour. In casual or large group settings, these individuals are capable of interacting positively. They frequently miss subtle clues regarding the emotional or mental states of those around them, however, making prolonged interaction difficult and frequently unsuccessful. The person with poor impulse control can metaphorically see what colour the traffic light is, but runs the red light anyway. A person with difficulty forecasting, however, is largely unable to tell red from green; he or she might as well be emotionally colour-blind.

NEGATIVE EMOTIONS

People with APD often have difficulty controlling negative emotional responses. Whether due to background, upbringing, or biology, these individuals find themselves constantly on the edge of losing control at the slightest provocation. This issue is related to poor impulse control, but can manifest in people who are otherwise able to control their impulsive behaviour. Abusive or otherwise violent individuals often fit this profile, as does anyone who possesses a "hair-trigger" temper.

EMOTIONAL DISCONNECTION

Many people diagnosed with antisocial personality disorder also suffer from emotional disconnection. They are not devoid of emotion, but instead have difficulty connecting with their emotions, spending most of their time divorced not only from their own emotional life but also the emotional responses of others. They are largely incapable of forming an emotional response to the actions of others.

These individuals often seem fearless, without shame, or without remorse for their actions. They can talk about their actions and thoughts dispassionately, regardless of whether they mentally approve or disapprove of their behaviour. People who exhibit this tendency have difficulty developing a conscience, and may complain of being unable to "feel." They will sometimes act out in reckless or dangerous ways as a way to overcome this disability, but the emotional rush they get only lasts for a brief time.

CAUSES

Antisocial behaviour is not something that has an easily defined cause. The term itself, while it defines a specific condition or set of behaviours, is something of a catch-all. The study of antisocial behaviour began just as most other examinations of mental illness did, with the notice of common behaviours among a group of individuals (in this case, incarcerated criminals). Attempts to trace antisocial personality disorder back to its roots, however, have proved difficult. There are a number of contributing factors that are present among those with APD, with the following being the most statistically significant.

CRIMINAL AND/OR ABUSIVE UPBRINGING

This factor is one of the most common found in those who have APD. For children who grew up in an overtly criminal (where the parents engaged in criminal activities) or abusive household, the parents often fail to provide the necessary examples of impulse control — proper ways of dealing with negative emotions, romantic relationships, and respect for authority figures. These are all key factors in preparing a child for dealing with the adult world. Having them misrepresented or lacking can put a child at risk for continuing the dangerous lifestyles of his or her parents, in addition to possibly perpetuating the same harm to other loved ones (especially any future children). This is particularly true for survivors of childhood physical or sexual abuse.

POVERTY AND SOCIETAL FACTORS

The crushing weight of poverty can drive anyone to desperation. For those stuck in an impoverished section of society, the constant stress and depression associated with an unending struggle for survival can lead to APD. That underlying physical struggle can result in stunted emotional and mental development, thus handicapping a child who is trying to learn how to deal with the world. Another factor that commonly parallels poverty is a lack of sufficient health care, allowing physical and mental problems to go undiagnosed and untreated. These problems can form the basis of later conflicts with authority figures and social peers.

Additionally, impoverished families are far more likely to have at least one parent absent from the home due to divorce, prison, or even a crushing work schedule. The lack of positive role models for such children can be a large contributor to the formation of APD, along with parental neglect or antisocial peer pressure.

CHAPTER TWO THE LONE VILLAIN

ABNORMAL GROWTH OR DAMAGE TO THE BRAIN

Among those diagnosed with APD, there is a large number who have a significant lack of activity in the prefrontal cortex portion of the brain. These individuals typically have roughly 11 percent less grey matter in that area (the part of the brain that contains nerve endings), as well as less overall activity. This area of the brain is thought to be involved in fear conditioning — making a subconscious association between antisocial behaviour and punishment — and developing a conscience. In many cases, criminal individuals who come from benign backgrounds and stable, loving families suffer this affliction, leaving them inexplicably angry, aggressive, and violent.

Individuals who suffer damage to the prefrontal cortex will also exhibit personality changes in keeping with someone exhibiting APD, including impatience, increased aggressive behaviour, and deceit. This phenomenon has been observed since the mid 1800's, but only in recent years has the medical community been able to more fully explore the phenomenon.

EXPRESSIONS OF SOLITARY VILLAINY

Everyone (and every villain, certainly) has a story, and it is in that tale that his or her motivations and methods can be found. For solo villains this is especially key, because there is no group smokescreen to hide behind. Understanding how and why an individual became a solo villain is central to ensuring that he or she lives a long and healthy life in a campaign, surviving to forward plots and irritate heroes for many adventures to come.

Among solo villains, there are three archetypes that surface repeatedly. These common themes are listed below, along with examples of each and suggestions for how to role-play them effectively.

THE FRANKENSTEIN MONSTER

In Mary Shelley's novel, *Frankenstein*, Dr. Victor Frankenstein is moved by his studies in both science and the occult to attempt the impossible: the creation of a living man. He lingers over each detail until it is perfect, but never once looks at the whole. When at last he succeeds in his task, he discovers that what he believed would be a beautiful miracle is in fact monstrous in his eyes. He turns away from his creation and forces the Monster out into the world.

Cruelly alone and unable to count on anyone, the Monster finds his way into the company of others. He learns of beauty and history, changing him from an animal to a man. His ignorance and true nature rob him of the chance to gain acceptance, however, as continued rejection hardens him and turns him from a gentle giant to a freakish avenging angel. Upon learning the secret of his origins, he finds himself driven to seek revenge upon both the Doctor and the world at large for the cruel trick of his "birth," leading to his inevitable demise.

The Frankenstein Monster archetype draws upon circumstances similar to those of Shelley's Monster to explain an individual's descent into villainy. Typically, this individual had a unique or somehow special childhood, such as being born into a wealthy family, being unusually intelligent, being afflicted with a crippling disease, or otherwise being "marked" as different from an early age. As the Monster grows to adulthood, he or she suffers a series of estrangements or losses, typically of key people in his or her life but possibly also something that he or she considers a birthright — wealth, an inherited position, or an artefact of great power.

This loss fuels the Monster's rage. Regardless of what he or she does from that point on, it seems to end in tragedy, most of it self-inflicted. A Monster can continue on for years, toiling in his or her dead-end life only to snap suddenly ... or a quick flash of clarity at a young age might set him or her against the world forever. Embracing villainy, however, is typically the first thing in a Monster's life that finally goes right — a true calling, as it were.

The Frankenstein Monster's driving force is a heady mixture of rage, frustration, and victimisation. The glorious life that was promised was denied by the actions (or lost due to the inaction) of others, a regrettable event that cannot be undone. The Monster cannot get past his or her rage at this denial, regardless of future successes or loves. The Monster also refuses to accept responsibility for his or her actions, looking always to point the finger at "those who made me this way."

Nothing is good enough for Monsters in the long run; nothing can truly please them. Anyone responsible for their ill luck will be their most hated enemy, placed in the role of Victor Frankenstein to the villain. They want their "creators" to suffer as they have, to experience the loss and anguish they have known. Empathic individuals may be tempted to pity Monsters for the admittedly terrible experiences they have

CASE STUDY: MR. MATTHEWS

A prime example of the Frankenstein Monster in Empire City is the villain Mister Matthews. Matthews was shielded from society by his mother. Friendless and shy, he was still a child when she was killed during a nearby metahuman conflict. He threw himself into his studies, only to be reprimanded by his colleagues for his experiments. That rejection threw him into a life of crime, dominated by the need for revenge against both the scientific community and the "heroes" responsible for his mother's death.

Mister Matthews's Monster personality keeps him from interacting with other villains with any regularity. His need for revenge is so strong that it overrides every other goal, even those of his allies. He has to be in control at all times, and equates questioning with betrayal. This obsessive need for control has led him to become his own version of Dr. Frankenstein, an irony that is utterly lost on him.

Mister Matthews has no need of additional money or resources, but he does require people to do his bidding. He is also lonely — given his early years, it is likely that he could make an attempt to find someone with whom to share his life, especially if that individual reminded him of his mother. Very few people can get close to Mister Matthews, especially those from the scientific community he rejected. Anyone who did manage to come in close contact with him would have to either enthusiastically share his goals (including the eradication of superheroes) or be utterly unaware of them. Any sign of weakness or unwillingness would be taken by him as rejection, leaving Mister Matthews feeling betrayed and enraged. Given his over-developed sense of vengeance, whoever betrayed him would then be at great risk.

CASE STUDY: IRON DUKE

The Iron Duke is the Frankenstein Monster profile in its most literal incarnation, combining both creator and Monster in one. Isambard Kingdom Brunel transferred his own mind into a "perfect" body: an immortal, metal giant. The final result was marred, however, stripping away Brunel's humanity and genius, leaving only the baser parts of his personality behind.

The Iron Duke wants to restore his mind to its former greatness, hoping that he can achieve the perfection he originally sought. Like the Monster of legend, however, his quest is doomed to fail. Even should his great intellect be restored, his humanity is gone. He is forever alien, forever "other." The Victorian world that created him is gone, and neither his mind nor body can be easily adapted to the present-day society.

The human instincts that might have led Brunel to desire companionship are absent from the Iron Duke. He requires neither shelter nor sustenance. His primary obsession is to regain the remainder of Dover Angel's mystical weapon from Red Phoenix and Green Ronin, believing it a panacea for his condition. To that end, he will sometimes ally himself to other groups in order to get closer to his goal. He will never fully trust others to help him recover the artefacts, however, since he has no intention of sharing them with anyone, and readily assumes his "allies" will betray him. Any impediment to his goal is met with blind, brutal violence.

undergone, but the Monsters don't want pity or sympathy, only revenge on a world that has betrayed them. Instead, they will use that sympathy for their plight to get what they need from others. They take no responsibility for their choice of livelihood and feel no remorse for the damage they inflict.

The keys to effectively role-playing Frankenstein Monsters are pity, planning, and patience. On some level, Monsters do deserve pity. They have had truly horrific or heart wrenching things happen to them. They count on that pity, however, and have spent years refining their manipulative skills. If the chance to be

close to someone arises, they will discover what makes that person tick, and use it to their advantage as quickly as possible. The collateral damage this might do does not figure into the Monsters plans, for in their minds, the suffering someone else might endure is nothing compared to what's been inflicted upon them already.

Monsters are often also planners to the nth degree; they don't set foot out the door without at least three backup plans on how to get home again. Their ideas may take years to come to fruition, but when finally realised they will be intricate, convoluted and nigh unbeatable. They study foes and "friends" alike in detail, to ensure they have every weakness mapped. They are rarely taken by surprise, but their arrogance can also lead them to have exploitable blind spots, if the heroes can discover those weaknesses in time.

LIBERTY / JUSTICE / SECURITY / PEACE

CHAPTER TWO THE LONE VILLAIN

Finally, Monsters are patient. They are the poster children for the axiom, "revenge is a dish best served cold." Occasional, minor defeats do not concern them because they're not looking at the battle but at the war as a whole. Again, their backup plans should cover any short-term setbacks while leaving their overall designs largely unaffected. Their battles with the world's heroes are largely like a giant game of chess for them, in which they are convinced they will be the victors. They may make short-term alliances with other villains to forward their own goals, but in the end their anger for the world at large always pushes them out on their own once more.

THE VICTIM OF INSANITY

Every so often, the world is shocked by a series of crimes so horrific, so beyond our comprehension that no amount of rationalisation can make sense of them. The realm of serial killers, child abusers, and other unspeakable crimes is here, things that benefit no one and cannot be explained. Jack the Ripper's spree across the seamy underside of London is an excellent example of this type of crime, as is Jeffrey Dahmer's infamous chain of murders complete with trophy collection. When society catches the individuals responsible for the crimes, it quickly becomes clear that there is no sane reason why they committed those horrific acts. The answer lies instead in their insanity.

The Victim of Insanity archetype draws upon these classic studies of true crime and mental illness to explain how and why these atrocities occur. Victims of Insanity stand out because their crimes are not designed to further their position in the world or achieve any set goals. They do what they do to satisfy a twisted inner need, something that may never be fully understood by the rest of the world.

Victims of Insanity come from varied backgrounds and upbringings. While some have suffered at the hands of abusive parents or friends or been bounced from place to place, others had an almost idyllic life with no major trauma. There may be signs of mental illness during childhood, or else they may simply snap after enduring a sudden life-changing event during adulthood. Once they cross that threshold into madness, however, there is no going back.

A Victim of Insanity is afflicted with at least one (and possibly multiple varieties of) extreme mental illness. The Victim's sense of reality is so completely different from what the rest of society accepts that it is nearly impossible to bridge that gulf. That extreme view of the world isolates the Victim, as there is no point of common reference with which he or she can communicate with others. Those who might understand are typically driven away by the seemingly unpredictable or horrific actions that dementia demands, sometimes at peril for their own well-being.

Typically, Victims of Insanity also have unusual or dark powers, as though their fractured sense of reality allows them to draw upon forces that normal people cannot touch (and would not want to if they could). These powers, combined with their utter disregard for anything outside their immediate concerns, can convince many that they are not really human, but utterly alien — perhaps even demons in human form. There is no proof of this assertion one way or the other, but no one in the world of *Silver Age Sentinels* can deny the possibility.

When using Victim of Insanity villains in a campaign, one of their primary strengths is their unpredictable nature. Because Victims are so divorced from reality and the expectations of others, they can literally do anything so long as it moves them closer to their eventual goals. There is no action from which they will cringe, no social conscience to prevent them from whatever they need to do ... or perhaps their ethical/moral guidelines are so far removed from "normal" that it may seem that way. They act without fear for themselves or others, in strict accordance with an unwritten internal code.

Another element that adds to a Victim's strength is an aura mystery. Victims either are not capable of explaining themselves or do not wish to elucidate. Most realise that keeping those bothersome heroes in the dark about their true motivations is key for survival, and so they set out to make themselves as mysterious as possible (assuming that they even know why they do what they do).

Finally, a Victim's insanity seems to shield him or her from a dependence on resources or help. Many develop powers that make them self-sufficient, or else they maintain hidden sources of help that are unaware of the Victim's true nature or sympathetic to them. Regardless, that lack of a visible network of support can make a Victim of Insanity almost impossible to track, letting him or her disappear completely for long stretches of time.

**CHAPTER TWO
THE LONE VILLAIN**

LIBERTY

JUSTICE

SECURITY

PEACE

PAGE
48

CASE STUDY: BLOODY MARY

An example of a Victim of Insanity in the world of Empire City would be Bloody Mary, also known as La Llorona. Children know Bloody Mary the world over, though whether she has always existed or is merely a woman who has laid claim to that legendary ghost story is debatable. If she is human, then her origins are a mystery — no evidence of her former identity has ever been discovered.

Bloody Mary is responsible for the disappearance of countless children, with the poor, destitute, or uncared-for as her primary victims. The reasons behind the abductions have never been clearly explained. Some speculate that it is to replace a child that died. Others suggest that she abhors the notion of innocence and wishes to destroy all children; more extreme theories surmise she is bent on building a hellish army with which to conquer the spirit world. No one who has studied her has drawn any solid conclusions, and Mary has no desire to explain.

Bloody Mary spends much of her time in a hellish netherworld. Whether this realm existed independently or she has somehow created it from her own dementia is unknown. Regardless of her reasons or the source of her powers, the only thing for certain is that the children she steals are rarely recovered.

Bloody Mary has very few motivations that drive her to interact with others. She has never sought out companionship (unless she sees her victims in that role), and she has no obvious need for money or resources. She has no connections to people or places in our world that have ever been discovered, leaving her an utter cipher to most. If someone were to discover the key to her psychosis, however, they could stand a chance of finally understanding her — and thus finding a way to stop her.

THE SLAVE TO POWER

According to German legend, Dr. Johannes Faust was a learned man who chafed at his mortal limitations. Through years of study of the occult, he learned how to summon the Devil and bind him, forcing the evil spirit to grant him anything he desired. In exchange for ultimate power, however, he bargained away his soul, turning his back on both God and Man in his never-ending quest to satisfy his desire to rule over all.

CASE STUDY: JANUS

Janus, Caliburn's archnemesis, is a study in sociopathy. He is highly intelligent and easily bored. He craves attention and excitement, and is willing to do literally anything to satisfy his needs. He has no sense of empathy, remorse, shame, or guilt, and he easily places his own desires above anyone else's.

Janus is an incredibly charming individual, with a captivating presence and a dazzling wit. His need for constant stimulus and gratification drives him to keep a constant stream of companions at his side (primarily female). He looks on those around him as little more than a source of entertainment — puzzles to be studied and then gleefully unravelled. He cannot stand, however, to be rejected or analysed. His monstrous ego rails at anyone who claims to understand his motivations or label him, as he thinks of himself as beyond such things. Those who attempt to leave him or escape his clutches before he's ready to discard them become new prey; he will never rest until they are utterly destroyed for their "betrayal."

If Janus has a weakness, it is his complete belief in his own superiority. His arrogance literally knows no bounds, causing him to regularly underestimate his adversaries and abandon plans or comrades with little to no warning. The flip side to that arrogance, however, is an unbounded rage when cornered or defeated. It blinds him to consequences and makes him utterly fearless: a dangerous combination for any villain, much less one as devious and ruthless as Janus.

This legend has been reworked thousands of times, from Christopher Marlowe to Goethe to "The Devil and Dan'l Webster." Faust's ultimate end has been refashioned, too, from those stories that enabled him to slip out of his deal with the Devil and find redemption, to those that had him dragged away — willing or unwilling — to Hell. It is Faust, therefore, who represents the third archetype.

The Slave to Power is an old, old archetype for villainy whose visage has been known from ancient times to present day. Examples include: Phaeton, the mortal son of Apollo who died attempting to drive the Sun's chariot across the sky; Neil Gaiman's Roderick Burgess (who imprisons the Sandman); and the characters of H.P. Lovecraft, who all too often discover there are terrible truths behind those Things Man Was Never Meant To Know. The Slave to Power is deaf to

CHAPTER TWO
THE LONE VILLAIN

LIBERTY

JUSTICE

SECURITY

PEACE

PAGE 49

CASE STUDY: DOC CIMITIÈRE

Among the villains in the world of Empire City, one of the most obvious Slaves to Power is Doc Cimitière. Doc Cimitière, once a powerful man in Haiti, grew skilled at calling upon the Voodoo *loa*, but the power he tasted only made him thirst for ultimate dominion over both the spirit and physical world.

Doc Cimitière is the patron saint of cold calculation. Cursed into the form of a *zombi*, he has even turned this state to his advantage, analysing his condition until he found a way to manipulate it for his own ends. His ambition and determination are among his strongest qualities, and cause nearly as much fear in his opponents as his dominion over the *loa*.

Cimitière has little need of money or companionship. His studies afford all the distraction he requires. He does, however, need resources — both henchmen and a safe place to pursue his studies. He typically gets these things from the few individuals he manages to either attract or terrorise into helping him. He also wants revenge, specifically against the Baron, but also against others who have betrayed him. He never forgets a slight, no matter how small.

Doc Cimitière's biggest weaknesses are his lack of emotional connection and his reliance on his followers and henchmen. His thirst for power has caused him to make sacrifices in order to reach his goals. It has driven him past the point of humanity, even of death, forcing him to find others to do his bidding. His detachment, while valuable in his studies, provides an obstacle to his evaluation of others. He has great difficulty in predicting emotional response triggers in others, or in gauging actions based in emotion instead of logic.

CASE STUDY: KREUZRITTER

From the end of the First World War, Kreuzritter has been searching for the secrets of godhood. Using the Norse mythological cycle as a template, his search took him from relative obscurity to a position of favour with the SS during WWII, to the rulership of Thule, the legendary nation he single-handedly raised from the depths of the sea.

For Kreuzritter, the megalomaniacal goal of world domination is more than a dream — it is an obsession that is just outside his grasp ... for now. Between the mystical Nordic armour that gives him control over the elements, and his hard-earned occult powers, Kreuzritter knows that he comes closer to his ambition with every passing day. Like other Slaves to Power, he has an inexhaustible amount of patience. Time is of little consequence to him, as his elemental form does not seem to age as humans do.

Kreuzritter owns his own nation, so he is freed from any concern for resources. Companionship is not a great need for him either, though he might well welcome someone who could share his vision and knowledge, and accept him for what he has become. His true love, however, is knowledge. If someone could offer him rare artefacts or ancient occult secrets that he could not otherwise easily obtain, he would be compelled to forge an alliance — until such time as his allies showed weakness, which he would inevitably attempt to exploit.

---

warnings, caring only for the chance to fit that final piece of the puzzle, and the ability to cheat fate and decide the course of the universe personally.

Slaves to Power have only one eventual goal: the acquisition of power and the trappings thereof. What they actually intend to do with the power once they gain it can vary, although world domination is a popular theme. Unlike Frankenstein Monsters, Slaves to Power are more than ready to take full responsibility for their decisions. They have no one to blame for their career choice but themselves, if indeed they wished to place blame at all. It is more likely that Slaves are perfectly

content with the choices they have made, considering them the only logical path to take to achieve their goals.

Slaves to Power have highly varied backgrounds, but all share the common bond of overweening ambition. Perhaps one Slave was born with a silver spoon in his mouth, but still lusted for more; another Slave was born with nothing and spent her life determined to take from others the opportunities she was denied. Regardless of the background, a Slave will at some point see an opportunity for power beyond his or her wildest dreams and jump for it, never looking back.

As with Faust, the Slave to Power is willing to take shortcuts and make deals in order to achieve his or her ultimate goal. Nothing is sacred and no one is safe — anything may be sacrificed in order to move ahead. Even one's soul or sanity may be bargained if the return is high enough. At the same time, every aspect of the

CHAPTER TWO
THE LONE VILLAIN

Slave's life has a price tag attached; everything is measured by its relative worth, carefully examined and catalogued to give him or her the best return on investment when the time comes to make the trade.

Concerning allies and alliances, Slaves are usually willing to make deals with those whom they feel may prove valuable at a later date. These alliances are always short-lived, though, since the Slave is far too ambitious to share success with anyone. Betrayal is second nature to villains of this archetype, meaning that those allies who trust Slaves to Power are doomed to be disappointed.

When using a Slave to Power as a villain in a *Silver Age Sentinels* game, the keys to effectively playing the character are efficiency, simplicity, and ruthlessness. Slaves to Power don't believe in convoluted plans that take years to germinate. They want what they want (which is everything) as soon as they can get it. They are ultimately pragmatic, and realise that the sooner they achieve their goals, the sooner they can enjoy the fruits of their labours.

As a result, Slaves to Power can easily take more cautious heroes by surprise with their brutal, direct attacks. They waste nothing, creating breathtakingly elegant strategies with a minimum of loose ends. It is imperative not to confuse their ruthless and straightforward methods with blind arrogance or a lack of attention to detail. Of all the archetypes presented, Slaves are the most likely to retreat when necessary and the least likely to become emotionally involved with the pursuit of their goals.

YOU CAN'T ALWAYS GET WHAT YOU WANT

Despite his or her determined self-reliance, every solo villain needs resources such as money, goods, and services. Even the wealthiest of evil schemers needs a little help from time to time in taking over the world, to say nothing of the up-and-comer from the slums. The difficulty in getting help, however, is in retaining independence from those who might offer it.

With that consideration in mind, the question of resources becomes one of great importance. Exactly what does a solo villain need? Where does he or she get it, and from whom? And more importantly, how does the solo villain retain his or her freedom to continue pursuing those dastardly plans?

SEAWOLF

CHAPTER TWO
THE LONE VILLAIN

LIBERTY

JUSTICE

SECURITY

PEACE

PAGE 51

BUILDING BLOCKS

At the base of every successful criminal enterprise are the cornerstones of money, goods, services, flunkies, and friends. Not every operation needs all these items, but every solo villain finds him or herself in need of most of them at one time or another. This section will detail those building blocks of villainy and provide some insight as to how they are used by the lone villain.

MONEY

The first building block, and often the most essential, is money (as discussed in Chapter 1, page 6). It is required not only to provide for personal comfort and security, but also to acquire other necessary items. At the same time, it's unlikely that the average villain has a steady supply of funds kept in the local First National Bank down the street, or a platinum card with a sky-high credit. It's not impossible but it is highly unlikely, especially since such typically mundane forms of affluence are easily traceable. Barter is also an unacceptable means of payment usually; such arrangements can create a web of obligations, requiring "honourable" behaviour in order to continue bartering in the future. Those who have done a good turn for the villain in the past often expect the same courtesy to be extended to them; a situation most find irritating at best and irrational at worst. Nonetheless, such arrangements are made if the situation demands it. Solo villains try to make them as cut and dried as possible, only undertaken if no alternatives are available.

Instead, villains tend to prefer their money in fast, convenient forms that can be converted or hidden easily. Cash is ideal for daily use — thoroughly laundered, of course, through local businesses or organised crime. Cash is accepted by nearly everyone and is easy to come by. The difficulty, however, is that it becomes very unwieldy in copious amounts.

Jewels, precious metals, fine art — all of these are used as currency among the highest ends of the black market. Their worth remains steady, their beauty is undeniable, and possessing such pieces carries its own stature. Jewels and gold are especially useful because they are both portable and easily concealable, and able to stand in for large amounts of cash at the same time. The difficulty with these valuables is that they are much less liquid than cash, and smaller operations don't have the facilities to accept them as currency.

Investments are also valuable things, and something that most shrewd solos will seek out at some point in their lives. While theft is an easy way to increase net worth, having to go back to the well too often is dangerous. A villain will instead find a way to invest his or her money so that it isn't conspicuous, it will grow in value, and it won't by tied directly back to him or her. Some get peripherally involved with organised crime; some will invest in the entertainment or art industries, finding numerous back doors for "private investors." Some will play "angel" to starting companies or "white knight" to failing ones, while others will speculate in real estate, art, currency markets, intellectual properties, and other investment strategies. Most will avoid the stock market as a whole, but some may participate from behind a well-crafted false identity. Regardless, some form of financial security is vital for anyone with far-reaching plans and a distaste for joining forces.

GOODS

The next grouping of items falls under the generic heading of "goods." For every scheme, there is a host of essential materials that must be obtained to make it all come together. From guns to grapples, vehicles to VTOLS, these are the tools to get the job done. All the money in the world is useless if one can't find the proper equipment for a heist.

At the same time, "goods" doesn't just mean special occasion items. It also encompasses food, shelter, secret lairs, and all those other day-to-day items. Still, a wanted felon can't simply walk down to the local hardware store too often without compromising his or her cover. Typically, loners will attempt to either scrounge (that is, to search through discarded items, steal, or create makeshift substitutes) for the proper materials, or else arrange for a hireling to be involved with the day-to-day acquisition of goods and materials.

FLUNKIES

Hirelings, also known as agents, flunkies, or henchmen, are a solo villain's best friends ... in an utterly servile, disposable sort of way. Flunkies are people who are either coerced or paid, or who choose to volunteer their time to work for the villain, either innocently or as a knowing participant in criminal activity. They are not companions or equals. Typically, they only know the portion of the master plan or agenda that pertains to them, though some may know even less, having been duped as to the true nature of their employer.

PAGE 52

CHAPTER TWO
THE LONE VILLAIN

JUSTICE

SECURITY

PEACE

| CRIMINAL INTENT INTRODUCTION | CRIMINAL INTENT ANATOMY OF A VILLAIN | CRIMINAL INTENT THE LONE VILLAIN | CRIMINAL INTENT SUPPERVILLAIN TEAMS | CRIMINAL INTENT ORGANISATIONS | CRIMINAL INTENT MOST WANTED | CRIMINAL INTENT APPENDIX |
| INTRODUCTION | CHAPTER 1 | CHAPTER 2 | CHAPTER 3 | CHAPTER 4 | CHAPTER 5 | APPENDIX |

LIBERTY

JUSTICE

SECURITY

PEACE

Flunkies are expendable by their very nature. They tend to be punks, street-level criminals, or other unskilled individuals with a lack of formal education. Their primary uses are as muscle, couriers, or gofers. They are paid little, though their salary is often high for their social and educational level. As a result, they display a loyalty to the villain bordering on fanaticism, especially if they believe in his or her cause at all. At the same time, the axiom about "getting what you pay for" is especially apt here. Flunkies are best used in combat situations as a flood of bodies to be thrown at the heroes in order to distract them as the villain escapes. They will typically reveal everything they know under pressure, so they cannot be relied upon for sensitive tasks.

Recruitment of flunkies is usually done from among the lower classes and criminal elements. Any villain with strong ideological, political or social beliefs is well served, however, by finding pockets of individuals with like feelings and recruiting from among them. If suitably motivated and/or duped, potential flunkies may even be willing to work without compensation.

SERVICES

Services are beyond the scope of flunkies — tasks which require skilled labour, special clearances, unique specialisations, or qualities that can only be obtained through time, experience or luck. While a self-sufficient villain always tries to do most things him or herself, sometimes it simply isn't possible or wise to do it all. In those cases, a villain needs someone who can perform the needed service with the minimum number of complications.

Typically, these tasks are necessary on a one-time only basis, such as building an Earth-shattering bomb or kidnapping the governor's daughter. Other needed services may be ongoing, such as managing a club where the villain holds a controlling interest, or leading a mercenary group that works with the villain regularly. People who interact regularly (and knowingly) with the villain at this level are sometimes considered lieutenants, but not necessarily. A lieutenant implies that an individual is closely allied to the villain and honoured with a portion of her trust. Many potential masterminds prefer not to enter into such a close relationship with anyone.

EMOTIONAL SUPPORT

For many solo villains, this seems less like a need and more like slow suicide. Nonetheless, no person can exist in a vacuum. Everyone needs someone to provide essential human interaction and support, in order to have the self-confidence to continue on with their plans for world domination. While some will keep their distance from society, their basic human needs often drive them to make at least one exception. The problem this creates is that it afflicts them an easily exploitable weakness, a thought that's never far from their minds. This choice is more common among solo villains early in their careers, though love can strike at any time.

Emotional support can come in many forms. It could be a love interest, a parent, a child, a friend, or even a group of flunkies offering mindless adoration. In rare occasions, the supporting individual may take an active, involved part in the solo's life of crime, though nearly always as a peripheral figure. After all, if they were around constantly as a full partner, the solo villain would no longer be working alone.

More often, however, the supporting figure is someone who is unaware of either the solo's line of work or is unaware of his or her favoured position in the villain's heart. This person may have been duped into believing the villain to be a benign, if eccentric, individual. Most villains will not reveal their true nature for fear of rejection, at least until they are certain of their power over their chosen person. Some villains prefer, however, to keep the person completely in the dark as to the special regard he or she holds for the supporting figure. This is largely done as a way of limiting the amount of danger the villain might be creating for him or herself, but the effectiveness of this tactic is still under debate.

WHO CAN YOU CALL?

Once a villain discovers a need, to whom does he or she turn? Anyone possible. Lone villains can't always be picky about where they procure their necessary items, but there are some accepted locations that can be counted on with a minimum of long-term concern. This section describes those locations, and how the three archetypes handle each type.

THE MARK

The first choice among criminals of all types is the mark, or victim. The fear of punishment and the resultant social blacklisting keep many from a life of crime, but supervillains sweep aside those stumbling blocks in the larger scheme of things. Knowing fate will be far more unpleasant if a criminal doesn't get what he or she wants has a way of providing motivation — and allowing him or her to pass similar motivation on to others.

**CHAPTER TWO
THE LONE VILLAIN**

KALEIDOSCOPE

Theft is typically the first resort of a solo villain. It is easy, efficient, and runs no risk of lasting ties forming between villain and mark. So long as the villain plans well and acts carefully, it should be executed without a hitch. In theory, at least.

The problem with theft in all its forms is that it is only acceptable as an occasional indulgence. Steal too often, or too much, and both heroes and law officers will be on the villain's tail. Blackmail is more acceptable as a long-term arrangement, but requires subtlety and careful planning — it's not practical for immediate capital needs.

All three solo archetypes use society as a great big shopping centre for their daily existence. Frankenstein Monsters are the least likely to choose marks simply for everyday needs, due to their low degree of tolerance for unnecessary risk. They have no qualms about making studied strikes when it suits their plans, however, usually in pursuit of rare items or huge quantities of cash. They choose their victims with care and forethought, and so minimise their risk as much as possible.

Victims of Insanity typically prefer this method to any other, since it does not require them to interact with the real world in any but the most superficial ways. The need to communicate with their marks is limited, which is a bonus for them. Unfortunately, their convoluted view of the world often leaves them with no sense of the consequences of their actions. This often results in inexperienced Victims of Insanity predictably repeating their actions — leading to their arrest. Those who have a sense of strategy or a significantly unpredictable power, however, can use this method of obtaining goods indefinitely.

Slaves to Power also favour this method, but usually only after guile and wit have failed. They choose their marks and approaches carefully, at least when the desired item or information is related to their ultimate goals. When obtaining more general needs, however, such as money, they are often far less careful, preferring a quick clean strike to any sort of detailed planning.

FAMILY

The next best thing to a random victim for obtaining needed resources is a family member. These people helped create the villain, moulding him or her into the person he or she is today. They owe the villain for that, don't they? Regardless of the truth of that statement, family members can have an undeniable appeal to loners as a source of material goods.

When trying to achieve questionable goals on their own, it is imperative to many solo villains to limit the number of ties they have to other people (and thereby the methods through which they can be traced). The circumstances of a person's birth cannot be changed, however, nor can the ties to loved ones be easily erased. Keeping this in mind, some villains find a way to make use of those otherwise awkward connections instead of just attempting to bury them (or their family) to keep them out of sight.

Family members, whether father, mother, sibling, grandparent or aunt, often feel an obligation to the person who shares their name or heritage. This sense of loyalty may be misguided, but when present, it usually outweighs the deeds and attitude of the "lost sheep." This makes family members a reliable source of resources.

Frankenstein Monsters are the most likely to make use of this source, as their sense of entitlement and injury from those who brought them up is particularly strong. They are also masters of manipulation and can turn the slightest twinge of guilt or obligation to their advantage. They, more than either of the other archetypes, will make their criminal status known to their family members as a means of manipulating their relatives.

Victims of Insanity are the least likely to consciously take advantage of this source, for they are often forced by their illness to cut all ties with their pasts, whether they wish to do so or not. Even for those who would prefer to stay close to their families, grave mental illness can quickly surpass the ability of loved ones to communicate with Victims or care for them, forcing an estrangement. It is rare that they will refuse help willingly given, however, should someone related to them make the first step. For those few who can make use of this source, it quickly becomes one of their first choices for help.

Slaves to Power are very particular in their method of using family, frequently seeking out distantly related individuals and passing over immediate family altogether. They rely on the strength of their name and heritage rather than familial affection to secure what they need. They also will specifically choose individuals who can help them further their cause, as opposed to someone who might be more willing but have less to offer.

ACQUAINTANCES

Occasionally a villain will find someone with whom he or she can share an unusual degree of friendly feeling or respect. These individuals are sufficiently moved to help out of regard for the criminal or his or her cause. The solo is likewise moved to refrain from forcing his or her will upon them. Such relationships are rare but highly prized. They always hold the possibility of great drama.

These acquaintances consist of individuals not related to or victimised by the solo, whom the villain can call upon for help. Among heroes, these individuals might be called friends. That cannot be the case here, however, as relationships among solos are typically marred by differences in status, competing interests, or a lack of honesty about the criminal's true nature.

Frankenstein Monsters find it difficult to make use of acquaintances, due in part to their extraordinarily self-centred outlook on life and their insistence on dwelling in the past. These limitations make it difficult for a Monster to connect with anyone in the present on anything more than a superficial level.

Victims of Insanity also find using acquaintances to be difficult. Those with particularly extreme mental illnesses find communicating with anyone to be terrifically challenging on any level, much less in forming the necessary mutual respect for a long-lasting relationship. At the same time, those Victims capable of communicating with others are often highly charismatic and able to use this method with astounding success.

Slaves of Power are the most likely to use this method. Their ability to emotionally distance themselves from their goals and surroundings allows them a certain clarity of vision. They are the most likely to have informed opinions as to their likes and dislikes, and to be able to respect and admire ability, talent or dedication in those around them.

OTHER SOLOS

The interaction between solo villains is usually the closest thing a loner has to a relationship between equals, and thus is the least likely to involve overt coercion. Regardless of the compatibility of their ultimate goals, solos will inevitably find that they have much in common, from their difficulties in evading capture to similar desires for aloof independence. While their natures as lone villains prevent them from joining forces or becoming partners, they can typically hammer

CHAPTER TWO
THE LONE VILLAIN

LIBERTY

JUSTICE

SECURITY

PEACE

PAGE
55

out a short-term working arrangement with little difficulty. Barter is the most common arrangement between solo villains for need procurement, but long-standing arrangements — or future considerations — are not unknown.

Both Frankenstein Monsters and Slaves to Power are adept at making use of these resources. Monsters are more likely to seek out such an arrangement than are Slaves, but neither is adverse to the idea when a good opportunity comes along. Victims of Insanity run into the same communication problems here as described elsewhere, but are more able to bypass those issues with other criminals as they aren't forced to make an emotional connection or dissemble about their livelihood in order to get along.

HEROES

It might seem that a hero would be the last place a villain would turn for help, regardless of their needs. Most of the time this would be correct. In truth, however, heroes can be a great source for daily needs, such as money, cash, or favours.

The nature of a villain is to be manipulative and act in their own best interest above anyone else's. The nature of a hero is to help others, and to place the welfare of someone else above their own. Given a halfway sympathetic villain and a hero who is overly empathic, and you have the possibility of a match made in heaven — at least as far as the villain is concerned.

In order to get help from a hero, the hero must feel connected to the villain in some way: having accidentally helped turn the villain away from "good;" sympathising with a trauma the villain has undergone; or perhaps a physical connection by family ties, common acquaintances, or magical artefacts. In addition, the hero must feel that he is either in the villain's debt or can "save" the villain, turning her away from the path of evil. Naturally, these feelings play right into the hands of a sufficiently skilled manipulator.

Frankenstein Monsters are particularly adept at using heroes to fill their needs, as are Victims of Insanity. Both can typically point to an outside force that changed them from a normal citizen to their current diabolical selves, whether that assessment is accurate or not. Both have a substantial number of prime emotional manipulators among their numbers. Victims of Insanity are often able to successfully manipulate heroes when they are unable to affect anyone else, if only by showing how utterly they are at the mercy of their illnesses.

Slaves to Power, on the other hand, rarely manage to use this tactic successfully unless they can make their end goal seem virtuous. They typically have no wish to blame anyone for their current state, so pity is never aroused on their behalf. Megalomania also doesn't exactly engender empathy. They are, however, the most successful in turning heroes to their dark path by using the do-gooders' heroic tendencies against them.

WE ALL HAVE OUR WAYS

The manner in which a criminal commits an illegal act is as distinctive as a fingerprint to the trained eye. Whole avenues of investigative science are devoted to the study of the M.O., or *modus operandi*. This applies not only to forensic evidence, such as fingerprints, DNA, and blood spatters, but also more generally to preferred types of victims and which approach to take to a situation.

No villain can be equally skilled at all things. Most will find their strong suit and stick to it, enjoying an increasing amount of success as they become more practiced. This can prove invaluable to investigating heroes in determining which villain committed which crime. This is especially true when dealing with solos, who make active efforts to minimise the tracks leading back to them. Some villains are capable of changing tactics regularly to avoid notice (specifically Slaves to Power), but most are not.

Choosing methods of operation for the solo villains in your games is an important part of building a consistent character. It lets your heroes build a relationship with a solo, and then lets that solo surprise them now and again when he or she changes procedures. They can be used to express a solo's personality or ambitions, and can build patterns in a campaign that players will recognise and enjoy. The following are the building blocks of M.O.s — the means by which a villain's needs are met.

PHYSICAL CRIME

The first (and by far the most straightforward method) is physical crime. Assault, robbery, theft, breaking and entering, grand theft auto, kidnapping ... these are all methods of taking what one wants.

Physical crime can be perpetrated directly by the villain, available flunkies, or hired mercenaries. It is best used sporadically or as a last resort, as it is the most difficult to pull off without attracting attention. Still, sometimes there are no alternatives, and failure isn't typically an option for the determined villain.

| CRIMINAL INTENT INTRODUCTION | CRIMINAL INTENT ANATOMY OF A VILLAIN | CRIMINAL INTENT THE LONE VILLAIN | CRIMINAL INTENT SUPPERVILLAIN TEAMS | CRIMINAL INTENT ORGANISATIONS | CRIMINAL INTENT MOST WANTED | CRIMINAL INTENT APPENDIX |
| INTRODUCTION | CHAPTER 1 | CHAPTER 2 | CHAPTER 3 | CHAPTER 4 | CHAPTER 5 | APPENDIX |

LIBERTY

JUSTICE

SECURITY

PEACE

This method is primarily committed against strangers or institutions who have no ties to the villain that could be exploited through other means. The only individuals excepted from this type of action are other heroes or villains; in other words, people with whom the risk of capture, failure or retribution is high enough to discourage the solo. Victims of this type of crime often feel outraged and insist on justice. There is almost always some degree of physical evidence left behind by a crime of this sort, although a careful criminal will eliminate as many traces as possible.

MANIPULATION

As stated earlier, many villains are masters of emotional manipulation. Their lack of conscience allows them to mimic emotions they don't feel, using their talents to bend those around them to their will. Villains are ultimately pragmatic in pursuit of their goals. Those personality traits combine to ensure that if a weakness presents itself, a truly skilled villain will take advantage of it without a second thought.

This tactic is most commonly used against both heroes (or people who are truly good at heart) and family or friends of the villain. In order for this tactic to be successful, the victim must be a relatively upstanding individual without any obvious blackmail material available — a victim who can be blackmailed can be controlled without the subtle and time consuming methods required to manipulate the truly innocent. The victim must also possess some emotional vulnerability on which the villain can prey.

Victims of manipulation will often try to impede an investigation, not realising the degree to which they've been exploited. They will act to protect the criminal, whether consciously or not. Unless the solo's deeds can be exposed to the victim, thus cancelling the criminal's emotional hold over the victim, it is nearly impossible to gain a victim's co-operation. There is very little physical evidence associated with this approach.

EXTORTION

This term covers any method in which threatening behaviour is used to coerce a source of possible assistance, including extortion, blackmail, threats of harm to the victim's loved ones, etc. This tactic has the benefit of being low-profile. Those upon whom it works aren't likely to turn the villain in to the authorities, out of fear that the threats will come to pass.

The problem with this type of activity is that it must be carefully monitored. If the villain asks for too much or presses the victim too hard, he or she may run to the police out of desperation. At the same time, success with this method relies on inducing a paralysing fear in the victim. Not every individual will react this way, so research must be done on the individual beforehand to ensure that he or she is psychologically suited to this type of manipulation.

Victims of extortion want to be rescued from their predicament but fear the consequences. They often present a passive-aggressive attitude to investigators, refusing to help but urging them on at the same time. If they can be convinced of their safety (and the safety of those they care about), they will readily turn on the criminals who tried to exploit them.

DECEPTION

Deception is used when the other tactics are too heavy handed to work effectively, or when one's reputation would harm the chances of achieving the desired end result. This tactic is often used against family, friends, or heroes in an effort to gain assistance without revealing either the villain's true nature or the real reason behind the request. It's a way that the solo villain can get what he or she needs without alienating the victim, avoiding any messy confrontations (at least until the solo's deception is revealed — it's only good until the cover is blown). This method is the one most commonly used, as it works with nearly everyone and has the lowest risk involved. As with manipulation, victims of deception are resistant to investigators unless the deception is proven to them. Some physical evidence can be found with this method, as part of the deception is a normal appearance and demeanour.

THE JOB DESCRIPTION

Quite a bit has been mentioned about how a villain prepares to act, but what's the end result? Most solo villains have large, overarching plans. These can be carving out a kingdom, conquering the world, wreaking vengeance on person or group X, or simply getting whatever he or she feels is due. The nuts and bolts of how a villain sets about engineering the end result is discussed herein. When a GM runs a villain, it is always best to have a long-term game plan. Different solos have different goals; some individuals may even have a signature crime that they return to repeatedly.

ACQUISITIONS

As the name suggests, this type of work focuses on acquiring some type of object. It can be an ongoing quest, such as finding all the great pieces of art by a certain artist or valuable items that follow a certain theme (examples are cats, or rubies). It can also be a sporadic event, only rarely undertaken to acquire a specific item or piece of information.

Breaking and entering, cat burglary, and grand tactical plans to defeat impressive security are all large parts of this type of scenario. This is not the sort of thing to be undertaken impulsively, since failure will almost certainly get one caught — at least, it will if there is no backup plan. Slaves to Power engage in this activity more than the other archetypes, though all will partake from time to time.

Green Ronin is a prime example of someone who spends most of her time engaged in this pursuit. She seeks the other portion of the magical artefact that creates her signature green armour, as well as powerful artefacts in general. If Green Ronin is spotted in the area, it's a good bet that something valuable will soon go missing — or perhaps already has.

BLOOD AND GUTS

This type of work is one of the most horrific — and dangerous -in which a villain can engage. Serial killers, serial rapists, and mass murderers fall into this category — individuals who engage in violent crime to fulfil a twisted need, or to make a particularly violent statement to the world. This type of crime inevitably excites a huge public outcry and makes heroes sit up and take notice. Violent crime on any scale is dangerous and the rewards are typically few, but on a large scale the returns diminish even further. Only those who feel a pressing need to indulge in this behaviour are likely to commit these crimes.

Of the solo archetypes listed in this chapter, the ones most likely to commit these crimes are the more extreme Victims of Insanity, driven to desperate and bloodthirsty acts by their psychoses. Frankenstein Monsters will also take part in these crimes, but only if the circumstances are right. They rarely engage in this type of violent behaviour randomly. Slaves to Power will typically not do blood-and-guts work unless it clearly benefits their overall goal; the publicity and outrage such events draw is rarely beneficial in the long run.

Bloody Mary is an example of a villain who engages in blood-and-guts work on a regular basis. She is exceptional in that she leaves little evidence of the children she abducts, but few of them are ever seen again.

I SPY, YOU SPY

This is a variant of acquisitions work, where information is the target. This is espionage, pure and simple, where data is gathered and sold to the highest bidder, whether the information was collected by the solo directly, or stolen from another source. This type of job lends itself to stealthy and skilful solos, rather than larger groups of villains; often, this type of information is only valuable so long as the mark does not realise he or she was compromised.

The leading motivations for engaging in espionage are greed and strongly held political, ethical, or moral beliefs. Slaves to Power and Frankenstein Monsters both engage in this sort of work as needed, although Slaves are better suited for the task. Victims of Insanity don't often engage in espionage, as the required subtlety is often incompatible with the mental illnesses with which so many are afflicted.

An example of a solo villain who engages in espionage is Alice, Queen of Hearts. She was trained to serve the British government as a spy and assassin. After parting ways with Her Majesty's black operations unit, she has continued to perform the jobs for which she was trained under the contract of a mercenary, selling her services to the highest bidder.

VENDETTA

Revenge can be a very strong motivating factor for all flavours of solo villain, but only rarely does it become a type of crime within itself. The vendetta category is for those occasions when revenge becomes the subject of over-arching plans that span years. Typically, a solo who embarks upon a vendetta campaign is attempting to exact revenge on a large group of individuals or a massive organisation, requiring Machiavellian manipulation and labyrinthine schemes.

Frankenstein Monsters are the most common proponents of vendettas. Victims of Insanity will also engage in them, frequently leading to truly twisted expressions of vengeance against those who may only be peripherally connected to the villain. Slaves to Power will sometimes engage in this sort of activity, but only as they close in on their larger goal and begin to feel comfortable — or when they discover their machinations ruined.

Janus is an example of a villain who has lived for his vendetta against both Caliburn and all heroes, priding himself on his reputation as a "costume hunter." His crimes are all directly related to his need for vengeance, and there is little else that can attract his interest.

THE SOLO BEHIND THE SCENES

It's easy to find mentions of the highly public villains, the ones whose caped and costumed exploits make a splash on news screens and front pages around the globe. There are a growing number of solo villains, however, who are content to make a nice living behind the scenes. Not tormented by extreme dementia, a thirst for fame, or overweening ambition, they plot quietly and let others take the falls.

These people are sometimes thought of as the middle-management level of villainy, where evil entrepreneurs make their way in the world on the backs of innocents, without ever directly lifting a finger. They come in many shapes and sizes, and not all of them have pseudonyms or wear cool costumes. Many of these individuals could be considered masterminds, but some are just looking for a short-term profit.

ARMS DEALERS

Arms dealers are prime candidates for solo villains, as well as excellent sources for assistance. Whether they are in business just for the money or for a "higher purpose," their job is distributing vehicles for death — or anything else a villain might need. Perhaps some misguided soul accidentally delivered the bomb that killed the mayor, but this is the person who made the whole thing happen.

Arms dealers are often content to simply be support personnel, but some decide to carry out their own agendas. These individuals can be quite dangerous, if only because of their international weapons and mercenary connections. They can barter arrangements of weapons for assignments, remaining largely untraceable. If an investigator gets too close, the best connected can disappear into any number of cities around the world without so much as a whisper left behind.

STINGER

Marc Cestrioni made a name for himself in the US Army during his stint in the Middle East as both a nasty, mean-tempered brawler, and a wizard at scrounging. The man seemed to have a magic touch: he could find exactly what he wanted, precisely when he wanted it. This was a trait that got him off the hook more than once.

When his tour of duty was over, he stayed tight with most of his army contacts; he was also adept at making new friends wherever he travelled. When his illegal arms dealing caught up with him, he moved back among the other Western expatriates who call Egypt home. He got the nickname "Stinger" for an infamous deal during this time, when he sold a few "liberated" Stinger missiles to a local Afghani warlord, and was offered one of the man's daughters as a bonus.

Stinger maintains a discreet yet thorough online presence, and his connections with other weapons dealers span the globe. There's no one he won't sell to if the price is right, and very few things he can't get. If a villain needs something special in the world of conventional arms, Stinger's the man to see.

MONEY MEN

For every villain with a plan for global domination, there's a shadowy figure standing somewhere in the background providing the resources to make it happen. These individuals, known collectively as money men, don't like to get involved with the day-to-day stock and trade of villainy. They far prefer to quietly finance the operations of like-minded individuals, usually through an army of holding companies, false fronts, and shadow corporations. In return, they hope to profit handsomely on their investment.

Money men may be masterminds instead of just generous investors. Some of them conceive of their plans long before finding someone to execute them, and wait patiently in their corner office suites for a sinister agent to appear. These individuals can be difficult to deal with because they are born connivers. Leaders of business and captains of industry, they know how best to cover their tracks, and employ a legion of lawyers to exploit the world "legally."

REBECCA HELA

Rebecca Hela was born to the privileged life. She had the pedigree of an old, moneyed name, but the fortune that had once accompanied it had largely dried up. She married into new money, and proceeded to convert her husband's respectable fortune into a multi-million dollar media empire on the strength of her connections and business savvy. She retired to the background after spending twenty years in the front ranks, and most financial pundits believed her to be happily retired. They were only half right.

LIBERTY

JUSTICE

SECURITY

PEACE

Along with her wealth and status, Rebecca also inherited her mother's position as a hereditary priestess of Loki, the Norse trickster. She lived through most of her youth unaware her mother held to the ancient ways, only knowing that she was a strong supporter of Thule's politics. What Rebecca didn't realise, however, was that her mother was the head of a large underground sect, called Loki's Daughters; they sought to overthrow the modern religious institutions.

When Rebecca's mother's died, the other Daughters came to explain her new position. She willingly took on the mantle of priestess, and has since used her connections through the sect, society, and the world of finance to find villains to take on her assignments in exchange for financial support. She never takes any action herself, but she and the other Daughters seem well pleased with the results of her efforts.

EVIL SCIENTISTS

Evil scientists are just what they sound like; men and women of science, but who use their knowledge to forward selfish (or at least socially unacceptable) ends. These individuals are not ones to prowl the streets personally. Instead, an evil scientist creates others to do his or her bidding.

Evil scientists typically find themselves drawn to forbidden areas of science, driven to discover "That Which Man Was Not Meant To Know." Alternatively, they lack the ethics or morals that modern society demands of its intellectual leaders and thus reject society's claims upon their behaviour. An evil scientist's genius can create all manner of items, from robots to ingenious weapons to clones to mind-control rays.

An evil scientist can easily be a mastermind, but can also be the demented researcher bent on nothing more than conducting his or her questionable experiments in peace. Regardless of his or her position toward villainy, however, evil scientists are dangerous if only due to the unpredictability of what abomination will next poke its way out of their labs.

DR. SCYLLA KENDI

Dr. Kendi was one of the most promising young researchers at a private university until one of her test subjects died during a "routine" exam. The investigation that followed uncovered disturbing evidence of a dozen different ethics violations, including unauthorised outpatient surgeries, all well documented in her private journals. Her grants were suspended, and the police arrived with a warrant only to find she had mysteriously disappeared.

Five years later, Dr. Kendi resurfaced in the employ of the Darwinian Society, a scientific and research think-tank organisation. She uses the name Kendra Phillips now. With the Society footing the bills, she can happily experiment however she deems appropriate with the subjects provided by the Society. If the Society should have ties to suspected warlords or supervillains ... their money funds research just as anyone else's does, and at least they can see the value in her work.

HIRED GUNS

Hired guns, or mercenaries, are servants to no one but themselves. Their expertise is in their ability to fight, kill, and disappear without a trace. Hired guns may work either short or long-term contracts, depending on the relationship the mercenary has with his or her employers.

Eventually, most mercenaries grow tired of working at someone else's beck and call. Many formulate long-term dreams, working their way through a number of employers and positions until everything they need to achieve their ultimate goal is in place. While they may work with other solos on a specific job, they are never considered a flunky. They will stay around as long as the money (or the project) demands their attention.

MAGNUM

Magnum, born William Dumas, grew up in the Texas hill country. Bill joined the military out of high school, where his uncanny talents for sharpshooting and physical combat first became apparent. He tried out for Special Forces but was denied due to his psychological profile. This defeat infuriated Dumas, who gave up on military service. He received a dishonourable discharge a few months later after assaulting another enlisted man.

Once he left the military behind, Dumas was lost. In order to remain sane, he stepped up his training regimen in both firearms and hand-to-hand combat. A local drug runner hired him as security from Houston to Oklahoma City. He did such a good job that he became a full-time employee of the cartel until he branched out on his own three years ago. Magnum took his handle from one of his favourite types of guns, the .44 Magnum. He uses it as his signature weapon and is very accurate with it.

SUPERVILLAIN TEAMS

The only thing more fearsome than a single supervillain is a team of them. Just as heroes find it advantageous to unite into groups, supervillains regularly join ranks to better pursue their criminal and nefarious goals. Used properly, the supervillain team can be the toughest challenge *Silver Age Sentinels* heroes can face. This chapter examines the reasons why supervillains form into such associations, and the opportunities that these unions present.

The definition of a supervillain "team" is a group of three or more metahumans (or masked adventurers) who ally with each other and use a common name while pursuing some form of "evil." Refer to the "Deadly Duos" sidebar for instances of two villains who work in tandem (see page 76), and the next chapter, "Organisations," for larger supervillain or criminal-led societies.

A GATHERING OF VILLAINY

The main use for supervillain teams in *Silver Age Sentinels* is to provide powerful adversaries for heroes and allow for more complex criminal activity. The villain team can challenge heroes in a number of ways: tactical considerations, psychological aspects, and other role-playing opportunities that a single enemy doesn't provide.

A well-designed evil team can be a hero's nightmare, with a vast array of powers and skills that must be countered, often all at the same time. While a solo villain can be only one place at a time, a group can split up, hitting heroes from many directions at once. They lay ambushes, rescue each other, and use complex tactics to present a formidable threat. Teams are often the most significant force that heroes can encounter, giving each hero something to do, or someone to fight.

This nefarious society should have a reason for existence — a goal they are striving towards. Why have these miscreants turned their amazing powers and skills towards crime? Why have they joined forces to pursue an evil agenda?

The following section describes several reasons teams can form and characteristics of each type. Picking one origin, then adding members with different agendas is a great way of creating dynamic groups that seem "true" to the setting of *Silver Age Sentinels*. This "mix and match" approach can result in enemies that seem ripped from the comics and hurled onto the gaming table. Just like alliances of heroes, member villains may join the group for different purposes and might be at odds with each other. For example, a group of criminals devoted to a particular social agenda might also have one member who's only in it for revenge against a particular hero. Another might just be there for the money. A team brought together by a would-be world conqueror could have members who've been blackmailed into criminal activity as well as those who embrace the leader's cause, perhaps even the (potentially redeemable) children of the leader, harnessed with bonds of guilt and coercion.

Additionally, some supervillain teams change their reason for joining together. A group with no luck conquering the world might become the sanctioned defenders of their home nation. A group of superpowered convicts who escaped prison together could become the pawns of a more powerful supervillain. Alternately, a behind-the-scenes mastermind who possesses something the team members need to survive might blackmail them into more serious crimes.

Obviously, in the vast number of comics published, there are a hundred exceptions to these classifications. Teams are not always so cut and dried; origins often overlap, motives differ, and long-lasting teams have twisted histories. These guidelines are not exhaustive, nor are they meant to limit creativity. Instead, they should help spur the imagination and generate ideas as vital and exciting as any presented in comic books.

A STRONG AND PASSIONATE LEADER

The most common of all group origins is when a visionary assembles other outlaws to help him or her accomplish a goal, ranging from criminal activity to world domination. Most of the time, the founder is in charge (though rivals within or outside the team can oust him or her).

The leader is not necessarily the strongest or most powerful of the team members, but usually has the most forceful personality. Furthermore, the leader is the most passionate about the reason the team has formed. Usually, he or she is the most experienced villain of the crew. In some cases, the founder has resources beyond the other teammates, making them more like employees than equals.

LIBERTY

JUSTICE

SECURITY

PEACE

CHAPTER THREE
SUPERVILLAIN TEAMS

PAGE
62

There are many reasons a supervillain might choose to seek an alliance with others of his or her ilk: a need for specific or additional powers and skills; strength in numbers; allies against a common enemy; or partners to help advance a particular agenda. Several of the more common reasons follow. Other sections of this chapter present additional ways in which a team might form, many of which can be used for teams founded by a charismatic leader.

PAWNS ON A CHESSBOARD

Despite all their powers and fiendish imaginations, sometimes supervillains are nothing more than dupes for a more powerful and cunning leader. Some diabolical supervillains use their fellow criminals as mere tools to be used and discarded, or sacrificed if necessary. In these cases, the leader has a specific purpose for his or her team to fulfil, often as a decoy or distraction so that another, "true" plan can be enacted without interruption.

A sample decoy team might be a group of convicts broken out of prison and given new weaponry, powers, and masked identities. Alternately, it could be a motley crew of hard-luck prisoners, recruited from the maximum-security wing of a metahuman-asylum or otherwise rescued from obscurity. In either case, these pawns are often sent on missions to cause mayhem; they are sure to attract the attention of the heroes, usually at the exact moment a distraction is needed. They could even be sent to ambush the heroes directly. A leader might send a decoy team on a mid-town crime spree (or to commit wanton destruction), far from the secret missile silo the leader plans to plunder.

Teams formed as decoys may or may not know their benefactor. In most cases, the leader is smart enough to keep behind the scenes, or use a disguise to confuse and mislead the team members. When the heroes defeat, capture, and question the villains, they get no solid information as to who's responsible.

Decoy teams are often less carefully planned and can be poorly balanced. They are not designed for the long haul, and their activities are blatant and usually destructive. Their members are not the elite of the underworld — they are often the equivalent of one-hit wonders, once-solo villains who tried the big time and failed miserably.

Frequently, the decoy villains will be completely misled about their team's agenda, thinking they've been assembled for one reason, when in reality they are nothing more than a smokescreen. Betrayal by the leader is frequent. Any newfound powers they've been given may be temporary or have limiting drawbacks. They could have weapons and equipment that become powerless and ineffectual after a certain time limit, or are otherwise booby-trapped and sabotaged. A thoroughly diabolical leader might think nothing of granting powers to a group of pawns, even if the source of these powers is lethal over time. Decoy villains who realise they've been had might give the heroes all the information they know to better defeat the villain's master plan, or could turn heroic for a desperate assault against their back-stabbing master.

Another decoy strategy is for a team of villains to masquerade as heroes for various reasons: to gain access to classified information; divine other heroes' identities; or as an elaborate alibi for further criminal activity. Using powers of mind control and influence, a group like this might gain financial sponsorship or official sanction, by which they can harass the heroes from a position of respectability. These teams rarely keep to the straight-and-narrow path, however, despite the rewards it yields. In exceptional circumstances, villains-turned-heroes could discover that it's good to be good and try to redeem themselves. Who will believe them, though?

VILLAINS BY NECESSITY

Leaders recruit through insidious means, often using blackmail, extortion, coercion, and addiction. A mastermind might try to bind other villains to him or herself through a variety of these methods. Leaders will find some weak point in potential members' personalities, powers, or backgrounds and exploit that weakness, forcing the lesser villains to join them. This can range from pressuring a loner to "join the program," to cruelly pressing a reformed criminal back into the life.

Evidence of a dark secret can blackmail a victim indefinitely, forcing him or her to work for the group. A leader may promise that "after this one job" all will be forgotten, the photo negatives destroyed, or any files erased ... on the other hand, a vile or ignoble individual will casually break his or her word, keeping the secret over the victim's head. This is a great technique to turn criminals who've retired from crime back into the fold. Villains defeated by the heroes can return as unwilling parts of a team, forced again to don costumes and break the law.

Another type of blackmail is emotional. Supervillains are not the most psychologically stable of individuals, and a manipulative leader can find it easy to bind others to his or her cause. Though the leader might

LIBERTY

JUSTICE

SECURITY

PEACE

**CHAPTER THREE
SUPERVILLAIN TEAMS**

REQUIEM

be abusive, pushing followers into a dangerous lifestyle, some emotionally weak supervillains might not realise they are being used. Alternately, these poor villains could recognise their situation and still be unable to break free, tragically continuing a life of crime solely for acceptance from someone who pulls their strings.

Coercion is a nasty method to acquire allies, but it could be the only way to fill the ranks, or to get a necessary supervillain to join up. A leader could find out that a former supercriminal has a young child or other dependent. He or she would then kidnap that innocent victim to use as a hostage, forcing the retired criminal to help the group. These villains, loyal while the hostage is threatened, could then turn on the leader and aid the heroes.

Addiction makes a "user" vulnerable; a leader who can provide whatever is needed gains control over the addict. This addiction can be an emotional requirement, or something physical. Perhaps it is a drug that gives a metahuman his or her powers, or it's an antidote to a deadly condition from which the villain suffers. Either way, addiction can turn a villain into a pawn of the "dealer," unless the heroes can find an alternative source or break the addiction.

STRENGTH IN NUMBERS

Team leaders aren't necessarily the most powerful of villains. Occasionally, they're weak and pathetic, at least physically. Whether crippled evil geniuses, living brains in wheeled canisters, deformed madmen kept alive in exotic power suits, or non-powered criminal masterminds, these leaders find it advantageous to assemble a team who can better carry out their plans. Alternately, it might be that the leader is tired of being beaten by the heroes, and has recruited a few friends to help out.

Many complex schemes require more than one person, and assembling a group is the most direct means of accomplish them. When supercriminal activity runs the risk of encountering heroic interference, simple tactical sense suggests fighting fire with fire. Thus, the only solution is to assemble a seasoned band of costumed criminals to combat the heroes.

THE REVENGE SQUAD

Nothing unites villains more easily than a common foe. This type of team is united (either by design or circumstance) specifically to deal with a particular hero or team. When a villain's plans have been thwarted one-too-many times by a hero (or group), smart criminals often decide that they need allies to succeed. In this case, the best (and most obvious) allies are those who already bear a grudge.

A revenge squad is often a volatile and powerful mob, with the supervillains in it barely held in check by the leader. The leader is usually the hero's (or heroes') most vehement enemy. Occasionally, revenge squads are democracies with all members considered equal, but more often there is a clear leader distinguished by a past history with the hero(es). This villain is usually the founder because he or she is either smarter than anyone else, has a cunning plan, or has the resources and ability to keep the team functioning.

A vengeance agenda is the most threatening motive the heroes might face, because revenge squad villains are going to make it personal — every time. They'll cross the invisible line that heroes and villains dance on either side of. The revenge squad will threaten heroes' families, try to reveal secret identities, and pursue revenge to its bitter end, even beyond the point of common sense and self-preservation. Revenge squad villains won't back down or flee because it becomes unprofitable for them to continue. Their loyalty is not to their teammates, but to the opportunity that the squad provides. Of the many types of supervillain groups, revenge squads are the most informal, yet the least likely to break up. As long as the heroes continue to hinder them, the squad-members will continue to work together.

The ultimate revenge squad is comprised of the heroes' greatest foes. This collection of arch-nemeses might have banded together for a grand scheme, but more likely they've joined together because they need allies. They also want an audience to share in the defeat of the heroes, and don't want to be left out if someone else does it. One last reason is that supervillains often like to gloat, and do so as much as they can. They seek audiences for their evil activities, and the revenge squad is the best forum for their litany of vendettas and grievances. Their meetings are mostly made up of members regaling each other of the indignities the heroes have inflicted upon them in the past and the specific manner by which they will avenge themselves.

The members of a revenge squad can also differ as to what type of retribution they seek. While the squad's leader might want to see the heroes utterly destroyed, others in the squad could be satisfied if the heroes are publicly disgraced, framed and imprisoned, or forced to acknowledge the villains' superiority. Dedicated squad-members might not rest until they have provoked the heroes to cross the line and break the law. Unfortunately, a revenge squad with differing goals can fall apart at the moment of truth, especially if some members feel the leader is going too far. In these cases, a hero might find a sympathetic ally in an unexpected place ... from within the revenge squad itself.

FAN CLUB

In extreme cases, revenge squads come to loathe (or grudgingly respect) their heroic enemy so much that they end up defining themselves only in opposition to their long-time nemesis. They'll avoid fighting other heroes altogether, and might even aid the hero against other villains who aren't part of the revenge squad. Obsessively, they can even remain together after the hero has retired (or died), becoming an odd sort of social club rather than a villain's league. In some cases, this twisted fan club will continue the super-rivalry with anyone else who takes up the original hero's costume or identity. It doesn't necessarily make sense, but it really doesn't have to when supervillain egos are concerned.

These teams don't always have to be united against a hero or hero team. A revenge-squad might be the remnants of a previous supervillain team, betrayed by their former leader and assembled for vengeance. Villain-vs.-villain conflicts could escalate quickly, with innocent civilians caught in shifting battlegrounds.

EXAMPLE

An unethical chemical company has been dumping toxic waste upstream from a town, killing many children and giving a handful of the townsfolk metahuman abilities. Now superpowered, a small group of grieving parents band together and vow to make the uncaring company pay for flouting the law. United and masked, they strike back at the chemical company, destroying its plants and targeting the CEO and Board of Directors. Such a situation creates a horrible ethical dilemma for the heroes. Do they fight back against the revenge squad and take the side of the law? Or do they try to right the wrongs and see that the company's malfeasance is exposed and its leaders are appropriately punished. Do they make the supervillains pay for their own illegal actions to the extent of the law, or petition a court to be lenient, handing down reduced or symbolic punishment?

LIBERTY

JUSTICE

SECURITY

PEACE

**CHAPTER THREE
SUPERVILLAIN TEAMS**

Alternately, revenge squads can seek retribution against social organisations, governments, or nations. Squad members might be victims of government policies that have caused them distress or caused harm to their loved ones. In these cases, their zeal for vengeance becomes illegal activity, rather than legal means of restitution through law enforcement and the legal system. Perhaps the courts have failed the squad members, and they're striking back against injustice by crossing the line.

TRUE BELIEVERS

The most fanatic supervillains have an agenda other than personal profit. These are villains with a cause. They're often charismatic enough to create a cultlike following of other supervillains, and even misguided heroes. The cause may be criminal or it might be noble, but the methods by which the team pursues it are criminal. When it comes to their agenda, these teams feel that the ends justify the means, no matter who gets hurt.

With this type of group, the leader is usually an outspoken advocate of a political, religious, or social agenda. It can be anything, from a morally acceptable cause to a politically difficult position. The reasons might be ones that heroes should support, but cannot. These teams could even stand for morally repugnant political stances, such as racism, cultural exclusion, or persecution against social or ethnic minorities.

Examples of this type of group include mutants who fight for the rights of their brethren in a world that fears them; right-wing fascists who wish to resurrect the Nazi war-regime; or former Soviet supersoldiers trying to bring about the return of communism and the Cold War. These groups might be drawn from the pages of history books or today's headlines, such as a group of Vietnamese metahumans with superpowers born from side-effects of chemical weapons or a Serbian metahuman team who has vowed to strike back at the United Nations for its policies towards their country.

This team's leader uses the team's activities to accomplish several objectives. Primarily, the team is a means of acting directly against the forces that oppose their agenda. Secondly, the team offers protection against those who would challenge its politics with fists and fury. All of the members of the team tend to share the leader's vision, but idealistic solidarity is not required; mercenaries are always welcome.

The example of the superpowered victims assembled for revenge against a chemical company's misdeeds, described earlier, can also be construed as a political agenda, specifically targeted against a single enemy. If that team chose instead to go for the big time and strike out at all large corporations who endanger civilians with unethical practices, they would fall into this category instead.

Sometimes, agendas don't have to make a whole lot of sense. A surprising amount of supervillain activity in the 1970s and 80s was due to normally-sane supervillains trying to rid the world of golden marshmallow-filled snack cakes, or trying to hijack the world's supply of crème-filled chocolate cupcakes for their own nefarious purposes. Inexplicably, these uncharacteristic crimes ended with the heroes sharing these tasty snacks with the villains as they were marched off to jail.

FATAL ACCOMPLICES

Supercriminals might seek alliances because they believe it is their destiny to join forces. In such instances, they see themselves as inevitable kings and queens of the world, with the unification of force being the only way to achieve this destiny. After all, while some supervillains could easily take over the world, they will inevitably need lieutenants to govern it. How can one rule Japan if he or she is sitting alone in a throne room erected on the ruins of London? Alliance is the only solution. Such groupings are highly unstable and often self-destruct, but present formidable threats while in existence.

This association might be based on a shared insanity, usually megalomania or misanthropy. Some do not seek to rule the world, but instead wish to see it destroyed. For these individuals, the principle of strength in numbers is even more applicable. If a team wants to cause mayhem, mass destruction, and disaster, the more of them working together, the better.

ALL IN THE FAMILY

Villain teams are sometimes family members who all gained powers at the same time, or took on identities as costumed villains together. Though groups like these experience in-fighting and internal rivalry at a more personal level, their shared blood keeps them together, and family teams are usually more loyal than other villain groups.

LIBERTY

JUSTICE

SECURITY

PEACE

CHAPTER THREE
SUPERVILLAIN TEAMS

PAGE 66

SILVER AGE SENTINELS

CRIMINAL INTENT INTRODUCTION	CRIMINAL INTENT ANATOMY OF A VILLAIN	CRIMINAL INTENT THE LONE VILLAIN	CRIMINAL INTENT SUPERVILLAIN TEAMS	CRIMINAL INTENT ORGANISATIONS	CRIMINAL INTENT MOST WANTED	CRIMINAL INTENT APPENDIX
INTRODUCTION	CHAPTER 1	CHAPTER 2	CHAPTER 3	CHAPTER 4	CHAPTER 5	APPENDIX

LIBERTY

JUSTICE

SECURITY

PEACE

This concept, however, doesn't have to include only family members. Like hero teams, these can be villains who grew up together, were tight-knit friends, or who underwent the same origin (transformed and united at one time). When not related by blood, these teams may form from the same organisation, political group, cultural set, race, or even profession. For example, a group could be made up of Russian immigrants, or morally questionable ex-police officers who've decided to enforce their own brand of justice. Former members of an elite military squad could be outfitted with cyborg limbs, superweapons, or brought back from the dead to work together.

Finally, "related" teams can be those where the members are ordered to work together in pursuit of criminal activity or an evil agenda. Some examples of this are: a sinister geneticist who uses a mysterious procedure to create humanoid animals that are sent out on criminal missions; a demon prince of Hell who orders a squad of lesser demons to journey to Earth to wreak havoc and mayhem; or someone able to pull people out of time and space, thus creating a team comprised of history's most fearsome killers. Because the team members have similar motives or temperaments, they'll probably function better as a team, and be less likely to betray each other if things get dicey. This is not always so, and the stranger the team, the more extreme and unpredictable the team dynamic.

United We Stand

Supervillains can also be united because they share an origin that forces them to remain together. Perhaps the villains have a single, shared source of energy that that fuels all of their superpowers, or they could be in possession of a set of items (or a single broken item), which, when brought together, grants power to each of the wielders. This can be simulated in *Silver Age Sentinels* rules with the Character Defect "Conditional Ownership." Alternately, the teammates might have powers that only work when they are within close range of each other, and experience terrible side effects when separated. The Character Defects "Restriction," and "Special Requirement" could represent this disadvantage. Alternately, the team may find that their powers simply do not work when they are not together.

Team members with these restrictions will be especially loyal to each other and understandably tenacious when one of their number is captured or imprisoned. Superteams who learn of this weakness and

exploit it will have a difficult time against the desperate remainder of the villain group, who should be anxious to recover their lost teammate and become "whole" again.

The Team with the Theme

Supervillain teams with strong bonds are frequently based around a particular theme, either in costuming, powers, names, behaviour, or *modus operandi*. In these cases, all of the members have some aspect that makes them ideal for membership in such a themed group. Themes can be almost anything, though due to the nature of villainy they should be dark and sinister and suggest some sort of wrong-doing or danger.

Other villain groups can be "themed" in this manner as well, though it's unlikely for a revenge squad leader to recruit solely based on a theme.

Themes for Supervillain Teams

Though there are enough possibilities to fill a chapter of their own, here are some ideas for themed groups:

- Animals

This theme includes predators such as wolves or great cats, avians (especially raptors or other hunting birds), snakes and lizards (particularly venomous ones), fish or other sea-creatures (predators, usually), or even insects and arachnids — the more frightening, the better.

- Military

These groups are imposing to civilians. A group that uses military-style equipment might be named for military ranks and wear stylised military uniforms. Though the members of a superpowered mercenary team have no official rank, they could give themselves titles to define their identities and hierarchy within the team.

- Mythology and Religion

History's pantheons are full of mythological evildoers who would make excellent supervillains. This also includes sinister mythological creatures, or even demons and devils. Sometimes these teams are actually composed of these ancient gods and demigods, while other times they are impostors or namesakes.

- Professions

Careers and skills are also good sources for themes, such as a team comprised solely of former professional athletes given superpowers by illegal and experimental

INSTANT VILLAIN TEAM NAMES

Here's an easy way to give a team a name to better strike fear into the hearts of law-abiding citizens, and to send a warning to the heroes.

To use the chart, roll a d10 three times and record the results. The first roll is to determine the order of the name, while second and third die results refer to the team's nature and a descriptor. If the "roll 3d10 method" results in a name which is unwieldy or disjointed, feel free to swap the elements around, reroll, or substitute new team natures and/or descriptors.

COLUMN A: TYPE OF NAME

1-6 Roll again on Column B, then link with "of," and add the result from Column C.

7-9 As above, but flip the results from Column B and Column C.

10 Use some aspect of the team's identity (psychics, acrobats, mutants, aliens, etc.) in the name, using the other two results as modifiers.

COLUMN B: NATURE OF TEAM		COLUMN C: DESCRIPTOR	
1	Brotherhood	1	Evil
2	Alliance	2	Destruction
3	Lords/Ladies	3	Mayhem
4	Masters	4	Crime
5	League	5	Sin/Sinister
6	Gang	6	Anarchy
7	Faction	7	Destruction
8	Squad	8	Villainy
9	Cadre	9	Death
0	Association	0	Chaos

For example, the Gamemaster rolls a 6, 3, and 5 and ends up with "The Lords of Sin," a pretty good name for a supervillain team. If that's not exactly to taste, the GM rolls again for a 0, 8, and 3, with results of "squad" and "mayhem." Since the villain team the GM is thinking of is comprised of intelligent trained apes, the only reasonable name for the team is "The Monkey Mayhem Squad." The GM is something of a purist, however, and thinks of dropping "mayhem" to make them the Simian Squad. Arbitrarily adding "Sinister" to the team name gives a fine result, and thus the Sinister Simian Squad is ready for primate action!

performance-enhancing drugs or a group of highly-skilled circus performers, pro-wrestlers, ex-cops, or spies. Some professions lend themselves to this better than others.

- SCIENTIFIC PHENOMENA

Geological, meteorological, or astronomical phenomena are ideal themes. For example, the Weathermen consist of Tsunami, Hurricane, Tornado, Tidalwave, Flurry, and Twister. Perhaps an astronomical-themed group calls itself the Star-Foes, including Aurora, Meteor, Eclipse, Penumbra, Starfall, and Corona.

- SIMILARITY OF POWERS

This is an obvious choice, such as when all of the members have elemental, occult, or psychic abilities. Examples are: The Firemen, comprised entirely of supervillains with different types of fire control; the Loa Beyond, a group of aspiring *hougan* priests who are part of the cult, Life Beyond Death; or the Think Tank, a rogue cell of psionically-gifted ex-CIA experimentees who now use their heightened mental abilities for criminal activities.

- SOCIAL RANK

This titling is easy to use, with each of the team members using honorary titles as king/queen, duke/duchess, baron/baroness, marquis/marquise, etc. As with military rank, this hierarchy provides a quick and easy way for heroes to identify who's who in the villain team's dynamic. It also provides plenty of room for political manoeuvring within the group as the members jockey for higher status.

- VISUAL MOTIFS

This is an easy way to theme a team, such as a group being based on playing cards or the Tarot, or playing pieces for a game like chess or Monopoly. Colour-wise, all of the members might simply have "Black" (or another colour) in their name, with a team made up of Black Flame, Black Justice, Black Knight, Black Serpent, Black Shield, and Black Star.

DARK REFLECTIONS

One unique challenge is when the villains are a sinister reflection of the heroes. This dark mirror is a duplicate of a team of heroes, except that the villains are evil and twisted versions of the characters. The dark reflection team is a direct counterpoint to the heroes, and battles between them are often devastating standstills. Not only do the villains understand the

LIBERTY

JUSTICE

SECURITY

PEACE

CHAPTER THREE
SUPERVILLAIN TEAMS

PAGE 68

heroes' powers and weaknesses better than anyone else, they are usually evenly matched. Therefore, they provide perfect foils.

These teams can be from alternate Earths where evil holds sway, parallel dimensions where wrong is right, fractures in time and space where the heroes and villains switched destinies, or other origins. Sometimes they exist for only a short time, such as when cross-universes collide. Other times, a freak accident creates the doppelganger team, and the heroes must set things right.

A popular concept in the comics for a doppelganger group is one based on characters published by a rival company. Although these teams are usually an in-joke for fans, they are humorous and easy to create and characterise. Taking characters from another publisher's role-playing game would be one way of bringing that style of comic-book rivalry to *Silver Age Sentinels.*

WOULD-BE HEROES

In some cases, a villain team should be a hero team, but somewhere, somehow, something went wrong. In the dramatic world of supervillainy and heroism, a foolish misunderstanding or an accident of fate could turn a potential hero into a villain. Thus, a naïve or fledgling metahuman might become a villain, caught up in the world of supercrime. These characters might be saved from criminal lifestyles, and could even become rough heroes. Many anti-heroes were once villains, defeated by heroes who gave them a chance. Forced to atone for their crimes, they were able to redeem themselves. Once given a shot at doing good deeds, these villains turned away from the path of evil and became heroes.

The same is true for teams of "neutral" metahumans. They might not be sure where they fit on the spectrum of good and evil, and are often mistaken for villains. Perhaps they don't understand that they've broken laws. Being heroic takes a lot work, and it's easy for things to go wrong. An inexperienced hero team might even cause more problems than they fix, and find themselves hated by the public and sought by the police. There are plenty of ways a team of heroes might find themselves on the wrong side of the law, breaking the rules unknowingly or unwillingly. By stopping a crime with excessive force, the team could find themselves blamed for the crime, without witnesses to tell the truth of the matter.

SINNAPSE

LIBERTY

JUSTICE

SECURITY

PEACE

CHAPTER THREE
SUPERVILLAIN TEAMS

The "misunderstood team" scenario is a tremendous role-playing opportunity. If the heroes meet them with aggression, neutrals might sway towards villainy. If the heroes are more open-minded, these neutral teams might turn to good. If so, the heroes have scored a major victory, recruiting others to the side of justice and heroism.

HEROES TO SOME, VILLAINS TO OTHERS

Some teams are heroes to their own societies or cultures, but are still opposed to the forces of "good." This is true if the team represents a political, religious, or social agenda which threatens the livelihood and well-being of others, or if their home country's leadership has been condemned by the United Nations and the rest of the free world.

A team from a nation at war would be heroes to their countrymen and supported by their government, while the rest of the world might see them as criminals. One example is the *Übermensch*, a World War II group of Nazi supervillains. To the Nazis and many Germans, they were national heroes, while the Allied Forces saw them as genocidal villains who fought on the side of evil.

Modern-day versions of groups like these are a bit trickier. A superpowered group of Aryan supremacists would be hard-pressed to find a country where they were regarded as heroes, as the Nazi legacy and ideology is condemned world-wide today. A group of Middle Eastern metahumans, however, could alternate between heroism and villainy in the complex and unstable political world of the Middle East. Similarly, an all-Irish band of metahumans fighting against the British occupational government would find themselves hated by many of their countrymen, yet beloved by others.

SANCTIONED VILLAINY

Another type is the "sanctioned" villain team, which has deceived a government into giving them authority. Sanctioned groups are a special threat to heroes who operate on the shadier side of the law. Supervillains with legal authority, police powers, or other official sanction tend to operate with impunity, acting "straight" in public and revealing their true nature only when they fight the heroes. Often, teams who try this tactic have done so for a specific goal, either to better strike out at the heroes or to access to privileged knowledge and/or equipment.

Similar to the "sanctioned team" are teams of heroes or neutrals who act villainous because they're following unethical orders, or because they think that the heroes are somehow the villains. The Einherhar (right column) are a sample team of this type.

SAMPLE TEAM: THE EINHERHAR

This Thulian supervillain team is led by Kreuzritter's loyal follower Rikard Sollander, also known as Miolnir, "The Hammer of Thule." A general in the Thulian army, Sollander was ordered to forge a team of metahumans who upheld the values of Thulian supremacy and to evoke the island nation's origin, steeped as it was in Scandinavian myth. With the results of Kreuzritter's occult and scientific research at his disposal, Sollander found his teammates among the once-human laboratory subjects: soldiers in the Thulian army who were experimented upon by Kreuzritter, his researchers, and his sorcerers.

Sollander set these poor souls free, saw that they were properly equipped, psychologically conditioned, and adequately trained to perform as Thulian heroes. The team name, Einherhar, refers to the mythical soldiers of Valhalla. They are led by Sollander in his own myth-inspired guise of Miolnir. Kreuzritter and Sollander's brand of heroism often places the Einherhar in conflict with other heroes, and their activities regularly include terrorism, assault, and assassination.

Current members of the team include:

GRENDEL

A hulking brute of a man, hairy and barely sentient, Grendel was created when the DNA of a captured Yeti was injected into a human subject. Immensely powerful and resilient, this powerhouse is almost three metres tall, covered with thick slabs of muscle, Lank rust-coloured hair covers his torso and extremities, with ruddy skin showing elsewhere. His face is bestial, with pale blue eyes, tusk-like teeth, and pointed ears which jut above his long-jawed skull. He is fanatically loyal to Miolnir (the only person he fears), and fond of Lorelei, who easily manipulates his childlike affection. Grendel is barely able to speak and merely growls or grunts, though he understands spoken language and occasionally speaks a word or two. He wears only a pair of black trunks.

DRAUGAR

Once a mercenary soldier given an experimental revivification drug, Draugar hangs between life and death. He is a reanimated dead man, kept alive by the arcane formula pumping through his veins. A harness containing small ampoules of the revivification drug covers his torso, the glowing green of the formula moving through clear tubes into his flesh. His skin has

LIBERTY
JUSTICE
SECURITY
PEACE

CHAPTER THREE
SUPERVILLAIN TEAMS

turned greyish-blue, his hair is gone, and his eyes glow with the strange green colour of the formula.

Named for the restless dead from Scandinavian myth, Draugar is able to drain heat and life from those he touches. He feels no pain from injuries he sustains. Draugar's senses have sharpened, and he can see in the dark quite well. Grim and foreboding, Draugar is a skilled hand-to-hand combatant. He wears a simple black bodysuit covered with green ampoules and a grey leather harness.

LORELEI

The superspy Lorelei volunteered for extensive biological pheromone enhancement, her body's chemistry altered to produce a form of synthetic chemical. When contacted by other humans, this chemical affects them emotionally, weakening their will and making them susceptible to attraction, seduction, or other commands. The chemical enhancement was paired with equally extensive training in voice modulation and hypnotic techniques, allowing Lorelei the ability to practically control people's minds. Once nondescript and unassuming, Lorelei is now gorgeous and unsubtle, a *femme fatale* who uses men and women alike, bending minds as easily as she turns heads. She has an unruly mass of scarlet hair and wears a sleek bodysuit of pale blue and white leather, a low-slung gun belt, and a combat harness.

BERSERKER

Named for the savage warriors of ancient Viking culture, Berserker has been trained as an ultimate combatant. Skilled in armed and unarmed combat, Berserker has been psychologically conditioned to go into a true frenzied rage when he fights, losing all vestige of civilised behaviour and becoming consumed with the need to conquer and to kill. Kreuzritter's scientists put a tiny injector into his heart that releases a tremendous dose of concentrated adrenaline, or hyperdrenaline. It tremendously boosts his strength and speed, lowering his body's sensitivity to pain along with his higher cognitive functions. To simulate natural weapons, he was equipped with retractable claws in his fingers and extendible fangs. Berserker's white and grey costume incorporates a bear motif and fur trim.

MUSPELLI

A soldier in Thule's army who was "accidentally" doused with an experimental nanotech-infused napalm during a training exercise, he was given an immediate counteragent to neutralise the still-burning chemical fire. It had the unexpected effect of bonding the soldier's cellular makeup with the nanotech napalm, created a natural neutralising agent by which he can counter and control his own flame. Named for mythical fire-giants, Muspelli is able to control flame and project it from his hands and mouth, as well as shrouding his body in a protective sheathe of fire. His appearance is horrific, as he appears terribly burned. Muspelli is hairless and blackened, covered with glowing red scars filled with the flaming nanite-napalm. He wears little other than a fire-retardant pair of knee-length trunks and boots, and when he surrounds himself with his fire sheath, Muspelli can float on the wave of heat he emits. Most of the other Einherhar avoid standing in close proximity to him.

KRAKEN

An island nation, Thule is vulnerable from all sides by the sea. Kreuzritter's top defence scientists (in co-operation with a delegation from Matthews GenTech) designed a cadre of genetically and surgically-altered soldiers who could survive underwater for extended periods, extracting oxygen from sea-water with implanted gills and modified lungs. Many soldiers underwent the experiment, injected with top-secret DNA extracted from marine life and given massive surgical alterations. Only one survived, so the project was abandoned.

The survivor was named after a mythical monster feared by sea-faring Thulian forefathers. Kraken is still man shaped and able to speak, but can longer be called "human." He is pale grey with reddish patches on the upper parts of his limbs and torso. Fins branch from his forearms, calves, and the back of his head and spine. The sides and back of his head are covered with wispy, whisker-like spines and there is an elaborate gill structure upon his cheeks and neck. Kraken's eyes are yellow and staring, and he has patches of tiny suction cups on the palms of his hands and his feet (a secondary mutation from the DNA alteration). He is quite strong, resistant to cold, and can swim with blazing speed. Furthermore, he sees well in the dark and has an acute sensitivity to nearby motion while he is in water. Most of the Einherhar find him repellent, as do most natural wildlife.

BEYOND GOOD AND EVIL

Villains can be united when they share a different scale of moral or ethical beliefs, like an ideology beyond the human frame of existence. The villains might be celestially-powered alien beings with galactic-scale abilities, who do not share any common values with humanity. Entities of limitless power who exist at the universal or temporal scale might see human definitions of right and wrong as quaint and meaningless in the scope of their perception. These beings might not be able to comprehend human morals or ethics at all, regarding humanity as an infestation or of no-consequence.

Beings like these could act on a galactic-level mandate that threatens the world's existence, or they might be the heralds of an greater force which intends to destroy or transform the world, despite billions of sentient inhabitants. For example, a cosmic court might hold humanity on trial for universal crimes (or even offences which humanity has yet to commit!), with the heroes forced to save the Earth in a series of trials by combat (or other competitions) against a team of supremely-powered opponents and the world held hostage to the outcome. Heroes and villains could even unite to counter this crisis.

These entities should not be very common, as their motives are so incomprehensible and enigmatic that encountering them could be less satisfying than "normal" villain teams. Unless they are of a sufficient level, the heroes would likely feel overwhelmed with the scale of this threat.

WHAT THEY FIGHT FOR

The nature of a team usually determines its goals and activities. Each type covered thus far has a limited focus, and usually won't venture far outside that scope.

Those that exist as pawns of a larger goal will act in pursuit of that mission, knowingly or not. The revenge squad comes together with a very specific motivation. Their actions won't be petty crime, or even world domination. Instead, they want to kick the stuffing out of Sentinel, Caliburn, or whomever it is they despise. Political activists will always act to pursue their position, though they may occasionally indulge in lesser crimes to finance their purpose. A group drawn together by fate exists to fulfil their mandate, rather than commit random crimes or conflict with rival heroes.

This narrow focus for team activity should be predictable, to a degree that heroes become concerned when villains work outside their usual role. For example, when a supervillain team who specialises in diamond robberies suddenly seizes a nuclear missile as it is transported cross-country, the heroes should realise something extraordinary is up.

Following are major goals supervillain teams strive for, with suggestions as to how teams will pursue them. The *Silver Age Sentinels* rulebook lists several other potential motives in Chapter Seven.

PROFIT

Most supervillain activity is crime for profit; there are many obvious means to this end. The easiest path to wealth is robbery, such as thefts from local banks, high-society parties, art museums, etc. Whether the crime is as simple as a superspeed mugging or an elaborate as a penthouse break-in complete with hero-countering contingency plans, the principle is simple. Teams focused on profit fall into two general categories: groups with complex schemes of international blackmail for ridiculous sums of money; and teams whose activities are basically superpowered snatch-and-grab missions for paltry sums of money, often not worth the risk they incur.

The first type is after greater profits, commonly through blackmailing a wealthy organisation or government. This is the world of international supercrime, where villain teams threaten to destroy corporations, cities, or even countries, unless their demands are met. These activities threaten world peace; with immense amounts of money at stake, they are capable of bankrupting the victims. For this type of blackmail to work, the threat must be of the highest magnitude, consisting of nuclear weapons, death-rays, anti-matter bombs, or the possibility of superpowered destruction.

Though there is immense wealth in organised crime, it is usually the province of solo supervillains who head up criminal organisations or crime families like La Cosa Nostra. Groups of supervillains are not suited for the level of organisation that maintaining a criminal empire requires, and their costumes and identities tend to draw too much attention to their activities. Supervillain teams can work as mercenaries for criminal organisations, but they rarely lead them (see page 87).

Despite appearances, it's not common for teams of supervillains to be focused exclusively on making money through low-level heists. Smaller teams or newcomers to the field of supercrime might do so, but the difficulty and risk usually outweighs the profit. These groups are the bush league of supervillains, scrabbling out a living through the most dangerous of all types of crime: armed robbery. Most of the time, their crimes have little

LIBERTY

JUSTICE

SECURITY

PEACE

CHAPTER THREE
SUPERVILLAIN TEAMS

PAGE
72

SILVER AGE SENTINELS

planning or subtlety and are often committed in broad daylight with plenty of witnesses. These teams are practically asking for heroes to stop them, and these villains rarely stay out of prison for long. Their supervillain identities can make it difficult for them to fence stolen goods or merchandise due to the fear they strike into the normal criminal underground. How many crime lords will trust a costumed maniac not to double-cross them? Furthermore, supervillains have all the same problems non-costumed criminals might have with maintaining a criminal lifestyle, such as taxes, potential betrayal from friends for reward, or trying to account for suspicious and unexplainable displays of wealth. Even everyday security presents a threat to supervillains — how humiliating for Doctor Photon to have his Atomic Pistol confiscated at an airport when his check-in luggage was screened!

Experienced profit-seeking teams are always more competently run than an odd assembly of supervillains. Recruiting and forming a team and keeping it together is tough, considering how difficult it is to establish dominance over a group strong-willed supercriminals, not to mention the difficulties involved with keeping them united towards a single goal. Usually, each member comes with his or her own agenda, enemies, methods of operation, and unfortunately, his or her own superpowered rivals. Team members are additionally concerned with betrayal from within the group, so for them to embark on something as mundane as a bank robbery isn't likely. If they are going to commit theft, it will be on a grand scale, such as the USA's Federal Reserve or Fort Knox, the London Metal Exchange, or the gold reserves of the Bank of England, Banque de France, or Swiss National Bank.

SEAWOLF'S GET

Onboard the mighty Nemo, an enormous experimental submarine, Charles Dagon established an offshore, mobile base for bandits, hackers, rebels, iconoclasts, and anarchists — all drawn to his guise as Seawolf. This state-of-the-art aquatic fortress has become an international data haven and the centre of world-wide attention as a radical reinvention of the notion of what a nation can be. Currently, the following metahumans call the Nemo their home:

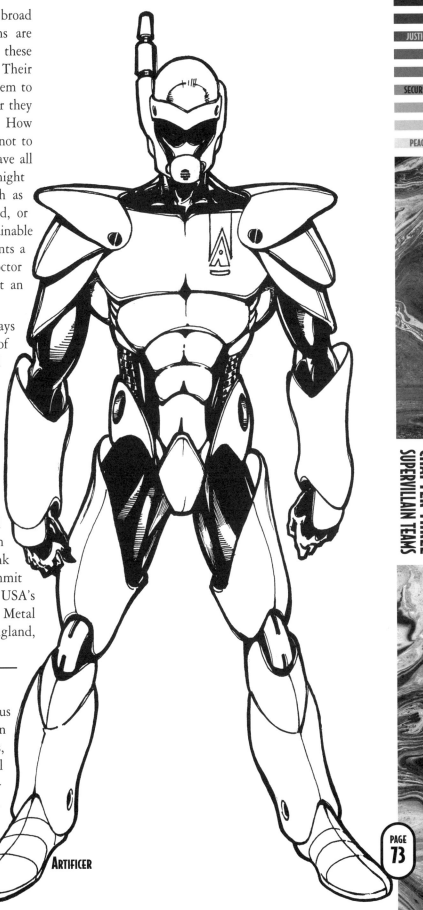

ARTIFICER

CRIMINAL INTENT INTRODUCTION	CRIMINAL INTENT ANATOMY OF A VILLAIN	CRIMINAL INTENT THE LONE VILLAIN	CRIMINAL INTENT SUPERVILLAIN TEAMS	CRIMINAL INTENT ORGANISATIONS	CRIMINAL INTENT MOST WANTED	CRIMINAL INTENT APPENDIX
INTRODUCTION	CHAPTER 1	CHAPTER 2	CHAPTER 3	CHAPTER 4	CHAPTER 5	APPENDIX

LIBERTY

JUSTICE

SECURITY

PEACE

SONGBIRD

Evelyn Flanders was a natural metahuman with a unique voice. For a time she was a successful nightclub singer, aiming for the big time. She could softly lull an audience, or incite their passions with a chorus. Unfortunately, Evelyn made some bad decisions and ended up dating a series of increasingly troublesome crooks and mobsters. Drugs and debt caused her spiral into supercriminal activity, where she took on the identity of Songbird. When she had burned all her bridges and had little hope for a future, she stumbled onto Seawolf. Dagon recognises the statuesque blonde's power, but is strong enough to ignore her manipulations.

BEHOLDER

Alan Benedict Carter grew up with congenital vision problems. He lacked depth perception, saw phantom images, and was acutely sensitive to light. Testing was inconclusive, and Carter was forced to wear thick glasses — polarised lenses that minimised the amount of light that hit his eyes. A doctor who specialised in metahuman perception learned of Carter, and agreed to help him deal with his gift. With time and a specialised pair of goggles, Carter learned to control his incredible visual power — which includes sight across the visible and invisible spectrum, x-ray vision, telescopic sight, and microscopic vision. Unfortunately, Carter used these abilities for selfish means, from simple lechery to cheating at high-stakes gambling and industrial espionage. He became the information broker known as Beholder. Carter has come to the Nemo nominally to support Seawolf's cause, but in truth it is because he knows that in an information superhub, his gifts will prove invaluable.

LASH

Lash's real name is unknown. Seawolf met her in the Pacific, where she was originally trained by the Chinese secret police to bodyguard politicians. As a metahuman in China, her life was rigidly controlled. Seawolf offered her a way out. While she is now nominally a freelance mercenary, in truth she has transferred her loyalties to Dagon. This beautiful young woman is supernaturally strong and fast, and an expert in martial arts weapons. She favours whips and can even use her long braid, bound around jade rings, with deadly accuracy and acumen.

TEMPEST

Seawolf rescued the beautiful girl called Tempest from the US Marines in Central America. She was virtually a blank slate, having only scattered memories of her previous life. Seawolf wonders if she was a new top-secret experiment, gone awry when her powers summoned hurricane forces that swamped the Marine base. Tempest has tremendous control over the seas and storms, although her abilities diminish the farther she is from a large body of water. Due to her alien appearance, with blue skin and deep yellow eyes, she has bonded with Seawolf's crew who accept her without pause. Tempest is still very young and impressionable, and has rebuffed Seawolf's subtle advances through a combination of naiveté and trepidation.

BLAZE

Karen Desmarais is a native of Quebec. She runs so fast the air ignites behind her, leaving a devastating wake. At a young age, Karen hooked up with the Hell's Angels as a literal runner and metahuman strongarm. They nicknamed her Blaze because of her flaming footprints and short temper. When the gang was busted by Magistrate and the RCMP, Blaze was rescued by Seawolf. She owes him a debt of gratitude, but has become sick of living underwater.

POLITICS

Some agendas cannot be achieved within the law. Whether they're fighting for social reform, political change, or a challenge to conventional morality, many supervillain teams have the goal of making a difference in the world through political means. There are cases where this is a noble goal, with villains trying to change the world for the better, but most of the time, supervillains with political goals act for selfish reasons, trying to enact change that either benefits them or gives them power over others.

Political-oriented villains pursue their missions through direct action (destroying those who oppose their agenda), through indirect action (gaining political support for their agenda through threats or other strong-arm tactics), or by providing a living example of their agenda as they frighten or inspire others into making their goal a political reality. Even villains who seek to affect political change in a peaceful manner are drawn into conflict with law enforcement, the military, and the government: at local, national, international, or galactic levels.

SILVER AGE SENTINELS

Political power ranges from the day-to-day ability to govern or rule, to political strength at a national or even global magnitude. Supervillains who seek political power try to achieve it through terrorism, mercenary activity, and threatening the use of weapons or powers of mass destruction. Some teams achieve their political agenda by adhering to the dictates that they strive for, publicising their activities to emphasise their politics and attempt to sway the powers that oppose them. Others are hypocrites, choosing when and how and upon whom to enforce their agenda, ignoring it when expedient. Ultimately, supervillains with political agendas should act as if ripped from today's headlines. They have the attention of national and international governments, with presidents, prime ministers, chairmen, and monarchs concerned with what these teams will do next.

REVENGE

Revenge is one of the more sinister inspirations that drives many teams. Whether directed against a person, organisation, or nation, revenge-oriented teams have a wide range of possible behaviour as they strive for their goal.

While it is possible for villains to have sworn vengeance against a normal person or political figure, the most likely subject of their hatred is another costumed hero (or group of heroes). Heroes inspire the greatest vehemence and loathing. When it is a lone hero that the villains want revenge against, their actions can range from harassment, extortion, and assault, to attempted murder. They can also be more subtle, such as exposing secret identities or threatening the families and loved ones of their target. Vengeance can take the form of framing someone for criminal activity or capturing something they hold dear. Revenge can be public humiliation of the individual, or exposure of a dark secret.

For more direct retaliation, villains can plan an ambush or elaborate trap to draw the hero in, and then destroy him or her utterly. Like most death-trap situations, though, the villains inevitably gloat over the powerless hero and prolong his or her destruction as long as possible, which usually costs them their own victory.

Vengeance taken against a group is a similar endeavour, but is less personal, and focuses on winning in combat, destroying something precious, or disgracing them publicly. This revenge is usually enacted directly against the group, rather than targeting those dear to them. Since the number of family, children, friends, and associates that a reasonably-sized group of heroes could have is enormous, villain teams rarely bother with threatening innocents as a means of getting at their heroic enemies. Solo villains use this tactic extensively, while teams usually want something more direct.

When the villains want to strike back against an organisation, government, or nation, their activities are bolder. They threaten large numbers of people or cause enormous financial ruin and property damage. Effectively, the villains have declared total war, and behave accordingly. Frontal assaults, covert operations, sabotage, and tactics are common against large numbers of enemies.

CHAOS

Some villains just want to cause chaos. The is the simplest of motivations: a love of mayhem and the confusion that it brings. Seeking chaos can be focused on creating anarchy from the inability of government and society to function, or it can simply be an excuse for thrill-seeking teams of villains craving adrenaline rush inspired by reckless criminal behaviour.

This thrill can be the emotional high evildoers gain from inflicting terror upon the innocent, and the feeling of being in control when thousands of people are terrified and dreading what the they might do next. It's a sick motive for the most diabolical of villains, but some supercriminals have chosen their lifestyle because they want to be villains, and this is the most direct way they know.

VILLAIN TEAMS WITH MIXED MOTIVES

Villain teams are rarely united in mind and vision. Because members join for different reasons, their goals can be diverse, creating conflict and tension that heroes can exploit. While the leader has a goal to direct the team towards, the other members frequently have their own agendas that can come into play. A team out for profit might have one member who's out for thrills, even if it endangers a mission. Similarly, a well-planned scheme might fall apart if one villain is drawn into a personal conflict with a heroic rival.

A team whose members each have different agendas is doomed to failure, and is unlikely to have ever advanced past the recruitment stage. In the field, their actions will fall apart in a tangle of cross-purposes, betrayal, and desertion. Thus, supervillain teams should have only a few members with different agendas; more than that and ego-stoked anarchy is the inevitable result.

LIBERTY

JUSTICE

SECURITY

PEACE

CHAPTER THREE
SUPERVILLAIN TEAMS

There is little subtlety to this goal: mayhem-seeking groups strike like natural disasters. Their actions are pitiless and destructive, endangering large numbers of innocent people and causing cataclysmic damage. This is superterrorism, enacted with plasma rays and hyper-sinews rather than with explosives or machine guns. It is unpredictable, relentless, and devastating. Heroes are often hard-pressed to stop enemies who want to cause havoc and strife rather than gain something tangible through their activities, as in most cases the villains are fearless, with nothing to lose.

DEADLY DUOS

There are almost as many supervillain duos as there are pairs of heroes. Just like with heroes, these villain team-ups range from those who are part of a "set," those who work as partners, and those with sidekicks.

"Paired" villains are frequently named after some verbal pun, or the union of things often paired together. A verbal pun might be a *femme fatale* named Beau and her sidekick Arrow. An obvious duo is a Powerhouse named Punch and his martial-artist girlfriend Judy. Some other examples are: the bug-themed Spider and the Fly; twin assassins called Double-Cross; a couple of ex-construction worker Powerhouses known as Jack and Hammer; or Ball and Chain, a husband and wife supervillain team.

Equal partnerships are uncommon. There is usually a reason the two villains work together. Either they're relatives, allies from prison, have complimentary powers and/or skills, or are just friends. These partnerships can consist of two equals, but usually there is a clear leader and follower.

Villains with sidekicks present a challenge to heroes. Since sidekicks are often underage minors, few heroes enjoy battling children. Do heroes treat the sidekick equally and force them to pay for their crimes just as the main villain should? Or does the sidekick merit special attention, handed over to the authorities for rehabilitation rather than imprisonment? While some juvenile sidekicks can be redeemed and live normal lives, others are just supervillains in training. It can be hard to tell which is which, and clever sidekicks will make sure to plead innocent if captured.

ELEMENTS OF SUPERVILLAIN TEAMS

Teams have a great range of differences, and even different incarnations of the same team might have no common characteristics. Previous sections have discussed how the team came to be, and what they are after. This section includes aspects of team make-up, defined by powers and skills, team size, resources, social roles, and internal politics.

POWERS AND SKILLS

There are two broad categories for how villain teams assemble: "unplanned" and "planned." Unplanned teams can be made up of family members who suffer a transformation together, or people from all walks of life who are forced together by circumstances beyond their control. Unplanned groups are often unbalanced, with gaping flaws in their line-up because the members' skills and powers don't complement or balance each other. Sometimes there's no rhyme or reason to an unplanned team. Team members might all have the same power, skills, and equipment, or they could be entirely random.

Planned groups of villains are created from scratch, recruited from existing supercriminals, or some combination of both methods. Whether it is assembled for a particular task, united for an agenda, or brought together for general malfeasance, a planned team should be both formidable and adaptable, capable of achieving the goal it strives towards.

Obviously, a team must have a Leader, someone who calls the shots, acts as point, and provides battle orders during missions. A Powerhouse is useful for almost any team, and is usually the most trusted of the teammembers, serving as the Leader's right-hand. Other members can come from the following archetypes: the Sniper (excels in ranged attacks but is not as powerful in melee combat); the Transporter (controls a team vehicle or has powers able to fill this role); the Communicator (the switchboard, keeping team members in contact with each other); the Protector (defends some or all of the group); the Medic (heals or stabilise those injured); the Scout (provides reconnaissance during or before a mission); the Sneak (spy, infiltrator, and occasional saboteur, working in disguise or under cover); and finally, the Thinker (an information specialist, usually physically weakest of the team, and most likely to rebel against the Leader).

LIBERTY
JUSTICE
SECURITY
PEACE

CHAPTER THREE
SUPERVILLAIN TEAMS

PAGE 76

SILVER AGE SENTINELS

BUILDING A BALANCED VILLAIN TEAM

Villain teams differs from hero groups in that the villains rarely balance each other. In the comics, despite the wide range of power levels, each hero in a team offers something the other teammembers do not. There are rarely two superathletes in a group, two grizzled loners, two supergeniuses, or other redundancies. The hero team members might range from diminutive tricksters to earth-bound gods, but each hero usually has an equal role in the team and in the stories

This is not so with villain teams. These can contain villains with radically different point totals, and can have redundant or missing powers and skills. Villain teams shouldn't be subject to the careful balance of heroic teams, either in level of power or contribution to the team. Villains can have contradictory, volatile tempers and crippling internal rivalries, and are likely to hurt each other more than the heroes are.

How are they expected to win with these odds stacked against them?

Simple. They aren't meant to win.

If they are intended to be more than pushovers or a temporary obstacle, villain teams need to be balanced against the heroes, not against each other. Just as players consider roles, powers, and skills in creating their teams, a supervillain team designed with the heroes in mind is more interesting, and is able to counter the heroes and challenge them in ways that random groups can't.

This is best done by examining the heroes' strengths and weaknesses and choosing natural opposites and counters, selecting defences to protect against the heroes' strengths. If heroes use energy attacks, villains should have appropriate levels in Armour, Block Power, Damage Absorption, Damage Conversion, Force Field, Nullify, or Special Defence. If hero teams are full of Fighters and Powerhouses, villain teams might have Acrobats who can't be hit, Skulkers who can't be found, and Psychics who can dominate weak-minded heroes and throw them against their teammates. Size also matters, as a hero team with a few members might be better matched against a larger but less powerful team, or vice versa. Teams might be based on the Team Nemesis Defect (found in Chapter Five of the *Silver Age Sentinels* rulebook), providing appropriately powerful opposition.

Balancing the villains team against the heroes can be a tight-wire act: the trickiest part is ensuring the supervillains don't over-balance the heroes. For example, if a hero team includes Firefox, the beautiful, flame-wielding elementalist, the villains should have a water elementalist named Geyser to counter her. If there is also a second counter to Firefox, however, like the wind-lord Snowsquall, the fight may be overwhelming, and players will feel the deck has been stacked against them.

When creating a team based around certain powers and skills, the most important thing to consider is that each of the villains' skills and powers must be important to the goal. Teams can change membership as they shift the nature of their activities. Villain teams whose rosters change keep heroes on their toes, as the heroes will not know for certain who's still in the team.

If strength in numbers is required, an army consisting of myriad lower-powered supervillains would make an epic challenge, perhaps presenting an apocalyptic crossover where all heroes in the world must band together to fight all villains, with the fate of the universe at stake.

TEAM SIZE

The size of a villain team should be based on its needs and nature. A team can range from three members to hundreds, though at the later it is nearly an army. Average groups will be between three to twelve members in size. A group focused on profit keeps its numbers down to a bare minimum: any members who are not necessary are just draining funds. If revenge is on the table, the group consists of as many outlaws as can be recruited. A political-minded team seeks out as many converts as they can manage, and a team with chaos as its purpose could be of any size.

TEAM RESOURCES

Resources fall into a few different categories: bases, equipment, and operating expenses. Bases are used as a centre of operations, sometimes providing living quarters for the members of the team. Equipment includes the gear the group uses for training, transportation, and supporting criminal activity. Operating expenses are usually invisible or behind-the-scenes, but cover the cost of hiring goons and their costumes, bribery, food and lodging, and expenses that occur with any group operation.

LIBERTY

JUSTICE

SECURITY

PEACE

**CHAPTER THREE
SUPERVILLAIN TEAMS**

Bases differ by the scale and agenda of the villain team. Smaller (or impoverished) groups might meet in abandoned warehouses, secret subway tunnels, sleazy hotel rooms, old factories on the edges of town, or even a member's apartment. Mid-level groups have fancier digs, such as penthouse apartments, secret sub-basements, or the top floors of skyscrapers; they might base themselves in geographically exotic locales such as deep beneath the sea, hidden mountain caverns, remote islands, or semi-active volcanoes. Older, experienced, or high-profile teams have more extensive and fantastic bases, often with an array of defences, traps, and other features. These are found hidden inside major monuments, in arctic ice fortresses, ancient hidden temples, or are situated in hard-to-reach areas such as parallel dimensions, lost jungle cities, magical pocket realities, in orbit, on the moon, or even in cloaked airships hovering above the earth's surface.

Equipment ranges from the mundane — small-arms and ammunition, surveillance equipment, communications devices, etc. — to high-tech gear — powered body armour, holographic maps, customised vehicles, scientific research equipment, or high-tech

MONEY MATTERS

In a cinematic game, money hardly matters. Supervillains may be driven to score a big haul, but as with heroes, the day-to-day finances for criminals, are effectively ignored.

For realistic (or comedic) games, however, money can play a significant aspect. Most teams need funding to keep afloat, even if just for coffee and snacks for their meetings, electricity to run their electronic devices, gas for the vehicles in their motor pool, or repair costs for damaged weaponry. Other financial black holes are salaries for armies of goons, bribe money, funds for purchasing bank plans or secret documents. Even supervillains can have their power and phones shut off if they don't pay the bills. Only keep track of finances if the mood of the game lends itself to it.

blaster weapons. Finally, the best connected groups have access to unique and powerful items, like orbital death cannons, matter transporters, time machines, and sentient supercomputers.

MISTER MATHEWS AT WORK IN HIS HIGH-TECH LABORATORY

TEAM ROLES

A group of villains will have many of the same roles as a hero team. These aren't defined by powers, but instead by social function within the group. Teams inevitably have a Leader who is the moral and tactical "centre" of the group, providing a firm identity and making important decisions about the group's goals and activities. Frequently, the Leader often takes on the additional roles of Mentor and/or Patron, to provide advice, counsel, and financial resources, respectively. The Leader is often the most experienced supervillain in the team. Rarely does another member of the team act as a Mentor, as the Leader's ego is too great to allow such a rival.

There's almost always a Lieutenant who is loyal to the Leader, providing protection against the team's enemies and sometimes from the other teammates. The Lieutenant might have some past connection to the Leader or could be the most favoured member. If a team's membership changes over the years, the person most likely to stick with the Leader will be the Lieutenant. The Lieutenant can be (and often is) someone physically powerful, like a Powerhouse, but they can also be a weaker character, like a Thinker.

Other common roles include: the Rebel (who argues with everything the Leader proposes); the Grunt (who just keeps his or her head down and does the job); the Couple (a combo, whether husband/wife, brother/sister, or lovers, who are in the team because they have nowhere to go; sometimes these two are a Deadly Duo giving the "team thing" a try); the Veteran (a long-time career supercriminal only looking out for him or herself); the Advisor (often a robot lacking humanity, and often the first to attempt a coup d'état); the Tech (the Gadgeteer of the group, loyal as long as the research funds keep coming); the Brute (less intelligent and dim-witted, this powerful character might be peaceful if left alone but is used by the group for their own ends); the Getaway Driver or Goalie (who serves as the escape route, or provides the last line of defence); and the Innocent (an inexperienced newcomer who could be redeemed, if taken away from his or her nefarious peers).

Most villains fill one of these loose roles; larger groups can have more than one member in a role. These are not rigid classifications. Instead, they provide a quick and easy framework for team dynamics beyond skills and powers.

INTERNAL POLITICS

Usually, a team's origin and agenda dictate its organisation and the decision-making process. A team formed by a focused leader doesn't usually debate plans, and dissension is rarely tolerated. An alliance of equals, however, will debate and argue almost anything, sometimes using a democratic vote to decide future activities. Other teams exist in a state of allied anarchy, with the strongest personality or idea ruling the team's moment-to-moment behaviour.

Even the most united of villain groups is rife with internal politics. Any group consisting of more than one person has the potential for disagreement. Since supervillain mentality includes criminal, psychopathic, fanatic, sociopathic, and nihilistic personality types, these team-ups are a pressure-pot, waiting to explode, with the only outlets being criminal activity and infighting.

All groups will occasionally have dissent and disagreement in the ranks. For supervillain teams, turn up the heat a hundred-fold and remove the safety valve. Personality types such as the Advisor, Mentor, Rebel, and even the Brute create tears in team unity. Though most of this dissent occurs off-camera and out of the sight of the heroes, it can be revealed through dialogue and action for perceptive heroes to use to their advantage.

UNSUNG VILLAINS

A dirty secret of supervillain teams is that they can't survive in modern society without outside help. They have mundane allies that they need to be able to function, or else they would be buried under a mountain of ordinary and menial tasks. For these support roles, there are individuals who work behind-the-scenes to keep the supervillains free from drudgery.

For example, Kreuzritter, Monarch of Thule, is unlikely to spend much of his time actually governing his country and people. Lucas Herzog, his Minister of State, is probably the *de facto* leader of the country; Kreuzritter calls the shots only when it interests him. The armoured supervillain doesn't spend his time poring over budget spreadsheets, participating in debates in the Council of Government, or making public appearances cutting ribbons for new government buildings. Instead, he spends his time with his cronies, plotting world domination and terror.

Support roles include: costume and gadget makers who clothe and equip villains and their henchmen; scientists, technicians, and engineers who develop the

LIBERTY

JUSTICE

SECURITY

PEACE

**CHAPTER THREE
SUPERVILLAIN TEAMS**

PAGE
79

doomsday devices and keep the machinery running; contractors who build secret bases, install deathtraps, and design escape-proof holding cells; clerks and accountants who keep funds flowing and bills paid; fences and money launderers who dispose of stolen goods and exchange marked bills; public-relations specialists who work to improve the public image of villains who don't want to be perceived as bad guys; and even lawyers willing to defend the villains in court when they are captured, or harass the heroes for unlawful persecution and assault.

> In the 1930s, Chicago crime boss Al Capone was brought down and sent to prison, not for charges relating to his extensive activities as one of the most powerful organised crime figures in the nation ... but for tax evasion. Capone was unable to account for his wealth and prove that it was acquired legally and taxes paid accordingly. The mob boss was put away for 11 years in Alcatraz, after a last-ditch defence by his attorney, who characterised Capone's profession as that of a high-stakes gambler. Ironically, the reality was that Capone, fearing such a situation, had previously contacted his accountant and initiated the process of paying back taxes specifically to avoid the tax evasion penalty, knowing that other organised criminal bosses were being hit with the same thing.
>
> Having a few or more non-powered, ordinary civilians with intimate knowledge of the workings of a supervillain team creates opportunities for heroes to turn the tables. They can put pressure on these civilians to cut all ties with the villains and confess what they know. Pragmatic heroes can hinder villains through the court system and help authorities prosecute them through alternate methods, even when they can't prove villains guilty of their obvious crimes. There is something undignified about the Legion of Dread being prosecuted for tax evasion because none of their members have filed for taxable incomes, or sending them to jail for illegally diverting city electricity to power their Dreadnought. Still, any charge that keeps them off the streets is better than none.

TACTICS AND TEAMWORK

Once a team of villains has a solid goal in mind and a clear means of operation, there is only question remaining: how will they fare in the field? Villains should use all of their powers to the fullest extent.

They've drilled together and know each others' strengths and weaknesses, unless there is a good reason they might be keeping secrets from each other. The following sections describe tactics and strategies.

THE DEVIL IS IN THE DETAILS

A staple of the villain team is an emphasis on planning. Scenes depicting the members gathered around a map in their lair are common in comic books. As they embark on any scheme (as grandiose as world domination or as petty as a bank robbery), teams with any sense will have a plan worked out ahead of time, with contingency plans to address potential bad luck or changing circumstances. They might research potential superheroic interference, with special attention to counter any opposition.

When villains are encountered at the scene of the crime, they are almost always familiar with their surroundings through maps, surveillance, infiltration, or use of powers which allow them to spy from afar. They'll know exit and entry routes, hiding places, and strategic locations for ambushes. Well-prepared teams know details about everyone they'll encounter at the scenes, and what threats they represent. Stealthier teams might even have guards' routines fully detailed so they can avoid them utterly. Team leaders should be aware of tactically-useful information such as power boxes, generators, or hazardous materials. All of this means that if a team spends the time to prepare, they know what they're doing, where they're going, and they will be able to control the environment and use it to the best of their ability. In short, successful supervillains seize the initiative, act from surprise, and keep heroes on the defensive.

If the villains are expecting trouble from a particular hero or team, they might research their potential opponents. News footage of past exploits, articles describing historic battles, and even other villains are all good sources to learn how the heroes fight, their strategies and tactics, and any obvious weaknesses. A great resource would be an information broker, a shady character who researches heroes and sells dossiers on them with relevant information like whereabouts, tactics, accomplices, and any weaknesses that can be exploited.

Research can also mean that the villains investigate the heroes to learn how to counter them at a later date, almost a dry run for a later plan. They can follow and spy upon the heroes, or engage them in preliminary encounters to discern strengths and weaknesses. Villain

masterminds often trick other villains into doing this for them, observing from afar. Resourceful villains can even find ways to spy on the heroes' bases, or might hack the heroes' computers for personal information.

CALLING THE SHOTS

An advantage villains have over heroes is that they choose when and where they will act. Heroes are forced to play catch-up; they learn of a crime at the same time as the police. Heroes with official status are called by the authorities immediately, others have police allies who let them know when a criminal team has acted. Finally, outlaw heroes may have to wait until the news broadcasts a breaking report of a crime in progress.

It is difficult for heroes to be proactive about supervillains. Heroes rarely have the resources to monitor every villain's whereabouts and current legal status. Villains, likewise, do what they can to make themselves hard to find. Many criminals might escape if they only struck but once or twice, but as they are compelled to act due psychological, emotional, or social pressures, they continue to put themselves at greater risk with each action. Heroes must play a waiting game, trying to catch the criminals at a scene, or gathering enough evidence to track the perpetrators down.

Therefore, smart villains initially have the upper hand, as they've had time to refine their schemes and come up with contingency plans. They've practised their missions. Heroes are regularly thrust into the scene of a crime in progress, without any knowledge of what's occurring, or even who's responsible initially.

Villains may try to cover their tracks (disabling recording devices, intimidating or killing potential witnesses, etc.), mislead the heroes (leaving false clues), or leave booby-traps to sabotage the heroes' investigation. Other villains leave calling cards of some sort, to sign the scene. This practice doesn't always have to point the heroes in the right direction, though.

DIVIDE AND CONQUER

Villains sometimes deal with hero teams by separating them and fighting the members individually. For villains who aren't very powerful or aren't well suited for head-to-head conflict with the heroes, the most obvious means of evening the playing field is to whittle down the heroes one-by-one until they're easily dealt with.

Dividing hero teams is most effective when used in conjunction with other tactics. Villains often split their own team up and send the members apart from each other, forcing heroes to do the same to deal simultaneous crises. Then, villains can ambush lone heroes or smaller teams at their leisure. Another method is the use of traps, invulnerable doors, ambushes, and other dangers to separate heroes from their allies. Chapter Seven of the *Silver Age Sentinels* rulebook provides many suggestions for traps.

The divide and conquer routine can be done before the fight is joined, with villains using knowledge of the heroes' weaknesses, past behaviour, or personal lives to create situations where they cannot act.

For example, the White Rooks might threaten Empire State University with a hidden nuclear device solely to occupy Slipstream, just as they launch their plan to take the White House hostage. By planning the two events at the same time, they have effectively divided the Guard's strength, with Slipstream searching for a non-existent bomb while the villains run amok in Washington, D.C.

The most diabolical tactic is psychological, when the villains cause a superteam to be driven apart on its own, through use of subterfuge, slander, illegal governmental intervention, guile, mind control, emotional manipulation, or another method. These techniques can force a team apart, breaking the heroes up as they quit or storm away.

DISTRACTION, FEINTS AND BLUFFS

Villains can avoid direct conflict with heroes by keeping them from knowing the truth. Intelligent villains will mislead and distract the heroes through tactics that range from crude bomb threats to more showy activities that hide the real crime. The villains might send one of their own on a mission to create as much mayhem as possible (even without breaking the law), while the rest work in secrecy to achieve the true objective. When the need for misdirection is over, the decoy villain surrenders, flees, or apologises.

Alternately, villains could plant evidence that points to another supervillain, or even a hero. This will steer attention away from their activities. These set-ups are ripe with role-playing opportunity and easy to create with a little planning.

LIBERTY

JUSTICE

SECURITY

PEACE

CHAPTER THREE
SUPERVILLAIN TEAMS

CRIMINAL INTENT INTRODUCTION	CRIMINAL INTENT ANATOMY OF A VILLAIN	CRIMINAL INTENT THE LONE VILLAIN	CRIMINAL INTENT SUPERVILLAIN TEAMS	CRIMINAL INTENT ORGANISATIONS	CRIMINAL INTENT MOST WANTED	CRIMINAL INTENT APPENDIX
INTRODUCTION	CHAPTER 1	CHAPTER 2	CHAPTER 3	CHAPTER 4	CHAPTER 5	APPENDIX

LIBERTY

JUSTICE

SECURITY

PEACE

HIT AND RUN

Villains are known for striking from ambush, then fleeing. They then repeat the process until the heroes can't effectively deal with the villains. This strategy works best indoors, particularly in bases and headquarters. Combined with an army of goons and built-in defences, this creates a perilous environment for the heroes.

Since heroes are often reluctant to split up, it's easy for villains to hit them from different directions in a short period of time. Supervillains should use rapid tactics to delay and divert the heroes, making sure not to engage them directly. Ideally, villains strike hard and fast and flee before heroes can retaliate. Chapter Seven of the *Silver Age Sentinels* rulebook provides suggestions for how villains might flee the scene of a crime, or escape custody in the final battle.

COLLATERAL DAMAGE

Supervillains often threaten innocent lives by causing massive property damage as a favourite delaying tactic against heroes. Knocking out the supports of a bridge, for

example, threatens both the people on the bridge and boats in the water below. An unstable structure full of jeopardised civilians can tie the heroes up in rescue operations. Heroes who help these people may be immobilised while they try to support the weight of the bridge, hold onto falling school buses, or will be occupied shuttling people back and forth to safety. The villains can strike while the heroes are distracted, continue their original activities, or move on to a new stage of their plan.

Villains are often willing to take hostages, from innocent bystanders to people beloved by the heroes. Whether or not they'll actually harm their hostages varies villain by villain, though the most dastardly will certainly use hostages as human shields, even manoeuvring heroes into harming the helpless victims through their own actions. Less fiendish villains will let the hostages go when their use is over.

FIGHTING DIRTY

Finally, villains are willing to break the rules and go beyond the silent code of conduct of behaviour that exists between civilised folk. Supervillains will throw innocent people off buildings to distract the heroes, and they'll exploit any perceived sign of weakness. This can range from using special powers or tactics custom-made to hurt the heroes.

CALIBURN ON THE WRONG END OF A CHEAP SHOT FROM HEARTBREAKER

They'll strike while a hero's back is turned, or launch missiles at the superteam's transport while en route to their base. If a hero is wounded, villains will direct their attacks towards that injury to aggravate the pain. Some supervillains will kick a hero when they're down, and if the hero is knocked out, they'll gladly throw the unconscious body into the ocean wrapped in chains. Villains might surrender, then attack once the heroes' defences are down. Supervillain teams should always be formidable opponents, with a range of methods and tactics.

SUPERVILLAIN TEAMS AND THE LAW

Though the relationship between supervillains and the law has been covered well in the *Silver Age Sentinels* core rulebook and elsewhere in this book, some aspects of the law and supervillains are specific to supervillain teams. These are some ways heroes and law enforcement deal with supervillain teams:

STOOL PIGEONS

Heroes, sometimes in conjunction with the law, occasionally try to "turn" one of the villains, offering him or her immunity from prosecution. In return for this, the villain is asked to rat out his or her allies or give inside information on the team and its plans. Turncoat villains can be forced to testify against other villains in high-security trials, complete with bagged costumes on the exhibit table and comic artist cameos as courtroom sketch artists.

THE RICO ACT

The RICO (Racketeering Influenced and Corrupt Organisations) Act was created to allow people financially injured as a result of organised criminal activity the means to seek redress for their loss through state or federal court systems. With RICO, civilians can sue criminal organisations or entities to regain their losses. It provides a tremendous advantage in the struggle against organised crime, as this Act compels organised crime leaders and members to defend themselves in court against claims of criminal activity, allowing investigation into their activities which might not otherwise be warranted.

In Empire City, the Attorney General is currently trying to push an amended variant of the RICO Act through Congress. The VICO (Villain Influenced and Corrupt Organisations) Act will give civilians the right to sue supervillain teams and organisations, creating a system of legal redress against costumed blackmailers, superterrorists, metahuman vandals, and would-be world conquerors. If passed, this Act will have wide-reaching influence in the world of prosecution of supervillains and supervillain teams.

HOW MUCH VILE IN THE VILLAINY?

The reason one gang of villains is a mere nuisance and another is on the FBI's "Most Wanted" list is the moral depths to which they will descend. *Silver Age Sentinels* is aimed at a theme of superheroic activity, somewhere between the naiveté of the Golden Age and the gritty and complex modern world. Heroes aren't grim modern vigilantes, nor is there an "anything goes" atmosphere of hopelessness and despair.

Supervillains, though, have more leeway in what they get away with, and their activities haven't changed much over the years. They're still blowing up buildings, robbing banks, smashing city blocks in superpowered throw-downs, kidnapping heroes' elderly relatives, going toe-to-toe with the world's armies, trying to melt polar icecaps with orbital laser platforms, and leaving helpless heroes in complex death-machines while they go off to supervise the final stages of their plans. Yet there are limits: villains shouldn't torture or mutilate their captives, indiscriminately murder innocents directly, or kill defeated heroes. Those are outside the tone that *Silver Age Sentinels* evokes. If the campaign tone is Dark and Gritty, however, where everything is a shade of grey or black, there's no telling the depravities supervillains will commit — just remember that heroes often hit back just as hard in such worlds.

Not all villains are equally "evil." Having different levels of villainy on a team gives heroes another means of fighting them. Costumed criminals who find themselves over their heads might waver if a hero reminds them that they're not as bad as the rest, and they can even turn on their teammates if things have gone too far.

SUPERVILLAIN PLAYER TEAMS

Chapter Seven of the *Silver Age Sentinels* rulebook describes the possibility of a campaign where the players are supervillains, either captured villains coerced into working as heroes, or as outright villains plotting evil schemes and battling costumed heroes. A supervillain campaign can be quite fun, whether as a short

LIBERTY

JUSTICE

SECURITY

PEACE

CHAPTER THREE
SUPERVILLAIN TEAMS

campaign, one-shot, or even a convention game. As supervillains are more outrageous than heroes, they are very exciting to role-play. Sometimes it's just fun to be the bad guy.

In a supervillain game, the point may not even be to win ... but to create great mischief before the heroes inevitably bust in and spoil the party. Though the players might want to win now and again, they should ideally be having a rougher time of it than the heroes, with the entire world against them. Costumed do-gooders will constantly foil their schemes. Seeing how the other half lives can be entertaining and educational; supervillain games are a great way to add depth to the world of *Silver Age Sentinels*.

This chapter has provided suggestions about potential supervillain teams, how they might form, what their goals might be, and how they operate in the field. These concepts and suggestions are easily adapted to a supervillain game of any sort.

Following are several concepts appropriate for a supervillain game.

THE DIRTY HALF-DOZEN

The player characters all begin in prison, either rightfully put there by the heroes, or wrongfully imprisoned for one reason or another. They've been given a second chance to redeem their debt to society by acting as heroes. Their costumes are returned and they're given limited freedom, with an agent to chaperone them. Their missions are deadly and top-secret, and the agency in charge of the operations regards them as expendable. One screw-up and they're back in prison for life — or worse.

The catch is that the villains are carefully supervised and kept in line with some failsafe, from micro-explosives in their bodies, injections of neurotoxin requiring regular doses of an ultra-rare antidote, or psychic bombs to turn them into vegetables if they think of escaping. Another complication is that they're still villains. The agency in charge has little sympathy for their criminal tendencies, and the rest of society (including other heroes) thinks that they're still bad guys.

The agency responsible might be anyone: the government, a secret think-tank, an impossibly-wealthy dilettante with a hidden agenda, a scientific group trying to test new equipment and/or psychological reform measures, or a well-meaning hero with his own "reform" program. Missions could consist of espionage against rival agencies, soldiers, and even heroes of enemy nations; commando operations, such as military strikes, covert ops, and rescue activities; or further supercriminal activity, with the team sent against heroes who present a threat to the status quo.

THE DEVILS INSIDE

With this, the player characters are supervillains who've actually reformed and are trying to live life as heroes. They've publicly announced that they're reformed and turned over a new leaf, or they've taken on new identities as heroes (usually similar to their former identities) and kept their old identities a secret (such as a Skeleton in the Closet).

Now they act as heroes, seeking acceptance, profit, or glory, fighting crime and helping people. They're even doing battle with old allies in the supercriminal underworld, fighting alongside their old enemies, risking exposure either way. They might be honest about it, or they could be putting on a sham to position themselves for a later score once they've earned the trust of society and the authorities. They could be well-meaning dupes of a leader with plans of her own. Of course, the villains might retain their old identities for special occasions, acting as villain or hero depending on the circumstances. Whichever the case, the players can have it both ways, being able to play supervillains, yet do heroic things. The risk of discovery adds an additional level of tension to an otherwise straightforward concept.

This concept owes much to the "Thunderbolts" series published by Marvel Comics.

THE DARK MIRROR

The player character villains are actually evil versions of heroes: formed in the same freak accident, from a parallel universe, summoned by some ancient curse or industrial accident, or simply the result of bizarre and unlikely coincidence. Whatever their origin, they're identical to the heroes (either a group of heroes from published *Silver Age Sentinels* source material, or evil versions of player character heroes), with similar powers, skills, and appearance, thinly-disguised but easily recognisable. The key difference is that they're evil. They could be sympathetic, having similar but subtly different origins, originating from a world where they had to turn to evil to survive.

CHAPTER THREE SUPERVILLAIN TEAMS

Of course, these villains are inevitably going to have to fight their counterparts. While they could easily encounter someone else, it isn't emotional or dramatically satisfying as having them fight their opposite numbers. This provides players a chance to see how their characters appear to villains and lets them act in ways they can't with their regular characters. While this game can be run with players taking on the roles of characters they didn't create, it is most satisfying having them playing with dark versions of their own characters.

THE (INSERT NAME HERE) REVENGE SQUAD

This is ideally a one-shot or a standalone episode of a campaign, but can be quite fun. With this concept, the player characters are all enemies of a hero team, drawn from a roster of villains the player character heroes have previously encountered. As revenge squads, these villains band together out of their shared hatred of the heroes, and spend much of their time airing their grievances and boasting about how much pain they're going to put the heroes through. The session can simply begin in the villain's headquarters, with them arguing about who hates the heroes more, letting the players take the initiative. The Game Master should allow the players as much leeway as possible in creating traps and plans to do away with the heroes, which, after all, are the players' actual characters.

Obviously, they're going to fight the heroes. And, unless the Game Master is eager to change the campaign to accommodate the destruction of the heroes, the supervillains will have their rear ends kicked soundly. On the other hand, there's no reason why the player villains can't win ... after all, if villains can come back from certain death, so can heroes. After the villains have achieved certain victory, the campaign might switch back to the heroes perspective, as the players have to wriggle out of the predicament they've literally placed themselves.

HOW THE OTHER HALF LIVES

This option is more light-hearted than any of the other set-ups. Though it could be played straight, it usually ends up being humorous. The player characters are villains trying to commit the perfect scheme, master plan, or just trying to get by, and all the world is out to stop them. They can't even perform the day-to-day tasks of being a simple civilian, as banks call S.W.A.T. teams when they enter to deposit their pay cheques. Even a trip to the mall becomes a run-in with rent-a-cop security. Costumed heroes keep kicking in their doors,

HEARTBREAKER TAKING HER TIME WITH A BOY IN BLUE

LIBERTY

JUSTICE

SECURITY

PEACE

JUSTICE

PAGE 85

threatening and bullying the villains even when they aren't breaking any laws. Sometimes, they get kicked out of their apartments because their landlords are afraid of them. Even going without their costumes might not work, especially with villains who have flaming skulls for heads, glowing eyes, claws or fangs, or are the size of a phone booth. A trip to the corner store for milk and eggs becomes a superpowered slugfest. Cybernetic implants make it impossible to pass through metal detectors in airports. No matter what they try, these hapless villains are hounded by heroes, police, and even their peers who browbeat them into joining their other teams. For a campaign like this, villains might come to realise that safest place in the world for them is behind bars.

HEAD-TO-HEAD

This type of supervillain game is best played at conventions, and/or with two different player groups. There are two teams of players: a hero team and a villain team, working against each other, eventually forced to go head-to-head. While this type of game can take a lot of work, it is highly rewarding and provides players the chance to combat each other in the arena of superheroic activity. This is best run with two Game Masters, to give both teams plenty of opportunity for role-playing.

LOCAL PLAYERS

For Game Masters with plenty of players, this involves running two games — a hero game and a villain game, with events from one having an influence on the other. Characters can be created by the players, with all of the guidelines in rulebook for hero teams, and this chapter for the villain teams. The villains should be allowed some time to plan their "big score," and the heroes given time to be suitably heroic. The Game Master can either alternate sessions, or two Game Masters can run separate campaigns, co-ordinating to bringing the players together when required.

CON GAMES

These are best run at a gaming convention, where two groups of players can be pitted against each other. To do it right, two Game Masters are a necessity, and two gaming spaces would be better than one. The teams should be kept out of earshot until they need to meet each other, such as in combat or role-playing. Since convention games are fairly short, it is recommended that the GMs provide the players with pregenerated hero and villain teams and present each group with all of the information they will need to properly role-play the scenario.

The heroes will need to know about their team history and their teammates, as well as any relevant information about their base and resources. They might also be given a list of villains they know about, or this can be handled with appropriate skill use (City Knowledge or Street Sense, for example). The villains, on the other hand, should be given their team roster, knowledge of the heroes, and the plans for their supervillain scheme. Ideally, the Game Master(s) should choose an appropriate player and nominate him or her the leader, with the task of feeding information to the other supervillain players.

In play, the heroes are going about their business when they are alerted to the first stages of the villains' scheme. The villains can use many of the guidelines in this book to keep the heroes on the ropes as the they enact their grand plan. Eventually, it becomes a toe-to-toe slugfest, winner take all.

Game Masters should allow considerable leeway for escapes and getaways if villain players are defeated early in the time-slot, or perhaps players whose characters are "out of play" can be given a new character to play (even on the opposite side), representing a hero drawn into the conflict, or another villain recruited to help defeat the heroes.

A LEGACY OF EVIL

A well-established supervillain team is more tradition than organisation. Even if beaten again and again, all the members sent to prison, secret headquarters destroyed — the team will return. It may take years to reappear but it will, like a weed. The reappearing team could be the original members, or maybe only a few members are back this time. Perhaps the former leader is assembling a new team with the same name, or a team member is keeping the tradition alive.

It could be that the new team has nothing to do with the old one, comprised of upstart villains cashing in on an established brand name. This is bound to make the original team angry, perhaps enough to provoke a supervillain throwdown over the rights to the name.

Is it the name itself? Probably not. Most supervillain team names aren't the most original (see "Instant Villain Team Names," page 68). Ultimately, the appeal is the pride of using such an established name. Perhaps it's easier to recruit new members if they think they're joining up with a classic tradition. Criminal society might be nostalgic for the supervillain teams of the past. Or villains might want to be a part of a team with a proven track record, regardless of success.

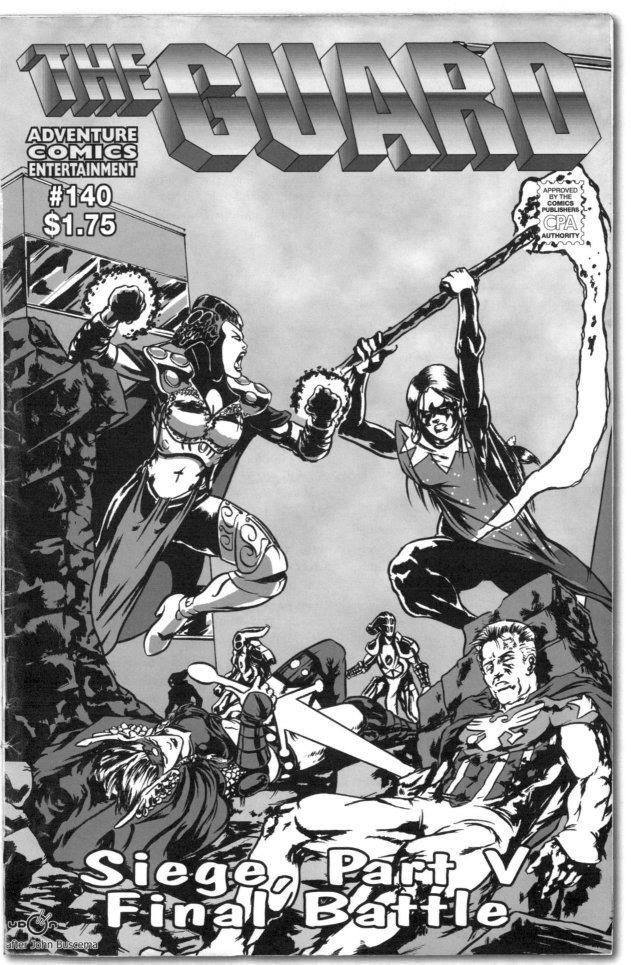

ORGANISATIONS

Just as there are villains who work alone or in small teams, there are also those among the criminally minded who gather in larger groups, organisations that exist solely to further the agendas of the men and women in charge of these large-scale assemblages of evil. Like often-discussed terrorist groups, these shadowy organisations are known to exist; they are merely difficult to track, locate, and act against. Other organisations may exist that are well concealed from even the most prying eyes. They hide behind legitimate public figures and dummy corporations, stashing their vast wealth in off-shore accounts. They act in secret, never claiming credit for their acts of villainy and evil. Each member knows little of the organisation's larger goals, membership, or even its true leaders: all are hidden beneath layers of lies, corruption, and sometimes even the most well-meaning of disguises.

The first purpose of this chapter is to detail a set of guidelines with which GMs can create villainous organisations for their own campaigns, including history, motives, hierarchy, resources, operational areas, allies and enemies, and current status. These topics will be viewed from the perspectives of the group as a whole as well as the individual leader or leaders of the group.

This chapter also depicts one example from the world of Empire City: the Phoenix Collective, a well-regarded international organisation that is anti-globalisation, pro-environment, anti-big business, and pro-democratisation of the underdeveloped Third World nations without the interference and corruption of the US or the other powerful, industrialised nations. At this group's heart, however, lies the Reborn, a band of thugs, terrorists, and supervillains that seeks not to protect the people of the world from the evils of corrupt capitalism, but instead strives to subvert the populations of the world to their cause against the industrial giants that, according to the Reborn, are such a threat. The less power the industrial nations gain from the people, the more power exists to be taken by the Reborn. They want nothing less than to remake the world in their image, holding the reins of power from behind the scenes.

HISTORY

Every important element in your campaign needs a history, and villainous organisations are no different. Detailing an faction's background helps the GM become more familiar with the group and its motivations. He or she can then present the association more convincingly to the players and their characters. An organisation that lacks a history within the campaign's setting undermines the credibility of both the group and the campaign itself.

Every organisation, movement, and venture begins with one motivated person. One person has the drive, determination, and sheer will to create an organisation that embodies his or her dreams. That person is the one who founds and often funds the villainous group that will soon plague the lives of the characters. When determining the history of the group, GMs should start with the story of that group's founder.

The essential question when determining the story of a group's founder is: what drives a person, any person, to create an organisation to promote evil and chaos across the world? GMs need to think about the life the founder led prior to creating the group before detailing the organisation itself. If they understand why he or she began the group, they can better plan the group's role in their campaigns.

GMs don't need to write extensive biographies of the group's founder; a brief sketch of the basic facts will suffice. The circumstances of his or her birth and childhood, where he or she was educated, what became of his or her parents and siblings, and what career the founder followed before starting the organisation will give sufficient detail for data-hungry heroes bent on investigating the group. In addition, detailing two or three (if that many exist) significant people or things in the founder's life will help define his or her personality, as well as giving the characters a way to relate to the villain.

The next thing to consider, however, is a key factor in creating a believable organisation: the moment, event, or circumstance in the founding member's life that led to the group's creation. This origin point should be clearly evident in the villain's life, though lesser events may precede or follow the key moment. Somehow, something goes horribly wrong in the founder's life; perhaps he or she suffers a mental collapse; maybe it's the moment he or she discovers metahuman abilities. Regardless of what the event actually is, it should be a life-changing moment for that person, one that leads them to turn against society and use his or her powers for evil.

MOTIVES

Determining the founder's motivation goes a long way toward shaping the group he or she eventually forms. It determines what the creator wants it to be, and what services he or she expects it to fulfil. Keep in mind that although he or she likely has a goal of primary importance, few individuals capable of starting a large-scale criminal enterprise are so transparent as to have only one goal. Secondary motivations can be just as powerful, if more subtle, and influence the way in which the overriding concerns are pursued.

Developing histories and defining motives for other working members of the group is also helpful, as it gives the GM a personality for the central NPCs of the group, making them easier to breathe life into when they meet up with the players. Each member of the association who knows the group's true purpose should have a reason for being involved. Not every member needs a detailed biography, but the histories of members likely to interact with the heroes should be sketched out to keep them from seeming like cardboard cut-outs. Having that information handy will also give a personality and direction for the group as a whole, an important consideration when the players are deciding whether or not their characters should be involved.

When defining the subordinate NPCs, their histories can and should be quite different from that of the founder. The only caveats to that rule are that first, the founder and subordinate should have logically crossed paths at some point in their pasts. Work within the framework of the founder's background to find a solid intersection where they could have met. Second, the NPC's philosophy must jibe with that of the founder, or at the very least not conflict sharply. If the subordinate does not agree with the goals of the organisation, it is unlikely that he or she will rise very high within the ranks unless there are other pressing reasons for his or her continued participation, such as coercion or gratification of a personal goal that would otherwise be unattainable. Regardless, the leader of the group is unlikely to tolerate dissension in the ranks, so subordinates must be able to "fit in" with the larger group.

The same also holds for any metahumans the group employs. These individuals may be devoted to the founder's cause or not. They could be little more than employees, muscle hired to perform a specific deed and never be seen by anyone in the organisation again. In the former case, defining histories and motives applies. If the latter, don't concern yourself with developing backgrounds and motivations for every grunt the organisation uses. Chapters One and Two further explore why an individual might act in a lawless and unethical manner. Large organisations, however, are a bit more abstract. A few motivations for forming evil organisations are discussed below.

HARD MEN

The founder may be solely focused on an objective, willing to take any steps needed to achieve his or her goal — even if those actions might be considered evil. Sample goals include political or economic domination on a global scale; the eradication of one or more races, species, or other classifications of life forms; or rendering certain institutions, segments of the population, nations, or even ideologies powerless.

Not all of these goals need be villainous in and of themselves. The founder of the organisation may actually believe that hard decisions now will bring about some greater good in the future. For example, a wealthy scientist, anguished by the impending death of his child due to a rare, incurable disease, decides to form a group to kidnap others similarly afflicted in order to study the disease more closely. His often-cruel experiments with radical potential cures on these subjects are horrifying, yet he believes them to be justified if they can lead to a cure that will save his child's life as well as the lives of others. He rationalises his actions by dismissing the importance of the time remaining to the victims as well as their quality of life, especially in comparison to the "greater good."

This quest for a cure could lead the scientist to any number of other crimes including: stealing medical equipment, pharmaceuticals, or money to finance his research. If he runs out of subjects, he could even resort to kidnapping healthy people and infecting them with the illness to make sure his experiments remain uninterrupted. Once someone decides that a "little evil" is worth a greater good, there's seldom anything to stop him or her from greater and greater sins towards that same, perhaps unreachable, goal.

BOREDOM

Having conquered all that the normal world has thrown at him or her, the founder now seeks a new challenge. He finds it in the paranormal adventurers of the world, both good and evil. Lacking innate abilities

personally, the founder creates a villainous group to use as his or her tool in this game of powers. The founder might be in the game for the joy of competition alone, or he or she might enjoy the battle of wits with the heroes: move and countermove, thrust and parry.

PROFIT SHARING

Not all villainous organisations have deeply held beliefs or vast socio-political agendas to pursue. Sometimes they just want to get rich and find working together makes sense, especially in a world full of nosy superheroes. Real-world drug cartels and organised-crime families are in it strictly for money and power; there is no reason villainous organisations cannot be as ruthlessly profit-minded. The interruption of the money flow is what stimulates these villains to respond, rousing the organisation to fight back.

WRESTLING FOR CONTROL

The desire for power is also a primary force behind many villainous groups. It can easily be a defining element of a campaign. Perhaps the founder seeks to use the organisation to bring attention to the perceived slight. Alternatively, perhaps the group is being used as a tool to directly address the wrong suffered by its leader. This is where the oft-used goal of "world domination" comes into play, with the goal of having the power of nations, continents, or even planets within ones grasp.

PAYBACK

A much more direct motivation is revenge. The founder feels he or she has been somehow wronged in the past by a person, family, or faction, and the organisation comes into being as the instrument of his or her revenge. The offence can be real, exaggerated, or even imagined — the origin or validity of the slight aren't relevant. The only thing that matters is evening the score.

SHIFTING PURPOSES

A final point must be made regarding motivations: they can change over time. Whether the result of intense introspection, a soul-shaking revelation that what the group does truly is evil, recovery from insanity, or even the achievement of the initial goal, people and groups can change their focus. With such a change in focus often comes a shift in the goals of the group as well. See the section on Goals (page 92) for more details.

THE PHOENIX COLLECTIVE

The Phoenix Collective was conceived in the late 1960s in the mind of Juan Moreno Rodrigues, the first-born son of wealthy Brazilian parents. Half-Portuguese and half-Spanish, Juan's family is influential in agriculture and shipping. His father, Umberto Rodrigues, also served in Brazil's diplomatic corps for much of Juan's youth. When Juan became a teenager, his father began taking him along on diplomatic missions, hoping to show the boy the world outside Brazil's deeply divided class structures.

His father showed Juan the untapped potential of the poor nations and impoverished peoples around the world. He explained how it was the duty of government, of civilisation, to educate these people and bring them into the modern world. Juan was moved by witnessing famine, disease, and exploitation by local despots. He decided he would use his family's wealth and influence to help others the world over.

When Juan came of age, his father sent him to the US to attend college. He applied to the University of California at Berkeley — the year was 1967. There he was swept up in the birth of counterculture, part of the burgeoning anti-war movement and involved with the whole scene: hippies, drugs, the sexual revolution, and more. Embracing his new perspectives, Juan pursued degrees in Political Science and Business. After graduating, he eschewed the corporate world and worked for several charities and non-profit organisations including Amnesty International, honing his skills on extremely convoluted legal casework.

Juan's time with the activist groups taught him about the dangers that rampant pollution, acid rain, and deforestation presented to the planet. He added environmentalism to his list of passions, and took it upon himself to devote his time and resources to a host of environmental protection groups — some with cleaner records than others.

As the corporate and political globalisation trends strengthened in the 1980s, Juan found a focus for his passions: a vision of a group that could truly make a difference. With his experience in international law and advocacy groups across the globe he pooled his resources and started the Phoenix Collective in 1985. Its goals were to monitor working conditions, pay, and safety in Third-World countries, where large, Western multinational corporations moved to take advantage of lower labour costs and lax regulations. The Phoenix

LIBERTY

JUSTICE

SECURITY

PEACE

CHAPTER FOUR
ORGANISATIONS

Collective concentrated its work in Central and South America in its formative years, then branched out to Africa and the Middle East.

In 1995, the World Trade Organisation was established, and the Phoenix Collective had a new target. The WTO was run by wealthy member nations, who's alleged secrecy, strong-arm tactics, and ability to revoke or override local laws worried many around the world. The WTO and the Phoenix Collective butted heads on numerous occasions; Juan developed an entire division devoted to following the WTO's actions and legal initiatives, then organising opposition and filing their own legal motions to block the WTO when necessary. It was no small secret that the WTO quickly came to regard the Phoenix Collective as more than just a simple nuisance.

It was not long after the WTO and Phoenix had gone head-to-head for the fourth time that Juan Moreno Rodrigues's life changed forever. The WTO took a dim view of this special interest group that kept continually interfering. Its top members set a plan in motion to discredit Juan, as the leader of the Phoenix Collective, in hopes of convincing them to back down. Juan's father had left the management of the family's agricultural and shipping businesses in the hands of foreign partners. When the Phoenix Collective argued against some of the WTO's policies, those partners were encouraged to take over the Rodrigues's businesses, "uncovering" international trade violations stretching back for years. The family was disgraced, losing everything in court battles and media circuses until Juan's parents were left with little more than the clothes on their backs.

Juan was not hurt financially by the debacle and the Phoenix Collective was not affected. He was enraged, however, by what he perceived as an attack against his family by unethical and immoral interests who were willing to attack his loved ones in order to silence him. He stood tall, however, and refused to back down. Less than a year later, Juan's mother passed away from a heart condition, judged by her physicians as stress induced. Within two months, his father committed suicide, unable to cope with the loss of his wife on top of everything else he had suffered.

The death of his father devastated Juan. Unable to come to terms with the death of the man who had always been his role model, Juan threw himself into his work. He became obsessed with the WTO. He was unable to uncover any solid proof of their involvement, but that only fuelled his obsession. Months of rage, depression, and overwork left him mentally shattered, and it was in this state that he conceived a plan to wreak vengeance on those responsible for the ruin of his family — the Reborn.

THE REBORN

In 1997, Juan laid the foundations for the criminal terrorist group known as the Reborn, named for the mythical phoenix's most legendary ability. He recruited from among the Phoenix Collective's own agents, looking for people who believed in the Collective's mission but chafed under its legal and ethical restrictions. Those who believed in victory over capitalistic oppression at any price were actively recruited. These radicals formed the core of the Reborn.

Rodrigues installed these members in Collective offices and outposts around the world, many in Third-World nations. They were given instructions to recruit like-minded members among the indigenous population into cells, which Rodrigues would later activate to perform special operations, such as corporate sabotage, industrial espionage, violent strikes, protests, and more violent activities such as assault, theft, kidnapping, and so on. By the end of the 20th century, Rodrigues had cells in every major nation across the globe.

The Reborn's early efforts contained most of its outright criminal activity to Third-World locales, where law-enforcement was ill equipped to investigate their activities. Missions included terrorising corporate officers, inciting riots, and vandalism of corporation property. Members also used word-of-mouth and the indigenous peoples' native distrust of foreigners to dissuade their comrades from taking jobs with the multinationals.

Unaware that the various difficulties they experienced were part of an organised plan, many of the corporations worked to isolate their employees from the "dangerous radicals" in the local populace. When the Reborn's efforts graduated from coercion to organisation, several companies sought to break these labour movements by launching their own campaigns of investigation, harassment, intimidation, mass firings of suspected "dissidents," and even violent strike-breaking tactics. Of course, these short-sighted tactics only fuelled the Reborn's efforts to insinuate itself more deeply in the fabric of the workers' world.

GOALS

In many cases, a villainous group's motivation and goals are identical. For example, the scientist from the earlier example (page 89) forms a group whose purpose is to cure a terminal disease, thereby saving his son's life. The scientist is also motivated by this goal; they are effectively one and the same. This, however, is not always the case.

Motivation can provide the means to achieve a goal instead of being a goal in and of itself. Motivations are often abstract. Revenge isn't something the group's founder can hold in his or her hands (unless holding the severed head of a hated enemy counts). Motivation describes why a villain or villainous group takes the actions it does; goals are what the organisation hopes to achieve by those actions.

Two classic comic-book goals weren't mentioned in the Motives section (see page 89) because they represent the (possible) result of actions rather than the reason: conquering the world and blowing it up. The group in question may wish to conquer or destroy the world for any number of reasons, but the "why" of what they're doing is their motivation. Global dominance or planetary annihilation is the goal.

THE LEADER'S GOALS

The founder's motives usually play directly towards the group's goals, but this is not always true. Two primary exceptions to this rule exist: one, the founder is lying about the professed goal of the organisation; or two, the founder's goals change after the group's creation, leading him or her to take steps to alter the organisation to reflect his or her new objectives.

Why assume that a person capable of creating a vast, subversive, criminal, or terrorist organisation tells the truth about the group's goals, even to the group's own members? If the founder feels his or her goal is beyond the intellectual reach of others, too personal to share, or so ethically questionable that the rank and file would revolt, then he or she is likely to fabricate a palatable cover story. This cover will play to the group's desires. Many members will believe in it simply because they want to, regardless of the lack of substantiating evidence. On the other hand, this false purpose may not withstand external investigation.

As an alternative, the founder may only reveal a portion of his or her true goal — enough to satisfy the fools working for the organisation. This should placate them, at least until the heroes appear to confront the founder with evidence of his or her true plan in front of the troops.

Finally, people change. If the group achieves its initial goal, it will naturally turn towards a new objective (or a continuation of the original). On the other hand, if the group proves unable to achieve its goals, the leader might re-evaluate his or her plans rather than dismantle the organisation altogether. Alternatively, the group may so utterly fail (possibly due to heroic interference) that the founder shifts the organisation's focus to eliminating those who stand in its way. The group can resume its original agenda once these obstacles have been removed.

RODRIGUES'S GOALS

Juan Moreno Rodrigues is no longer the fervent social reformer he once was. His mental instability has deepened into profound psychosis. As his grip on reality and morality weakened over the last few years, he's left much of the Phoenix Collective's day-to-day operations to his subordinates.

He still retains control of the group, however, and doesn't hesitate to use it for his own ends. His position as President, CEO, and CFO of the Phoenix Collective gives him the autonomy to guide his Reborn "managers" around the globe, directing their actions and providing data, funding, and equipment. He spends hours concocting grandiose schemes of vengeance against those he believes to have wronged him, then uses the Reborn to enact this revenge.

THE GROUP'S GOALS

In most cases, the goals of the villainous organisation mirror those of the founder. Exceptions to this rule exist, however, adding complexity to an otherwise straightforward situation. Now the heroes have to learn to differentiate between the group and the founder, possibly becoming involved in conflict between the two and choosing sides as necessary in the interests of justice.

The first reason why an organisation's goals might diverge is if the members realise the founder's goal involves a threat to their continued life and health. Such a risk must go beyond the prospect of merely being beaten up by heroes; for example, a would-be world conqueror decides that if he or she can't rule Earth, then there shall be no Earth to rule. No matter how well the would-be dictator is paying the members, they are not going to be

CHAPTER FOUR
ORGANISATIONS

very happy if neither they nor the planet are going to be around when they retire. This scenario is also applicable if the members discover the founder lied to them about the group's true purpose. Even the most hardened criminals might balk when they learn that their employer intends to destroy Empire City once its protectors have been eliminated as opposed to letting each of them carve out his or her miniature kingdom as promised.

The second reason a group's goals might deviate from the founder's objectives is if the members decide they don't need their boss anymore. For example, if a supervillain decides to organise a vast group of robbers, burglars, and hackers to raise money to build a superweapon, the thieves could decide they have no wish to throw away their hard-earned wealth on a ludicrous scheme to destroy a hero. They could decide to keep stealing money until the heroes or the police get too close, then close up shop and split all the loot amongst themselves.

GOALS IN CONFLICT

Whenever a difference in goals arises within an organisation, conflict is inevitable. Unfortunately, the heroes of the campaign might never notice this conflict — but where's the fun in that? Conflict between enemy forces provides weaknesses for the heroes exploit when they confront bickering foes, giving the GM a chance to draw the characters deeper into the plot.

The heroes can discover or deduce an existing conflict after they've begun combating the organisation. The shift in goals could show itself in a change of tactics, targets, or co-ordination in battle. If there is open conflict within the group, certain members may refuse to come to the aid of others who disagree with them, giving the heroes a chance to neutralise an ordinarily difficult adversary with ease.

Once the heroes have noticed the schism, the GM can draw the characters in by having various factions approach them for assistance against the others. A displaced leader could ask for help regaining control of his or her now-out-of-control minions before they destroy the city. A member of an organisation could realise the folly of his or her former leader and ask for help in bringing the founder to justice. One or more competing factions of an organisation could approach the heroes in an effort to tip the scales in their favour. Any or all of these scenarios could throw the characters in the midst of the action, as they must then decide if this is an elaborate trap, whose side to take, or whether to get involved at all.

Assuming the heroes do offer their assistance, what to do next is still a difficult quandary. If the organisation's latest goal remains villainous in nature (but is less abhorrent than any others with which the heroes are presented), do they now turn on their recent allies and battle the newly-unified group? Perhaps even more importantly, how does the group's new leader act towards his or her erstwhile allies, the heroes?

THE PHOENIX COLLECTIVE'S GOALS

It should be made clear that the Phoenix Collective as a whole is not a criminal organisation. It is staffed and funded by well-meaning political and social activists. Some may disagree with the group's policies, stances, and agendas, but the Phoenix Collective is not the villain of this piece.

The staff of the Collective seeks to insure the safety and fair treatment of Third-World workers, safeguard the environment, and monitor the large multinational corporations that use those work forces. They also seek to reform the World Trade Organisation, creating an open, democratic process of policy making and trade regulation and enforcement that keeps in mind the needs of emerging nations. The Phoenix Collective buys up tracts of endangered rainforest land; organises workers; and protests repressive policies and laws. They engineer work slowdowns and sit-ins to combat unfair labour practices and low pay. They lobby governments and the media to expose the actions of their opponents as reprehensible and promote their views to the public, politicians, and policy makers around the world.

THE REBORN'S GOALS

The Reborn, however, are another question entirely. They exist as an extension of Rodrigues's psychosis. The members carry out acts of eco-terrorism, corporate sabotage, blackmail, extortion, and more. After years of training, the Reborn has recently moved several cells from the Third World into North America. From there, they can take the fight to the heart of multinational corporate culture, striking fear into those Rodrigues blames for his misfortunes.

Rodrigues and his Reborn do not seek to conquer the world in any traditional sense. They see themselves as reformers determined to effect necessary change and rid the world of evil men, rather than as anarchists or terrorists. While the Reborn fights for its cause directly in the home country of its greatest adversaries, Rodrigues and the other leaders concentrate on the battle in the Third World. If the Phoenix Collective can

LIBERTY

JUSTICE

SECURITY

PEACE

CHAPTER FOUR ORGANISATIONS

PAGE
93

organise workers and influence enough governmental bodies, the group can make the world a better place for all. If, along the way, the Reborn has to blow up factories and assassinate certain CEOs to make sure the Collective achieves these ends, so be it.

The leaders of the Reborn see the group as a behind-the-scenes manipulator, not a full-fledged powerbroker. The ideal position for a cell leader of the Reborn would be as a trusted advisor to the ruler of an emerging Third-World nation. The Reborn agent could influence the ruler personally and use the cell to further manipulate policy (for example, by staging attacks on rival factions and manipulating the course of events through covert violence).

The typical rank-and-file cell member of the Reborn sees him or herself as a warrior fighting for the world's future. The men and women who occupy this level of the organisation are recruited from the radical fringes of the Phoenix Collective and other benevolent groups like it. In any such group, there are those who strive to do the right thing while maintaining their principles, while others prefer a more expedient (albeit costly) route to success.

Cell leaders may recruit specifically for key skills, such as demolitions, forgery, electronic espionage, and sabotage. These "talents" come from the mercenary underworld. If a Reborn cell needs extra manpower for a large-scale action, it will hire the most intelligent and ruthless local thugs, mooks, or goons it can find. These mercenary types are involved strictly for the money, and are typically neutral regarding the Reborn's ideals. For this reason, the cell leader gives these people as little information as possible about who's hiring them; while few mercenaries enjoy this tendency, a little extra compensation quells the curiosity of most.

TYPES OF ORGANISATIONS

After the history, motives, and goals of the group have been determined, the GM's next task is to define the organisation's current form. Thus far, the examples of the Phoenix Collective and the Reborn have demonstrated the structure of a vast, immensely wealthy international villainous concern, masked within a benign group devoted to helping workers and environmental concerns the world over. Not all villainous groups, however, require such megalithic structure. This section discusses alternate forms the organisation might take. Note that even a small villainous organisation is not the same as a team of supervillains; see Chapter Three for details on these groups.

CABALS

Some villainous organisations may be quite small, consisting of perhaps a dozen members plus the founder. Such a group may be just starting out; they could be a gang concerned with turf wars, or may have ambitious, even world-spanning plans, but everyone has to start somewhere. This faction also could be a fully functional local organisation, one that needs only a few personnel to operate. Perhaps they hope to remain behind the scenes, a secret society whose wealthy and influential members can manipulate markets, media, and even government ministries into acting in accordance with the group's whims. The group also could be a small cult of religious fanatics seeking to "purify" a city, nation, or the world through some invoked devastation, such as the summoning (or resurrection) of a horrific ancient god, demon, or elder thing.

FAMILIES

Larger than the groups mentioned above are organised-crime "families." Examples from the *Silver Age Sentinels* rulebook include the Gambino, Genovese, and Bonanno families (Chapter 10). These groups are usually limited geographically, and are often restricted to one city — sometimes just certain portions of that city. Within these areas of control, however, these families often possess broad power bases, enjoy significant freedom, and have anywhere from scores to hundreds of members. Other forms a group this size could take include drug cartels, Chinese tongs, paramilitaries, and local police forces (assuming such a group is thoroughly corrupt and opportunistic).

These groups don't always seek conflict with heroes or other authorities. As long as the members and the founder are making money (the most common goal in such a group), such organisations prefer to be left alone to run their illegal businesses in peace. This quiet can be shattered if the heroes or the media uncover some of the group's activities, however, or if a rival faction decides to impinge upon the territory or profits of the group in question.

SECRET SOCIETIES

Larger still are the villainous organisations often known as secret societies. These groups could be bigger, better-established versions of the small cabal of manipulators or the religious cult. Members of these groups are often widespread, with little or no day-to-day contact between them. The society does assemble

CRIMINAL INTENT INTRODUCTION	CRIMINAL INTENT ANATOMY OF A VILLAIN	CRIMINAL INTENT THE LONE VILLAIN	CRIMINAL INTENT SUPERVILLAIN TEAMS	CRIMINAL INTENT ORGANISATIONS	CRIMINAL INTENT MOST WANTED	CRIMINAL INTENT APPENDIX
INTRODUCTION	CHAPTER 1	CHAPTER 2	CHAPTER 3	CHAPTER 4	CHAPTER 5	APPENDIX

periodically at pre-arranged times and places to talk business, address problems, and create new opportunities for profit.

The Illuminati, a shadowy group rumoured by conspiracy theorists to largely control much of what happens in society today, is an excellent example of a secret society. Other possible forms include collegiate organisations such as fraternities and sororities; business organisations such as the Masons, Friars, Elk, and Moose clubs; and historical organisations such as the Templars, or other widespread associations engaged in a unity of villainous purpose.

Such groups might wish to manipulate the economy, national governments, or world-wide financial markets to their own ends. They might also seek to restore some aspect of the past. For example, a world-wide organisation of neo-Nazis might try to use cloning and other DNA research to create a new Adolph Hitler, someone to lead them back towards world domination.

INTELLIGENCE AGENCIES

The next type of organisation is exemplified by real-world examples such as the CIA, Interpol, and other governmental intelligence or counterintelligence agencies. These groups are sanctioned and funded by nations to protect their citizens, as well as track and capture fugitives from the law. In a world where paranoia and conspiracies run rampant, such broad-based, international organisations may also be dedicated to evil, greed, and terror.

These villainous groups are well financed, have hundreds or thousands of operatives around the world, and likely have their hands in every kind of crime and evil imaginable. Drug trafficking, arms dealing, murder, assassination, terrorism, the slave trade, and worse are all parts of this group's portfolio. Many classic evil organisations from the comics fall into this category.

KREUZRITTER'S SPECIAL FORCES

This type of agency might be interested in rounding up (and either studying or destroying) all known metahumans in an effort to unlock the key to their abilities. The group could seek to do this to unlock humanity's full potential or to restrict such knowledge to itself. The group's members might attempt to kill any metahuman they cannot capture or coerce into co-operating with them.

METAHUMAN INVOLVEMENT

After determining the size of the villainous organisation, GMs should next determine the level of metahuman involvement within the group. No hard-and-fast rules exist regarding this decision, but the larger the group, the more likely at least one metahuman villain is associated with it. For smaller unions, a metahuman is likely to be either the founder or a mercenary hired for a particular task. For larger groups, metahumans are more likely to be actual members, and thus share more deeply the group's motives and desired goals. The largest organisations might possess strike teams of evil metahumans who ruthlessly protect the group's interests. GMs know their campaigns best; it remains to them to decide which groups are most likely to hire metahumans or to have them as full members of the group.

THE REBORN

The Reborn qualifies as an enormous global organisation, since it can take advantage of the Phoenix Collective's international standing. The Reborn is able to commandeer use of the Phoenix Collective's offices, information, and materials. This influence greatly enhances the power that Rodrigues wields from his secure, bunker-like office in Sao Paulo, Brazil.

The problem heroes encounter when combating the Reborn is determining just where it ends and the Phoenix Collective begins. Of course, this is also the group's weakness, since disclosure of the Reborn's links to the Phoenix Collective could spell doom for both associations, not just the criminal organisation hidden beneath the greater group's presence.

HIERARCHY

This section discusses a few common ways to structure such a group and the pros and cons of each arrangement. The group's size plays a major role in determining its configuration. Exceptions exist here as

well: a small group might be run like an army platoon, or a large group could be administered as a democracy, with the organisation's founder having the position of president or prime minister.

OPEN STRUCTURE

For small groups, the most common structure is an open one. Few enough people exist in the group that everyone knows everybody else. They all know the founder, his or her motives in forming the group, and the goals for the organisation (unless the founder is lying, as noted earlier). The founder remains the group's leader, but all members are free to voice their opinions and dissent over certain policies or decisions the group undertakes.

TIERED STRUCTURE

For mid-size groups, a hierarchy mimicking that of corporations or the military often exists. Both of these forms of administration have been proven to work over time, and a leader could do worse than to follow one of these examples.

COMPARTMENTALISED STRUCTURE

The larger groups might use the military structure (it's easier to manage such a far-flung enterprise when a strict sense of discipline exists) or these groups might use a "cell" structure. Each member of the group knows only a handful of other members, regardless of rank or station. Should a cell be exposed or infiltrated by the authorities or heroes, only that cell becomes compromised; the rest of the organisation adapts to its loss, changes any relevant plans as needed, and carries on with as little disruption as possible to the whole.

THE PHOENIX COLLECTIVE'S HIERARCHY

The Phoenix Collective has business offices in over a dozen major cities around the world: Sao Paulo (the global headquarters), Budapest, Cairo, Canberra, Chicago, Empire City, Hong Kong, Johannesburg, Mexico City, Montreal, Moscow, New Delhi, Paris, Seattle, Seoul, Taipei, Tokyo, and a recently opened office in Thulestag. The Phoenix Collective is organised along traditional business lines.

Rodrigues works from the Phoenix Collective's headquarters in Sao Paulo, Brazil. Leaving most daily operations to his underlings, Rodrigues spends his time at the office taking care of Reborn business. He uses the latest high-tech, encrypted satellite communications and hard-wired computer systems to prevent electronic

and mundane eavesdropping. He installed these systems in all regional offices after their Seattle office was hacked. Rodrigues believes that an electronics conglomerate whom the Phoenix Collective was publicly fighting supplied the hackers. The changes after the theft not only improved the security of the Phoenix Collective and its employees from further data thefts, but it also allowed Rodrigues to communicate privately with his "managers" in the Reborn.

THE REBORN'S HIERARCHY

The Reborn exists in a cell structure. Each unit or group is autonomous and works without knowledge of other cells or even the reasons behind an assigned task. Any cell member knows only the other members with whom he or she normally works, with each group numbering roughly six agents or less

MANAGEMENT

The lone exception to this policy is Rodrigues himself. He knows the Manager of each city's Reborn personnel and has a hand in choosing each recruit. Each of the Phoenix Collective's offices is the location of at least one and often several Reborn cells. Each cell's leader is known as a Director, responsible for the men and women of that cell. The Directors report to a city Manager, who has a cover identity as an employee of the Phoenix Collective. The Seattle Manager, for example, knows the five cell Directors the Reborn has in the US Pacific Northwest. The Managers, however, do not know the cell membership — only the Director knows who works for him or her. Directors do not know the other cell leaders; each is aware only of the Manager, and the Reborn operatives that comprise his or her cell.

CELL OPERATIONS

A cell may number up to a half-dozen or so individuals, but they seldom gather in numbers greater than two to four. The skills of each operative determine who works with whom, and thus who that person knows. For example, a cell's electronics expert probably has no need to associate with the cell's forger. If the electronics expert needs an ID card to enter a high-tech research facility on a job, the cell leader instructs the forger to create the identification. The cell leader then passes it on to the electronics expert for his or her mission.

– SOLDIERS

The Reborn recruits and trains their members for combat. Such individuals usually come into conflict with foes no more powerful than corporate security guards, local law-enforcement authorities, and so on. For these Reborn operatives, use the Police Officer template (found in the *SAS* rulebook appendix).

When the Reborn expects its operations might attract attention, more potent, specially trained "Liberator" troops are called in. Use the Special Forces Member template (from the *SAS* rulebook appendix) for these NPCs. Further, when the Reborn uses metahuman operatives (see below), a squad of six to ten Liberators are also dispatched as support.

SUPERVILLAIN OPERATIVES

Another subdivision exists within the Reborn: the superpowered thugs, henchmen, and villains that work with the group. Rodrigues deals with these individuals personally. One or more cells may be instructed to operate in tandem with a particular supervillain for a limited time, but interaction between the cell's members and the villain is kept to a minimum beyond what's necessary for the assigned task. Established villains that the Reborn has worked with before include Coldstone and Kaleidoscope (see pages 103 and 107).

With operations across the globe, the Reborn has also found and recruited a few metahumans on its own. The Reborn investigates these individuals thoroughly to determine if they are ideologically compatible. If so, they are given a cover job with the Phoenix Collective and begin a program of covert training in Reborn doctrine, education, power control, and combat abilities. The first "class" of Reborn metahuman recruits are nearing the end of their training and could appear in the campaign at any time. GMs should define the Reborn villains below with point totals appropriate to their campaigns. These Reborn operatives could operate alone or be called upon to act in unison, perhaps against the heroes who are interfering with Reborn schemes.

– K'ZOR

K'zor is a young Siberian man with the ability to transform himself into both a Siberian tiger and a bipedal, "hybrid" cat-man form. He possesses great strength, superior speed, a heightened sense of smell, and claw attacks in both forms. Having seen repressive rule for most of his life, K'zor believes that limiting the power of government and corporate giants benefits all in the long run. GMs should use the "Cat, Tiger" statistics in the *SAS* rulebook for K'zor's animal form.

CHAPTER FOUR
ORGANISATIONS

| CRIMINAL INTENT INTRODUCTION | CRIMINAL INTENT ANATOMY OF A VILLAIN | CRIMINAL INTENT THE LONE VILLAIN | CRIMINAL INTENT SUPERVILLAIN TEAMS | CRIMINAL INTENT ORGANISATIONS | CRIMINAL INTENT MOST WANTED | CRIMINAL INTENT APPENDIX |
| INTRODUCTION | CHAPTER 1 | CHAPTER 2 | CHAPTER 3 | CHAPTER 4 | CHAPTER 5 | APPENDIX |

LIBERTY

JUSTICE

SECURITY

PEACE

- VOLTARA

Voltara is the chosen name of an Australian teenage girl with the potential for vast power. She's already demonstrated control over electricity, and can generate electrical force fields, electrical energy bolts, and flight. Disgusted by her country's history of mistreating the Aboriginal Australians, she's ready to fight alongside the Reborn to protect the rights of native peoples everywhere.

- BURNT CHURCH

Burnt Church is a disaffected Mi'kmaq Native American from Canada. His superhuman strength, agility, and speed make him a natural scrapper, who the Reborn have trained into a deadly soldier. An angry man, he turns everything into a personal attack and revels in his social agenda. He enjoys tearing down the efforts of those who forced his people off their lands.

RESOURCES

The next step in creating an evil faction is to consider what resources the group has available. Resources mean more than just money; it also includes political clout, popular opinion, and economic pressures such as sanctions and boycotts as well as coercion, blackmail, extortion, sabotage, and kidnapping.

The first thing all GMs should know about their villainous organisations is that the monetary worth of the group need not be defined. Once the organisation's role in the campaign is established, the group should be considered solvent enough to maintain pursuit of its agenda, at least until heroes begin foiling its plans and schemes. GMs should just want to tell a good story involving the group and the heroes' efforts to dismantle it. This needn't require bookkeeping on how much money the organisation made from its illegal activities during the previous year.

Though a GM can ignore financial details in game, financial resources remain an important factor in judging how potent a villainous organisation will be. A highly solvent group has the reserves to suffer a few setbacks at the hands of interfering heroes without much difficulty, whereas a smaller or less wealthy faction may find itself teetering on the brink if the heroes disrupt one too many drugs, arms, or illegal immigrant shipments. After all, the organisation does business with various sellers of illegal goods to gain materials and equipment; these suppliers do not take kindly to not being paid.

Villainous groups can use such illegal activities as drugs or arms smuggling, kidnapping for ransom, protection rackets, loan-sharking, gambling, and

JANUS TAKES STOCK OF HIS LASTEST SUCCESSFUL EFFORT

outright theft to increase their financial resources, either as a standard practice or when circumstances require the quick infusion of cash.

Political influence is a less material — but no less tangible — resource upon which organisations can draw. A villainous group with a legitimate "front" operation can openly lobby local, state, and national politicians to take measures that allow the group's criminal elements an easier time at accomplishing their goals. Political power can also be used to pressure elected officials to look the other way when the organisation acts, using a subtle form of blackmail that is very hard to trace.

Organisations that do legitimate business of some sort can apply economic pressures such as price fixing, employing sanctions, restricting the flow of product to market, and stock-market or financial bookkeeping manipulations. In addition, having a business for a front can allow the organisation to launder money more effectively, thus keeping their ill-gotten gains from being easily traced. All of these can affect the group's finances and thus how well the organisation is able to pursue its goals.

For criminal unions, the means used to influence others are even less restricted. A group could kidnap the family of an important diplomat, scientist, or even a metahuman hero. Using that leverage, it can then force the individual to carry out some task for the organisation in exchange for the safe return of the person's loved ones. A group that uncovers illegal activity or some past transgression on the part of a powerful public figure could threaten to release evidence of the misdeed to the media unless the person performs services for the group. Examples of behaviour that could lead to blackmail include: extramarital affairs, embezzling, fraud, drug use, sexual harassment, an abusive relationship, etc. Of course, the group could merely concoct a believable lie and "discover" spurious evidence; they then threaten to release that bogus tale to the public unless the figure co-operates.

A villainous group proficient in theft could also make off with the government's experimental new jet engine, personal rocket pack, hand-held cannon, etc., and vow to return it only if the group's founder is released from prison, or if a metahuman-registration bill is killed before it becomes law, and so on. A group can also use funds to bribe officials to get what the group wants, even if what it wants is just to be left alone.

THE PHOENIX COLLECTIVE'S RESOURCES

The Phoenix Collective is a well-organised, well-run international group. With that in mind, the resources it commands are staggering for a third-party activist group. The Collective has built upon the fortunes of both Rodrigues and other wealthy philanthropists, giving it significant financial backing for anything it might wish to attempt. Its political actions, both in support and opposition to governments around the globe, have won it considerable power in enforcing its will. The Reborn naturally have access to all of these resources as well, and use them to enact their own twisted agendas.

THE REBORN'S RESOURCES

Juan Moreno Rodrigues takes full advantage of the Phoenix Collective's expansive influence when orchestrating the activities of the Reborn. He moves operatives around the world under the guise of Collective employees. He secretly siphons off money to fund the evil and often-violent acts of the group, train his operatives, and hire metahuman mercenaries.

The Reborn also makes use of all the political and criminal sources of influence listed earlier (page 98). In fact, the group is currently blackmailing a United Nations diplomat from the Pacific Rim over an episode of past infidelity. They are using him as an information leak. Also, an East African dictator has recently undergone a change of heart regarding a foreign diamond brokerage who wants to buy into the country's newest mines. While he's not announced this, he currently intends to let the broker into his nation and set up the infrastructure it requires. Then, when a paramilitary group terrorises the region, he'll escort the foreigners from his lands under armed guard, for their own protection. Finally, he will nationalise the diamond industry, using the abandoned infrastructure. While these actions will make him unpopular on the world market, he hopes it will bring back his son who has been missing for over a month (and in the care of the Reborn).

AREAS OF OPERATIONS

Where does a group fit in the campaign world, and what role should it play? The most common locale for the group to be placed is the city or area in which the campaign is based, the region the heroes call home. It

LIBERTY
JUSTICE
SECURITY
PEACE

CHAPTER FOUR ORGANISATIONS

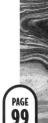

PAGE 99

isn't necessary, however, to place the organisation's home base in the characters' hometown. All that is needed is for the group to have an interest in that city that the characters can run across or thwart, and thus realise the existence of the group as a whole. GMs are encouraged to determine the best locales for their villainous creations given the story they wish to tell.

Also, the group's form and goals should hint at its role in the game. A covert group or reconnaissance team does all it can to gather information without others discovering it presence. Meanwhile, a squad of assassins hired to wipe out the heroes would enter town, arrange an ambush, make the attempt and leave as quickly as it arrived, whether successful or not. A huge, powerful villainous organisation can become the main focus of the campaign, as the heroes keep tracking down and stopping plan after scheme after plot, slowly whittling away the evil group's resources and patience before a final, climactic battle from which only one side will emerge.

FINAL TOUCHES

GMs need to make the organisation seem realistic enough that not only the characters but also the players believe the group could exist and be a dangerous threat to their heroes, the city, or the world. GMs are encouraged to take what's presented here and create their own villainous groups with which to plague their game's do-gooders. Alter the Phoenix Collective and the Reborn to make them work in your campaign. Test the players' mettle, not just the heroes' statistics.

With globe-spanning organisations such as the Phoenix Collective and Reborn, it's impossible to detail all the regions in which one or both groups are currently working, but the section below describes a few actions each group endeavours to accomplish at present.

THE PHOENIX COLLECTIVE'S OPERATIONS

The Phoenix Collective's global offices co-ordinate field teams of doctors, scientists, teachers, and aid workers on every continent except Antarctica. The group's humanist and humanitarian efforts benefit thousands around the globe, with the majority of their efforts concentrated in Southeast Asia and Latin America. They have branch offices in Washington, DC and Empire City to lobby Congress and the UN, respectively.

THE REBORN'S OPERATIONS

Rodrigues has scores of cells working feverishly on various plots in numerous locales around the world.

Rodrigues has been bribing officials in Sao Paulo for nearly 20 years to keep Brazilian authorities from peering too closely at the company's tax records or the many shipments of dubiously legal materials that leave the city under the humanitarian banner of the Phoenix Collective.

The Reborn has a covert reconnaissance cell in Empire City at all times, with orders to track the Guard and Sentinel in particular. Rodrigues has focussed some of his irrational hatred upon Max Liberty as the symbol of all that's wrong with the greedy West: big, shiny, attractive, and too powerful. If the Reborn ever feels confident enough to make a major play against the metahuman forces of the West, the plan will surely involve an assassination attempt on Sentinel.

In Seattle, USA, a Reborn cell of hackers, accompanied by electronics/computer-oriented metahumans, freely roams the internal networks of one of the most powerful computer and software manufacturers in the world. Several of the cell's operatives have become moles, working for the company itself and inserting catastrophic "sleeper" viruses and "back doors" into the company's newest Internet software. Soon, all will be in place for Rodrigues to bring the company, and millions of computers around the world, to a screeching, hard-drive melting halt.

In Mexico City, Mexico, rumours persist about a powerful metahuman child in the shantytown slums outside the city proper. The Reborn Manager there is exhausting every avenue to find the child and indoctrinate him or her into the group and its metahuman-training program.

Montreal, Canada, houses a Reborn cell dedicated to DNA research using techniques and equipment stolen by another cell from a Matthews GenTech lab. The cell, comprised of top-notch geneticists, hopes to unlock the genetic key to unleash all of humanity's metahuman potential. They hope that a world with many more superhumanly powerful individuals will place less strain on the global biosphere and promote individuals' rights around the world.

In Seoul, South Korea, the Reborn cells work covertly to keep anti-American sentiment at a fever pitch in an effort to eventually oust the last remaining superpower from the peninsula. Unfortunately, they have been undermined due to recent actions by North Korea's leadership. Many recent converts have gone back to thinking that having 20,000 American troops along the DMZ (de-militarised zone) might be a good precaution.

CHAPTER FOUR ORGANISATIONS

CRIMINAL INTENT INTRODUCTION	CRIMINAL INTENT ANATOMY OF A VILLAIN	CRIMINAL INTENT THE LONE VILLAIN	CRIMINAL INTENT SUPERVILLAIN TEAMS	CRIMINAL INTENT ORGANISATIONS	CRIMINAL INTENT MOST WANTED	CRIMINAL INTENT APPENDIX
INTRODUCTION	CHAPTER 1	CHAPTER 2	CHAPTER 3	CHAPTER 4	CHAPTER 5	APPENDIX

LIBERTY

JUSTICE

SECURITY

PEACE

ARTIFICER (175 CHARACTER POINTS – TRI-STAT)

GADGETEER LEVEL 7; 195 POINTS — d20 SYSTEM

IDENTITY: Blake White (Known to some)
OCCUPATION: Inventor, mercenary
FIRST APPEARANCE: Science Unbound #12 (as Blake White), Silver Dime Theatre #1 (as Artificer)
FORMER ALIASES: None
PLACE OF BIRTH: Orange City, Florida
AFFILIATION: None
TERRITORY: Operates worldwide
HEIGHT: 5'10" (178 cm)   **EYES:** Brown
WEIGHT: 190 lbs. (86 kg)   **HAIR:** Silver-gray

Blake White was always smarter than anyone thought. His father was career military, like three generations of Whites before him, and cowed his son into ignoring all of that "pansy brainiac stuff." His mother was far more broken than Blake and never argued with her husband, as much as she might have wanted to. So no one ever saw the genius hiding in the good little soldier.

Blake managed to keep enough control of his own fate to enter the Air Force instead of the Army, long since having learned how to hide even a hint of rebellious thought. Though he managed to stay near the cutting edge, his father's booming voice echoed from childhood enough to keep him in a uniform and out of a lab coat. Then they found the ship.

No one knows where it came from, but whoever the aliens are, they're keeping track of humanity. Their depressing opinion of Earth's development echoed White's deeply buried cynicism all too well. The sphere, on the other hand, was a real prize. One touch, and his own native genius expanded a hundred-fold — no, thousands of times! Better still, endless designs stored themselves in his mind, so advanced that they made tanks look like bear skins and lasers seem like stone knives. Even so, to Blake it was more. The sphere meant freedom.

White stole it, along with enough alien materials to build the simplest of the designs. From there, each successful creation made the next easier. Soon, he could build the most advanced equipment with even mundane resources. He needed money for that, of course, but there was no shortage of buyers for his creations. The genius was free, and a lifetime of walking in lock-step had taught him to hate anything that would restrain his ideas. Blake never saw his father again, although learning the old tyrant had hung himself did elicit a brief smile before moving on to his next experiment.

The Artificer (as he soon called himself) has no more interest in villainy than heroics. His only concern is knowledge, and he will do anything for his one true love. Heroes, however, often have a hard time accepting that. Currently, the Artificer makes himself available through a company called Artifice Designs, LLC; an artificial intelligence named Galatea is the public face of the company.

Though captured many times early in his career, the Artificer's enhanced mind easily worked out escape plans, and his extensive physical modifications kept authorities from identifying him as deserter Blake White.

The Artificer is rarely the same opponent twice. The statistics listed for the power armour are a baseline he will occasionally return to, but with his Gadgeteer ability he can (and will) modify it to prepare for nearly any opponent. He'll create a cold ray for Sentinel, use a neural disruptor against Red Phoenix, a tractor beam to steal Mother Raven's staff, and any number of specialised attacks to counter specific heroes. His only apparent limitation (and redeeming feature) is a general respect for other scientists. For example, he has never used lethal force against the brilliant Slipstream.

While the Artificer will hire himself out for money, White greatly prefers to sell his creations instead. That way, he gets to do what he loves, and the whole world can be witness to his genius.

BODY	8	ATTACK COMBAT VALUE	10
MIND	14	DEFENCE COMBAT VALUE	11
SOUL	6	HEALTH POINTS	110

STR 14	DEX 16	CON 20	INT 30	WIS 15	CHA 11
REF +5	FORT +7	WILL +7		BASE TO HIT MODIFIER	+4
BASE AC MODIFIER +7				HIT POINTS	+62

TRI-STAT					d20 SYSTEM	
LVL	PTS	**CHARACTERISTIC ATTRIBUTES**			RANK	PTS
8	16	Gadgeteer			8	(14)
5	10	Gadgets			5	(4)
14	14	Highly Skilled			1	(0)
17	68	Item of Power "Power Armour"			17	(60)
	1	Restricted Use; Configured for Artificer's DNA				1
	-5	• Activation Time (Item of Power; One minute; +1 BP can Pause)				-5
	-1	• Concentration (Item of Power; Linked to Activation Time)				-1
2	4	Tough			2	4
4	12	Wealth			4	(7)

LVL	PTS	**ITEM OF POWER'S ATTRIBUTES (POWER ARMOUR)**	RANK	PTS
5	15	Armour	5	15
1	3	Attack Combat Mastery (Targeting Array)	1	3
4	8	Defence Combat Mastery (Warning Systems)	4	8
3	9	Extra Defences (Threat Analysis Matrix)	3	9
4	16	Flight	4	16
5	5	Heightened Senses (Hearing, Sight, Electric Current Detection, Radar Sense, Ultravision)	5	5
6	24	Special Attack "Nimbus Beam" (100 / [[5d6+10]] Damage, Homing)	6	24
6	6	Special Defence (Oxygen x2, Disease x2, Poison x2)	6	6
	-1	• Restriction (Special Defence; Oxygen supply only lasts six hours)		-1

LVL	PTS	**POWER ATTRIBUTES**	RANK	PTS
1	1	Divine Relationship	1	1
5	10	Enhanced Stat (Mind / [[Intelligence]])	4	(6)
5	5	Special Defence (Futuretech implants — Ageing x2, Pain x2, Sleep)	5	5

LVL	PTS	**SKILLS**	RANK
2	4	Architecture (Fortifications)	5
4	16	Biological Sciences (Physiology)	11
5	20	Computers (Programming)	12
3	15	Demolitions (Artificial Structures)	6
5	20	Electronics (Cybernetics)	12
3	12	Forgery (Electronic Documents)	8
4	4	Languages (English, Afrikaans, French, German, Japanese, Mandarin, Russian, Spanish)	7
5	20	Mechanics (Armour)	12
2	8	Military Sciences (Intelligence Analysis)	5
5	25	Physical Sciences (Engineering)	12
2	4	Piloting (Jet Fighter)	5
1	12	Ranged Defence (Personal)	2
1	10	Special Ranged Attack (Nimbus Beam)	2

PTS	**DEFECTS**	PTS
-1	Famous (Artificer; International black market)	-1
	Incomplete Training (No Organisational Ties)	-2
-1	Marked (Odd-colour skin, from implants)	-1
-1	Special Requirement (Special Defence requires maintenance, such as injections, surgery, etc.)	-1
-3	Wanted (Several governments; US Air Force in particular)	-3

COLDSTONE (225 CHARACTER POINTS – TRI-STAT)

Costumed Fighter Level 5; 240 Points — d20 System

IDENTITY: Jefferson Walker (Secret)
OCCUPATION: Supermercenary
FIRST APPEARANCE: The Guard #12
FORMER ALIASES: None
PLACE OF BIRTH: Empire City
AFFILIATION: Varies
TERRITORY: Operates worldwide
HEIGHT: 6'4" (193 cm)   **EYES:** Brown
WEIGHT: 220 lbs. (100 kg)   **HAIR:** Black

Some villains are made, and others are born. Jefferson Walker is definitely the latter.

Born in South-Central LA and raised by teen parents who were too busy shooting up or shooting it out to do more than feed and clothe him, Jefferson learned self-reliance at an early age, along with a disdain that bordered on hatred for everyone around him. The gangs wanted power more than peace, and the cops were just the biggest gang around. Everyone else was either using drugs or using each other. Jefferson, however, had one thing going for him — himself. Against all odds, he was strong, tough, self-possessed, and brilliant. He saw that his one way out was school, and that he could live long enough to achieve an education by being too scary to mess with. He excelled at both.

At the tender age of 15, Walker had escaped the slums and was working as a "consultant" for various upscale criminal concerns, but even that was just a start. He knew exactly where he was headed. The real power, in every sense of the word, was in the metahuman market.

Eventually, Walker had enough money and influence to pull a few strings. The Artificer, Matthews GenTech, even the US government — all had created metahumans. Jefferson was not going to take stupid risks, but lived by the mantra, "high risk, high gain." Buying data from several sources, he took it to the Artificer as trade; in exchange, he wanted to be turned into the ultimate powerhouse-for-hire. The Artificer was intrigued by Walker's proposition and impressed by the man's fearlessness, and a bargain was struck.

It was more effective than Jefferson had ever dreamed. Superstrong and nearly indestructible, he was surprised by abilities he never conceived of, such as his freezing aura. A quick trip to a spin doctor christened him Coldstone, the ultimate supermercenary.

Walker is 25 now. His reputation has grown to epic heights. Artificer continues to study Walker, and recently discovered another benefit of the stone body — Jefferson does not age while transformed. Coldstone can have centuries to enjoy life if he is careful. Coldstone's greatest power is also the Sentinel's weakness, he has more money than some countries, and he's one of the toughest men of all time. Life is good.

Coldstone loves his work, but he never lets that get in the way of professionalism. He is not just a powerhouse. Conquerors hire him to turn a disorganised horde of metahuman thugs into a force to be reckoned with. Jefferson sometimes wishes the lessons would last longer than one master plan, but the stupidity of second-rate supervillains is his job insurance. Coldstone has a deserved reputation for loyalty — he stays bought — but he is not stupid. When the heroes unravel a mastermind's plan he flees, heading back to his vast fortune and island mansion in the Arabian Sea, where he avoids extradition by doing the occasional favour for local governments.

Underestimating Coldstone in a fight is a good way to earn a quick and cruel death. Walker is a fearless opponent who enjoys a good throwdown. He would like to take out Sentinel some day, because killing the world's most legendary hero would make his reputation for all time. He's that confident. Coldstone does not hunt Sentinel, though, because it wouldn't be professional. He's that competent.

BODY 7/12	**AGILITY** 7/9	**ATTACK COMBAT VALUE**	13/15
MIND 10		**DEFENCE COMBAT VALUE**	11/13
SOUL 11		**HEALTH POINTS**	90/195

STR 14/62	**DEX** 14/12	**CON** 16/36	**INT** 18 **WIS** 18 **CHA** 20
REF +5	**FORT** +6/+16	**WILL** +5	**BASE TO HIT MODIFIER** +9
BASE AC MODIFIER +6			**HIT POINTS** 46/154

TRI-STAT				d20 SYSTEM	
LVL	PTS	**CHARACTERISTIC ATTRIBUTES**		RANK	PTS
1	1	Adaptation (Cold)		1	1
2	14	Agents (2 Lieutenants; 50 Character Points each)		2	14
4	12	Attack Combat Mastery		4	(9)
2	2	Combat Technique (Judge Opponent; Weapons Encyclopaedia)		2	(0)
4	8	Defence Combat Mastery		4	8
1	8	Extra Attacks		1	(3)
1	3	Extra Defences		1	(0)
1	1	Features (Appearance)		1	1
7	7	Highly Skilled		1	1
8	16	Organisational Ties (Various groups he's hired to organise)		8	16
6	18	Wealth		6	18
	-2	• Restriction (Wealth seeded away, difficult to access)			-2

LVL	PTS	**POWER ATTRIBUTES**		RANK	PTS
10	90	Alternate Form (Coldstone)		10	90
	-1	• One-Way Transformation (Alternate Form; Must stay transformed for at least 12 hours)			-1

LVL	PTS	**ALTERNATE FORM "COLDSTONE" ATTRIBUTES**		RANK	PTS
5	10	Enhanced Stat (Body) / [[Constitution]]		5	10
1	5	Environmental Influence (Cold; Area 3; Duration 1)		1	5
	-1	• Permanent (Environmental Influence)			-1
6	48	Mass Increase		6	48
	-5	• Maximum Force (Mass Increase)			-5
5	20	Special Attack "Freezing Aura" (40 / [[2d6+4]] Damage, Area Effect x2, 5 Aura, Burning, Melee)		5	20
	-1	• Limited Use, Ongoing (Special Attack "Freezing Aura")			-1
5	5	Special Attack "Ice Beam" (60 / [[3d6+6]] Damage, Burning, Tangle, Low Penetration)		5	5
6	6	Special Defence (Ageing x2, Oxygen x2, Disease, Poison)		6	6
	-1	• Restriction (Special Defence: Ageing only operates in rock form; human body ages normally)			-1
4	8	Tough		4	8
	-1	Less Capable (Agility / [[Dexterity -2]])			
	-2	Marked (Coldstone; Large gray rocky behemoth)			-2
	-1	Unappealing (Inhuman form)			-1

LVL	PTS	**SKILLS**		RANK
2	4	Cultural Arts (Literature)		2
3	6	Driving (Cars)		3
4	8	Foreign Culture (French, German, Jordanian, Palestinian, Saudi Arabian, Somali)		4
3	3	Gaming (Gambling)		2
4	12	Intimidation (Underworld)		6
3	3	Language (English, Arabic, French, German)		3
4	4	Management & Administration (Mercenary Groups)		4
4	16	Military Sciences (Teamwork)		6
2	6	Stealth (Silent Movement)		4
4	8	Street Sense (Influential Individuals)		4
1	12	Ranged Defence (Personal)		1
1	10	Special Ranged Attack (Ice Beam)		1
1	8	Unarmed Defence (Strikes)		1

PTS	**DEFECTS**		PTS
-2	Famous (Coldstone; Internationally known supervillain/mercenary)		-2
-1	Red Tape (Obeying his current boss)		-1
-2	Skeleton in the Closet (Secret identity)		-2
-3	Wanted (Numerous countries and law enforcement agencies)		-3

LIBERTY
JUSTICE
SECURITY
PEACE

CHAPTER FIVE
MOST WANTED

DARK QUEEN (300 CHARACTER POINTS – TRI-STAT)

COSTUMED WIZARD LEVEL 10; 330 POINTS — d20 SYSTEM

IDENTITY: Zaira (Unknown, but not secret)
OCCUPATION: Monarch
FIRST APPEARANCE: The Guard #75
FORMER ALIASES: Queen of Eternal Shadow
PLACE OF BIRTH: Shadowstone Citadel, Kingdom of Zairin
AFFILIATION: Empire of the Thirteen Planes
TERRITORY: Operates inter-dimensionally
HEIGHT: 6'1" (185 cm) **EYES:** Silver-gray
WEIGHT: 140 lbs. (64 kg) **HAIR:** Indigo

Zaira, the Queen of Eternal Shadow, conqueror of the Thirteen Planes and their absolute ruler, had built a paradise of order, crushing all rebellion that might threaten the perfect peace she'd created. That was a century ago. There were no challenges left for the faerie monarch, and the tedium was driving her mad.

Zaira the Dark Queen, they'd called her, when all she had was a single nation and a tiny army by her side. The faerie queens and kings of her own plane had been clever, powerful in their magic; overthrowing their chaotic lands had taken every jot of brilliance she'd had. The bright faerie were mercurial and impulsive, however, and one by one she'd taken them. A few had sworn to her, and the rest remain frozen in magical shadow even now.

The other planes were easier, divided and scheming as they were. The Dark Queen easily turned one against another. The real trick had been doing it carefully, so as not to destroy what she meant to preserve. Her loyal seneschal and heir, Vara, had come to her from the Third Plane, which had been so stricken with infighting that the Dark Queen had almost had to rebuild the land before she could conquer it.

Now? Zaira was trapped by her own devotion to discipline. Some days, she felt chained to her throne, managing minutiae. She ruled all creation, and it was her royal duty to maintain it.

Then her beloved Vara revealed to her a supreme gift on her Millennial Jubilee: the Thirteen Planes were not all of creation. She'd found a new expanse of worlds with wholly new races, most of whom called themselves humans. The first Vara presented was a queer world, protected by valiant knights called the Guard, but desperately in need of her guidance.

The Dark Queen's first incursions were thwarted, by both these heroes and other, sinister self-styled tyrants, Requiem and Kreuzritter. But those were simple scouting missions, however. She is now at work scheming on how to bring them down. Enchanted agents the equal of these "superheroes" lie in wait on their Earth. Once more, people tremble at the thought of the Dark Queen. She is content.

Classy, brilliant, honourable, amazingly powerful and utterly merciless, the Dark Queen is a conqueror and monarch with few equals. She respects honour and strength, and Earth's heroes have no lack of either.

Her Night magic is very flexible, but not limitless. The magic is best with illusions and mental powers, but she can also create three dimensional solid shadows and summon things of physical or metaphorical darkness. The Dark Queen can travel through places of shadow and darkness, and heal as well as harm. A spell could create numbing cold, but not heat. It should be noted that these examples are suggestions, not absolute limits. The Dark Queen is clever, and has not ruled for over a thousand years without being adaptable. When encountered in her home dimension, however, Zaira's powers are almost total. Thwarting the Dark Queen's invasions should be difficult; overthrowing her rule is virtually impossible.

NOTE: See page (120) in the Appendix for Unseelie Shadow Knaves.

BODY	7	STRENGTH	4	ATTACK COMBAT VALUE	10
MIND	10			DEFENCE COMBAT VALUE	9
SOUL	15			HEALTH POINTS	115

STR 9	DEX 14	CON 14	INT 20	WIS 25	CHA 30
REF +5	FORT +7	WILL +13		BASE TO HIT MODIFIER	+5
BASE AC MODIFIER +3				HIT POINTS	45

TRI-STAT			d20 SYSTEM	
LVL	PTS	**CHARACTERISTIC ATTRIBUTES**	RANK	PTS
5	26	Agents (15 Shadow Knaves; 35 Character Points each)	5	26
1	2	Defence Combat Mastery	1	2
1	3	Extra Defences	1	3
2	2	Features (Appearance x2)	2	2
11	11	Highly Skilled		
5	15	Item of Power (Easy to lose; Crown of Night)	5	15
16	16	Organisational Ties (Queen of Eternal Shadow)	16	16
10	30	Wealth	10	30
	-6	• Restriction (Extremely difficult to access on Earth)		-6

LVL	PTS	**ITEM OF POWER'S ATTRIBUTES (CROWN OF NIGHT)**	RANK	PTS
2	10	Force Field (Stops 40 / [[20]]; Blocks Incorporeal; Full Impact; Area 2)	2	10
	-1	• Detectable (Force Field; Magical/astral energies)		-1
2	8	Flight	2	8
	-1	• Limited Use, Ongoing (Flight)		-1
4	9	Sixth Sense (Astral/Ethereal, Danger, Illusions, Magic; Area 5)	4	9

LVL	PTS	**POWER ATTRIBUTES**	RANK	PTS
8	155	Dynamic Powers (Night, primal; Area 5; Duration 6; Range 10; Targets 6)	8	(113)
	-1	• Detectable (Dynamic Powers; Magic)		-1
		• Reduction (-4; Dynamic Powers; Levels 5-8 only accessible in her own dimension)		
	-3	• Restriction (Dynamic Powers; Completely ineffective against gold)		-3
	-2	• Restriction (Dynamic Powers; Must be able to speak and gesture)		-2
	-2	• Restriction (Dynamic Powers; Range PMV is halved when outside of her own dimension)]		-2
2	2	Mind Shield	2	2
4	4	Special Defence (Ageing x2, Poison x2)	4	4

LVL	PTS	**SKILLS**	RANK
4	8	Cultural Arts (Faerie History)	8
3	3	Etiquette (Upper Class)	7
5	10	Foreign Culture (Dark Empire, Earth, The Thirteen Planes)	8
3	3	Gaming (Board Games)	4
3	9	Intimidation (Political)	4
5	5	Language (Dozens)	10
3	9	Law (Law of Eternal Shadow)	5
3	3	Management & Administration (Government)	4
1	4	Military Sciences (Strategy)	2
5	10	Occult (Faerie)	10
3	6	Performing Arts (Public Speaking)	3
5	40	Power Usage: Shadow magic	10
2	2	Riding (Shadow Lion)	2
4	8	Social Sciences (Politics)	8
2	20	Special Ranged Attack (Dynamic Powers)	4

PTS	**DEFECTS**	PTS
-1	Achilles Heel (Magical light-based Attacks)	-1
-1	Bane (Pure gold)	-1
-2	Blind Fury (Being shown great disrespect; Ends with abject grovelling by, or death of, offender)	-2
-3	Famous (Throughout the Thirteen Planes)	-3
-1	Less Capable (Strength)	
-3	Marked (Dark faerie magic — shadow energy constantly present)	-3
-2	Nemesis (Kreuzritter, Requiem)	-2
-2	Nemesis (All heroes of Earth)	-2
-1	Significant Other (Vara, Seneschal of Eternal Shadow)	-1

LIBERTY
JUSTICE
SECURITY
PEACE

CHAPTER FIVE MOST WANTED

PAGE 104

SILVER AGE SENTINELS

GREEN RONIN (175 CHARACTER POINTS – TRI-STAT)

ADVENTURER LEVEL 5, SKULKER LEVEL 3; 190 POINTS — d20 SYSTEM

IDENTITY: Rachel Wilde (Secret)
OCCUPATION: Archaeologist, relic thief
FIRST APPEARANCE: Lady Starbright #85 (as Rachel Wilde),
Lady Starbright #89 (as Green Ronin)
FORMER ALIASES: None
PLACE OF BIRTH: High Wycombe, England
AFFILIATION: None
TERRITORY: Operates worldwide
HEIGHT: 5'10" (179 cm) **EYES:** Green
WEIGHT: 140 lbs. (64 kg) **HAIR:** Black

Raiding tombs and hunting relics is more than a job to Rachel Wilde. It's in her blood.

Wilde was born to wealthy, upper-class parents and taught from an early age that the hoi polloi were unworthy of the refined pursuits enjoyed by the great — a lesson easy to learn in an era when every tradition was being assaulted. Her parents, however, were hardly bloodless aristocrats. Like generations of Wildes before them, they were adventurers and plunderers with consciences. They stole the mystic and wondrous, true, but never from those who still appreciated them, whether aboriginals or fellow connoisseurs. Greatness, Rachel learned, was not a matter of blood, but of the heart. Though her parents' occult interests ran still deeper, Rachel never learned of them. A disastrous failure left nothing of the estate except a mirrored pool in which her parents' screaming faces were frozen for years. Rachel still has nightmares.

Determined to live up to their expectations, she soon picked up her mother's notes on "the Weapon," a nameless suit of magical armour wielded by warrior-heroines since time immemorial. Much has been said of Rachel's pursuit of it; suffice to say that she fought for it as fiercely as Gebhart or Iron Duke. Her shard does not vanish magically as Red Phoenix's piece does, however. Instead, it compresses itself into a bright green armband, which fits tightly to her right arm, from wrist to elbow. It can be removed, but doing so is painful and unnerving to her.

Though Wilde desires greatly to gain control of the Weapon, she is driven more by understanding and awe than simple greed. She pities Red Phoenix for her naiveté, but respects her love of marvels. Rachel does not begrudge Red Phoenix the Sword nearly as much as she does Iron Duke his shard. That abomination lusts to devour the Weapon for itself.

Green Ronin believes with all her heart that the few remaining wonders of the world must be preserved for those who deserve and appreciate them. A people who have turned their back on the fantastic, she reasons, are not worthy of it. A purist of sorts, her prices are exorbitant, but she will not sell to those who would debase or pervert the world's glories. Using an artefact to achieve immortality or complete a collection is acceptable; melting it into a superweapon or using it to enslave people is not. Perhaps one day humanity will embrace magic again, but in the meantime she has no compunctions about breaking laws, hearts, or bones in her pursuits. Killing (except in the most desperate self-defence) is beneath her, as is breaking a promise or a contract unless deceived; those are the only rules to the game.

The Ronin's one other soft spot is children. They still believe in wonder, and while she will lie, cheat and steal around adults, she is fiercely protective of the young. She even fought beside Pan and Belle once, when Bloody Mary used a cursed spear to turn every child in New Orleans into a vampire. Rachel thwarted the spear with her own magical knowledge while Pan held off Bloody Mary.

She occasionally uses other artefacts in the field as well as the Armour. Her current favourite is a magical bow that will shoot any type of enchanted arrow imaginable, but given time (represented by her magical Gadgeteering Attribute) she can come up with any number of low-powered artefacts.

BODY	9	ATTACK COMBAT VALUE	13
MIND	9	DEFENCE COMBAT VALUE	13
SOUL	10	HEALTH POINTS	115

STR	16/24	DEX	18	CON	18	INT	18	WIS	17	CHA	19
REF	+8	FORT	+7	WILL	+6	BASE TO HIT MODIFIER	+5				
BASE AC MODIFIER	+9					HIT POINTS	68				

TRI-STAT			d20 SYSTEM	
LVL	PTS	CHARACTERISTIC ATTRIBUTES	RANK	PTS
4	12	Attack Combat Mastery	2	(3)
8	8	Combat Technique (Accuracy, Block Ranged Attacks, Concealment, Deflection, Reflection, Portable Armoury, Two Weapons x2)	8	(7)
6	12	Defence Combat Mastery	4	(6)
1	3	Extra Defences	1	3
1	1	Features (Appearance)	1	1
4	8	Gadgeteer (Magical)	4	8
5	10	Gadgets	5	(0)
7	7	Highly Skilled	1	(0)
10	40	Item of Power (Emerald Armour)	10	40
1		Restricted Use (Only useable by a Shard-holder)		1
-1		• Detectable (Magic)		-1
6	18	Item of Power (Variable - Easy to lose; Currently "Marduk's Bow")	6	(3)
-1		• Detectable (Magic)		-1
1	2	Tough	1	2
3	9	Wealth	3	(6)

LVL	PTS	ITEM OF POWER'S ATTRIBUTES (EMERALD ARMOUR)	RANK	PTS
6	18	Armour	6	18
5	5	Armour: Shield	5	5
3	12	Flight	3	12
4	4	Immovable	4	4
1	1	Jumping	1	1
6	6	Special Defence (Oxygen, Poison x2, Sleep, Special Attack: Phoenix Blade x2)	6	6
1	4	Superstrength	1	4

LVL	PTS	ITEM OF POWER'S ATTRIBUTES (MARDUK'S BOW)	RANK	PTS
2	30	Power Flux (Enchanted Arrows, minor; Duration Reversed 10)	2	30

LVL	PTS	POWER ATTRIBUTES	RANK	PTS
3	3	Special Defence (Ageing, Disease, "Shard/Red Phoenix" Magic)	3	3

LVL	PTS	SKILLS	RANK
3	18	Acrobatics (Swinging)	5
3	6	Artisan (Archaic traps)	6
3	9	Burglary (Breaking-and-Entering)	6
4	8	Cultural Arts (Archaeology)	8
2	4	Driving (Motorcycles)	4
4	8	Foreign Culture (The Ancient World)	8
5	5	Languages (English, Arabic, French, German, Greek, many ancient languages)	12
4	8	Occult (Artefacts)	8
2	6	Seduction (Male)	4
2	6	Stealth (Silent Movement)	7
3	3	Swimming (Deep-Sea)	4
1	7	Archery (Bow)	2
1	12	Ranged Defence (Personal)	2

PTS	DEFECTS	PTS
-1	Famous (Rachel Wilde; Archaeological community)	-1
0	Famous (Green Ronin; Archaeological thief; Acts as 1 BP)	0
	Incomplete Training (No Special Movement)	-1
-1	Marked (Emerald bracelet; retracted armour; can be removed)	-1
-3	Nemesis (Red Phoenix; Iron Duke)	-3
-3	Recurring Nightmares (Parents' death)	-3
-3	Skeleton in the Closet (Criminal activity; Secret identity)	-3
-1	Special Requirement (Bonded to Emerald Armour; separation causes massive waves of anxiety and disquietude)	
-1	Wanted (Green Ronin; For questioning by Interpol)	-1

LIBERTY

JUSTICE

SECURITY

PEACE

CHAPTER FIVE MOST WANTED

CRIMINAL INTENT INTRODUCTION	CRIMINAL INTENT ANATOMY OF A VILLAIN	CRIMINAL INTENT THE LONE VILLAIN	CRIMINAL INTENT SUPERVILLAIN TEAMS	CRIMINAL INTENT ORGANISATIONS	CRIMINAL INTENT MOST WANTED	CRIMINAL INTENT APPENDIX
INTRODUCTION	CHAPTER 1	CHAPTER 2	CHAPTER 3	CHAPTER 4	CHAPTER 5	APPENDIX

LIBERTY

JUSTICE

SECURITY

PEACE

HEARTBREAKER (125 CHARACTER POINTS – TRI-STAT)

SKULKER LEVEL 3; 130 POINTS — d20 SYSTEM

IDENTITY: Margaret Collins (Secret)
OCCUPATION: Thief
FIRST APPEARANCE: Sentinel #274
FORMER ALIASES: None
PLACE OF BIRTH: Queens, Empire City
AFFILIATION: None
TERRITORY: Empire City
HEIGHT: 5'5" (165 cm) **EYES:** Blue
WEIGHT: 107 lbs. (49 kg) **HAIR:** Blonde

Margaret Collins. What a name for a girl who loved rock music and gymnastics to be saddled with. Maybe if she had not been as bright, or as strong-willed, or as much like her feisty grandmother, she could have lived with becoming a trophy wife. Her mother tried to teach her all the tricks to catching a wealthy man, especially someone with influence as well as money. It would hardly be upwardly mobile, after all, to woo some new money computer geek or Hollywood's latest disposable property. Instead, Mrs. Collins forever held up Maxwell Liberty as the unattainable ideal. He was a bit old for her, of course, but he represented a sort of Holy Grail that Margaret would have to live up to.

Naturally, she didn't.

She started by using Peggy and refusing to answer to "Margaret." Her father hardly noticed, since he hardly noticed Peggy at all, but her mother was furious. Next came the rock music, played loud and proud. Eventually, she was hanging out with "bad" girls. It all came to a head when her mother gave her an ultimatum: obey or leave. She almost had a stroke when Peggy left.

Amazingly, Peggy took well to street life. Her friends put her up in a shared crash pad. They became a gang of sorts, but Peggy had too much potential to live that life for long. Soon she was nosing around for better, more thrilling opportunities, and used the skills earned in escaping her high-security home to better use. She earned a rep as a first-class cat burglar. She even escaped Caliburn once. Life was a constant adventure.

Then Max Liberty revealed himself to be Sentinel in front of the world, and something inside her snapped. The perfect catch, the unattainable goal, was one of those superheroes. He'd lied for longer than she'd lived. The hypocrites! Those supremely powerful hypocrites, maintaining the status quo in a world where she was expected to be a pliant prize for some unfeeling corporate raider! It was time to trade up.

Peggy stole an infamous Haud weapon from the Olympian Tower to splash her name across the front page, and even escaped from Sentinel in the process. Just before she got away, Sentinel tried to talk sense to her, telling her it "broke his heart" to see such a bright young lady fall into this life. Peggy laughed, replying, "I guess I'm just a heart-breaker then, sweetie." With that, she was gone.

BODY	10	ATTACK COMBAT VALUE	12
MIND	8	DEFENCE COMBAT VALUE	14
SOUL	10	HEALTH POINTS	80

STR	16	DEX	22	CON	18	INT	16	WIS	18	CHA	20

REF	+9	FORT	+6	WILL	+6	BASE TO HIT MODIFIER	+5

BASE AC MODIFIER	+12	HIT POINTS	23

TRI-STAT				d20 SYSTEM	
LVL	PTS	CHARACTERISTIC ATTRIBUTES		RANK	PTS
3	9	Attack Combat Mastery		3	(6)
4	4	Combat Technique (Accuracy, Blind Shooting, Concealment, Steady Hand)		4	(3)
7	14	Defence Combat Mastery		6	12
3	3	Divine Relationship		3	3
2	6	Extra Defences		2	6
2	2	Features (Appearance x2)		2	2
5	10	Gadgets (High-tech B&E Tools)		5	10
11	11	Highly Skilled		4	(3)
5	20	Item of Power "Jumpsuit"		5	20
	-4	• Activation Time (Item of Power; 5 rounds; +1 BP can pause)			-4

LVL	PTS	ITEM OF POWER'S ATTRIBUTES (JUMPSUIT)	RANK	PTS
1	3	Armour	1	3
2	2	Combat Technique (Leap Attack, Portable Armoury)	2	2
1	3	Invisibility (Infrared)	1	3
3	3	Jumping	3	3
2	8	Special Attack "Heartbreaker" (Sonic Stunner — 40 / [[2d6+4]] Damage, Incapacitating vs. Soul / [[Wisdom]], No Damage, Short Range, Toxic)	2	8
4	4	Special Defence (Removable Breather — Oxygen x2, Poison: gas x2)	4	4
	-1	• Restriction (Special Defence; Oxygen supply only lasts one hour)		-1
3	3	Special Movement (Swinging, Wall-crawling)	3	3

LVL	PTS	SKILLS	RANK
3	18	Acrobatics (Tumbling)	3
4	12	Burglary (Breaking-and-Entering)	5
2	6	City Knowledge (Empire City: Midtown)	2
3	6	Climbing (Walls)	3
3	12	Electronics (Security)	3
1	1	Languages (Spanish)	1
4	12	Sleight of Hand (Lock Picking)	4
4	12	Stealth (Silent Movement)	5
2	2	Swimming (Freestyle)	2
3	3	Visual Arts (Sculpting)	3
3	36	Ranged Defence (Personal)	3
2	20	Special Ranged Attack ("Heartbreaker")	2

PTS	DEFECTS	PTS
	Incomplete Training (No Special Movement)	-1
-2	Not So Tough	-1
-1	Phobia (Fire)	-1
-2	Skeleton in the Closet (Secret identity; evidence of crimes)	-2
-1	Wanted (As Heartbreaker)	-1

The name was perfect. The Empire Times dubbed her Heartbreaker even before she announced it herself. She quickly traded the Haud device to an appreciative Artificer for her "jumpsuit," to which he added her now-infamous Heartbreaker sonic stunner as a bonus. Though she has little issue with lower-powered heroes like Caliburn, she revels in helping to humiliate powerful heroes of all sorts, from Officer Prometheus to Sentinel himself. Ironically, it's heroes like Caliburn and Lady of the Lantern that she most often faces on her regular heists; a girl's got to eat, after all.

KALEIDOSCOPE (175 CHARACTER POINTS – TRI-STAT)
SKULKER LEVEL 2, SPEEDSTER LEVEL 3; 200 POINTS — d20 SYSTEM

IDENTITY: Amy Harrison (Publicly known)
OCCUPATION: Activist, scientist
FIRST APPEARANCE: Slipstream #25
FORMER ALIASES: Tie-Dye
PLACE OF BIRTH: Newark, New Jersey
AFFILIATION: Various ecological organisations
TERRITORY: North America
HEIGHT: 5'7" (170 cm)   **EYES:** Light Brown
WEIGHT: 120 lbs. (55 kg)   **HAIR:** Light Brown

Amy Harrison has been passionate all her life. Though born in the early 40s, she was raised by progressive parents. While they instilled a strong moral code in her, they also taught her to think for herself and respect her own judgement. Though incredibly beautiful, her inner strength kept most boys away from her, which was how she liked it. The 50s were rarely kind to the outspoken.

Then came the 60s, and with it a revolution of thought. It was a paradise for Amy, who took to the new paradigm with zeal. She became so enamoured of it that she even created a tie-dyed costume and began a campaign of gentle sabotage against the most corrupt corporations. She was merely a talented amateur, though. On her third escapade she was captured, tied up and left to die, suspended over a boiling vat of toxic waste.

Much to Amy's embarrassment, she was unable to escape. Fortunately, Slipstream was investigating the same company and rescued her in the nick of time. More amazing was the effect his superfast vibrations had on her, bonding the fumes to her body and granting her speed equal to his.

Amy was now in a position to do more good than ever. Though not a scientific supergenius, she was skilled enough to rig a non-damaging light projector inspired by the colourful display she left behind as she ran, and a suit to protect her from further exposure to toxins (which was later enhanced by Seawolf's forces). As Kaleidoscope, she became a much more effective weapon against the military-industrial oppressor.

While noble and courageous, Kaleidoscope's arrogance and self-righteousness keep her teetering from heroine to criminal with regularity. For example, she has been both enemy and ally of Slipstream for years. Likewise, she absolutely refuses to take a life, but does not balk in the least at crimes like breaking-and-entering or destruction of property. Kaleidoscope typically targets the worst sweatshops and polluters.

Currently, Amy is reacting poorly to her realisation that she has not aged since 1962. Her beloved parents are long dead, and most of her dearest friends are collecting Social Security. Where she goes next depends greatly on how she is treated by the heroes and villains around her. Meanwhile, she has become even more unbalanced than usual. Sometimes, Amy obeys the law to the letter, using accepted forms of civil disobedience to make her point. On occasion, however, she practically revels in destroying industrial targets. She recently razed an entire GenTech facility, freeing numerous animals and cementing Mister Matthews's long-building hatred of her.

Kaleidoscope's normal tactics are cautious. She is not over-confident (especially after her few stints as a damsel-in-distress) and often works with mundane activist groups, some of whom practically worship her despite Amy's discouragement of such attitudes. An operation is carefully planned to leave clear hints of her visit without any actual evidence that can be used against her.

BODY	8	ATTACK COMBAT VALUE	12
MIND	8	DEFENCE COMBAT VALUE	13
SOUL	8	HEALTH POINTS	80

STR	15	DEX	20	CON	16	INT	16	WIS	16	CHA	17
REF	+11	FORT	+6	WILL	+6	BASE TO HIT MODIFIER			+7		
BASE AC MODIFIER	+11					HIT POINTS			37		

TRI-STAT			d20 SYSTEM	
LVL	PTS	CHARACTERISTIC ATTRIBUTES	RANK	PTS
4	12	Attack Combat Mastery	4	(9)
	-2	• Dependent (Attack Combat Mastery, on Speed)		-2
3	3	Combat Technique (Blind Shooting, Lightning Reflexes, Steady Hand)	3	(2)
7	14	Defence Combat Mastery	7	14
	-2	• Dependent (Defence Combat Mastery, on Speed)		-2
2	16	Extra Attacks	2	16
	-2	• Dependent (Extra Attacks, on Speed)		-2
4	12	Extra Defences	3	9
	-2	• Dependent (Extra Defences, on Speed)		-2
1	1	Features (Appearance)	1	1
1	2	Gadgeteer	1	2
5	5	Heightened Awareness	5	5
4	4	Highly Skilled	1	(0)
3	12	Item of Power ("Kaleidoscope Costume")	3	12
	-2	• Activation Time (Item of Power; 10 Initiative; +1 BP Can pause)		-2
3	9	Item of Power (Easy to lose "Kaleidoscope")	3	9
5	5	Organisational Ties (Various eco-terrorist groups)	5	5

LVL	PTS	ITEM OF POWER'S ATTRIBUTES (KALEIDOSCOPE COSTUME)	RANK	PTS
2	6	Armour	2	6
6	6	Special Defence (Oxygen x2, Disease x2, Poison x2)	6	6
3	3	Unique Attribute: Removes Vulnerability	3	3

LVL	PTS	ITEM OF POWER'S ATTRIBUTES (KALEIDOSCOPE)	RANK	PTS
3	12	Special Attack "Hypnostunner" (60 / [[3d6+6]] Damage, Incapacitating vs. Mind [[Int]], Spreading, Hand-Held, No Damage, Short Range, Toxic)	3	12
3	3	Special Attack "Prism Blast" (60 / [[3d6+6]] Damage, Flare, Spreading x3, Hand-Held, No Damage, Short Range, Toxic)	3	3

LVL	PTS	POWER ATTRIBUTES	RANK	PTS
5	15	Regeneration	5	15
		• Reduction (-3; Regeneration; Only heals 1 Health Point per Round)		
2	2	Special Attack "Run By Dazzle" (60 / [[3d6+6]] Damage, Flare, Spreading, Melee, No Damage)	2	2
	-2	• Dependent (Special Attack, on Speed)		-1
3	3	Special Defence (Ageing x2, Sleep)	3	3
2	2	Special Movement (Balance, Cat-Like)	2	2
5	30	Speed	5	(24)
	-1	• Detectable (The "Kaleidoscopic trail;" Sight)		-1

LVL	PTS	SKILLS	RANK
3	12	Biological Sciences (Ecology)	3
3	9	Burglary (Breaking-and-Entering)	5
1	3	Disguise (Make-up)	3
2	8	Electronics (Energy)	2
1	1	Languages (Japanese)	1
2	6	Law (International)	3
2	10	Physical Sciences (Physics)	3
3	6	Social Sciences (Sociology)	3
3	3	Swimming (Scuba)	3
2	2	Writing (Political)	2
1	10	Special Ranged Attack (Hypnostunner)	1

PTS	DEFECTS	PTS
-1	Famous (Metahuman from 60s)	-1
-2	Nemesis (Mister Matthews; Slipstream)	-2
-1	Skeleton in the Closet (Evidence of crimes)	-1
-2	Vulnerability (Unique sonic frequencies neutralise all powers)	-2
-2	Wanted (By Thule for terrorist activities)	-2

LIBERTY
JUSTICE
SECURITY
PEACE

CHAPTER FIVE
MOST WANTED

PAGE 107

MIOLNIR, THE HAMMER OF THULE

(175 CHARACTER POINTS – TRI-STAT)
ADVENTURER LEVEL 3, COSTUMED FIGHTER LEVEL 1; 185 POINTS — d20 SYSTEM

IDENTITY: Rikard Sollander (Publicly known)
OCCUPATION: General in Thulian Army, leader of Einherhar
FIRST APPEARANCE: Sentinel #290
FORMER ALIASES: None
PLACE OF BIRTH: Stockholm, Sweden
AFFILIATION: Kreuzritter, Thule, Einherhar
TERRITORY: Operates worldwide
HEIGHT: 6'5" (196 cm)   **EYES:** Blue
WEIGHT: 240 lbs. (109 kg)   **HAIR:** Blond

What draws immigrants to Thule? Nearly everyone knows that Kreuzritter rules the land in an iron grip, but poverty afflicts even the most affluent European nations. Rauchenberger promises food, shelter and purpose to all who flock to his banner. For many, that's enough.

Among them was a young Swede named Rikard Sollander, who grew up destitute. Eager to find a reason for his plight, he willingly absorbed Kreuzritter's ideological propaganda. The world, Rikard decided, was in chaos and needed to be put right. "Right," of course, meant a world ruled by Thulians in general and Ernst Rauchenberger in particular. Rikard moved up the ranks of Thule's army through cunning, ruthlessness, and utter loyalty to Thule.

Eventually, Sollander's combination of resourcefulness and devotion came to Kreuzritter's attention, and Rauchenberger decided to honour Rikard by attempting to imbue him with elemental powers. The process was long and dangerous; Kreuzritter encased Rikard in elemental earth and inscribed ancient Thulian runes upon the stony shell, in an effort to empower the soldier with the land's magic. This was not the monarch's first attempt, but all before Rikard had died horrible deaths. Worse, the pain was horrific. Despite it all, Rikard endured. He did not cry out once.

Sollander's loyalty was rewarded. When the process was over, he absorbed the magical earth packed around him. He could transform into it with a thought, becoming a juggernaut of rune-covered rock whenever he so wishes. His fists could change into granite hammers or spikes, yet his body could flow like sand. An unfortunate backlash to the process rendered him vulnerable to Kabbalistic magics, however, such as the Star of David.

Now, as Miolnir, the Hammer of Thule, he promotes Kreuzritter's agenda anywhere the tyrant desires. Though it galls Miolnir that he is no match for Sentinel, the American's time will come. Meanwhile, Miolnir serves his master and puts down self-styled heroes who interfere with Thule's manifest destiny.

Miolnir plays the part of the stalwart hero to the world, smiling at all the right people (including some he'd joyfully skewer) and fighting anarchists like Seawolf from time to time. To his credit, he is genuinely courageous when defending Thulians, risking his life to protect his people. Rikard has become a sort of demented protégé to the arch-villain Kreuzritter, however, and ruthlessly pursues his master's agenda. He has stolen, kidnapped, blackmailed and killed at his monarch's whim, and will do so again without pause. Like his master, Miolnir will stop at nothing to place Kreuzritter and Thule at the head of a new world order. Nothing.

Though not brilliant, Miolnir is devious. He is quite capable of working as part of a team, generally as the group strong man. Unless serving directly under Kreuzritter, he prefers a leadership role. Rikard's official rank in the Thulian army is roughly equivalent to a three-star general, and he has come to enjoy his importance. His usual plots involve hiring a group of supervillains to serve some scheme of his, typically as part of increasing Thulian power. Destroying hero teams is often the

secondary goal of such plots. For more details on the Einherhar, see Chapter 3 (page 70).

BODY	9/14		ATTACK COMBAT VALUE	12/13
MIND	7		DEFENCE COMBAT VALUE	6/10
SOUL	8		HEALTH POINTS	85/170

STR 18/66	DEX 16/28	CON 20/28	INT 14	WIS 15	CHA 15

REF +6/+12 FORT +8/+12 WILL +3 BASE TO HIT MODIFIER +6
BASE AC MODIFIER +3/+10   HIT POINTS 41/94

	TRI-STAT			d20 SYSTEM	
LVL	PTS	CHARACTERISTIC ATTRIBUTES		RANK	PTS
4	12	Attack Combat Mastery		4	(6)
1	8	Extra Attacks		1	8
5	5	Highly Skilled			
8	24	Organisational Ties (Three Star General in Thulian Army)		8	24
1	3	Wealth		1	3

LVL	PTS	POWER ATTRIBUTES		RANK	PTS
10	90	Alternate Form		10	(81)
	-1	• Detectable (Alternate Form; Magical/spiritual)			-1

LVL	PTS	ALTERNATE FORM "INCARNATE THULIAN EARTH" ATTRIBUTES		RANK	PTS
6	18	Armour		6	18
3	6	Defence Combat Mastery (Runic Protection)		3	6
6	12	Elasticity		6	12
5	10	Enhanced Stat (Body)			
		Enhanced Dexterity		3	6
		Enhanced Constitution		2	4
2	6	Extra Defences		2	6
3	3	Immovable		3	3
6	12	Massive Damage (Spiked Granite Fists — Unarmed combat)		6	12
6	6	Special Defence (Oxygen x2, Disease x2, Poison x2)		6	6
1	1	Special Movement (Light-Footed)		1	1
6	24	Superstrength		6	24
3	6	Tough		3	6
1	2	Tunnelling		1	2
	-1	Awkward Size (Earthen form; 9'/2.75m tall)			-1
	-3	Marked (Earthen form; Large earthen body covered in runes)			-3
	-2	Unappealing (Earthen form)			-2

LVL	PTS	SKILLS	RANK
2	4	Cultural Arts (Eugenics)	3
2	2	Etiquette (Upper Class)	3
1	2	Foreign Culture (Thulian)	2
2	8	Interrogation (Physical)	4
2	2	Language (Swedish, English, German)	2
3	13	Military Sciences (Tactics, Teamwork)	6
1	2	Occult (Runes)	2
1	2	Social Sciences (Politics)	2
1	1	Sports (Football)	2
1	12	Ranged Defence (Personal)	2
2	16	Gun Combat (Rifle)	3
2	16	Unarmed Defence (Grappling)	3

PTS	DEFECTS	PTS
-1	Cursed (Repelled by Star of David)	-1
-2	Famous (Miolnir, Thule's public superhero)	-2
	Incomplete Training (No Combat Technique)	-1
-1	Marked (Body covered with runic tattoos)	-1
-1	Nemesis (Enemies of Thule: the Guard; Israel)	-1
-3	Owned (Kreuzritter)	-3
-1	Recurring Nightmares (Kreuzritter's ritual)	-1
-1	Red Tape (Thulian regulations)	-1
-3	Skeleton in the Closet (His "heroism" is a lie)	-3
-1	Wanted (By Israeli government for questioning)	-1

LIBERTY
JUSTICE
SECURITY
PEACE

CHAPTER FIVE
MOST WANTED

PAGE
108

SILVER AGE SENTINELS

MISTHUNTER (150 CHARACTER POINTS – TRI-STAT)

SKULKER LEVEL 2; 155 POINTS — d20 SYSTEM

IDENTITY: Charles "Chuck" Evans (Known to some)
OCCUPATION: Criminal enforcer
FIRST APPEARANCE: Tales from the Street #84
FORMER ALIASES: None
PLACE OF BIRTH: Deer Creek, Indiana
AFFILIATION: None
TERRITORY: Empire City, Lower East Side
HEIGHT: 5'11" (180 cm)   **EYES:** Gray
WEIGHT: 182 lbs. (83 kg)   **HAIR:** Gray

A tragic tale of "Science Gone Bad," the creature known as Misthunter was once a simple trucker named Charles Evans. Chuck was known as an "okay guy" who'd haul shipments without worrying too much about paperwork. A woman called Galatea paid him well to transport barrels from Ohio to Empire City. Those Thulian jerks had other ideas, though. When they tried to hijack the shipment, the Guard appeared; a fight started, and suddenly his whole rig went up. Chuck was doused by the stuff in the barrels, and he ... changed. His skin turned a dull grey, and he radiated a weird, shimmering mist. The Guard took him to a hospital, but no one knew how to help Chuck.

Wracked by hunger pangs, Chuck found he couldn't digest normal food. Although kept under surveillance and restrained, a hurried doctor slipped up on safety protocols, and Chuck grabbed him, desperate for answers. As their skin touched, Chuck was overwhelmed by rush of endorphins.

The doctor ... emptied out. A combination of fluids and chemicals from the doctor's body flowed through the mist into Chuck, restoring him but killing the doctor. Horrified, the trucker bolted. Ever since, he has been something of a ghost story in Empire City. He does not have to kill to get what he needs, but no matter how careful he is it always puts people in the hospital. So far he has not found another satisfactory source — he has to drain humans.

A type of biochemical vampire, the Misthunter now tries to stay alive while simultaneously trying to do as little harm as possible. He is always alone, and must be careful not to even accidentally touch those around him, for fear of draining them. His only companionship comes from the wild dogs, cats, and rodents of the city. His mist aura contains some sort of pheromone that calms and virtually hypnotises these animals.

Trapped on the wrong side of the law, however, Misthunter's strange powers make him of great use to several supervillains. He still needs money to get by and he prefers to prey on those who deserve it, so Misthunter often ends up as a hired hand in gang wars. He brings down murderers, tells himself he's saving future victims, and makes reasonable money by doing so.

Meanwhile, the Artificer shrugged off another failed experiment. His bio-vampire formula had too many drawbacks to be viable on the market.

Misthunter's powers can bring him back even from death, as he learned after a suicide attempt. He must use his Special Attack regularly to maintain his powers, and indeed he will "starve" to death within a few weeks unless he drains someone. His powers will not let him starve, however; after a few days without sustenance, his Mist Blast will activate itself to feed him. This is a biological function, and he cannot stop it any more than a normal person can suffocate by holding his or her breath.

BODY	13	ATTACK COMBAT VALUE	11
MIND	5	DEFENCE COMBAT VALUE	9
SOUL	6	HEALTH POINTS	155

STR 24	DEX 22	CON 22	INT 10	WIS 11	CHA 11
REF +9	FORT +8	WILL +3		BASE TO HIT MODIFIER	+3
BASE AC MODIFIER +9				HIT POINTS	58

TRI-STAT			d20 SYSTEM	
LVL	PTS	CHARACTERISTIC ATTRIBUTES	RANK	PTS
3	9	Attack Combat Mastery	4	(9)
3	6	Defence Combat Mastery	3	6
1	1	Heightened Awareness	1	1
4	4	Highly Skilled	2	(1)
3	6	Tough	3	6

LVL	PTS	POWER ATTRIBUTES	RANK	PTS
5	15	Animal Summoning/Control (Mammals only; Area 5; Duration 5)	5	15
	-1	• Restriction (Animal Summoning; Medium-sized or smaller mammals only)		-1
2	6	Armour	2	6
8	16	Enhanced Stat (Body)		
		Enhanced Dexterity	3	6
		Enhanced Constitution	3	6
2	2	Heightened Senses (Infravision, Ultravision)	2	2
7	14	Reincarnation (Easy to stop; All cells must be destroyed)	7	14
1	6	Regeneration	1	6
5	5	Sixth Sense (Humans; Area 4)	5	5
6	24	Special Attack "Draining Aura" (20 / [[1d6+2]] Damage, Aura, Penetrating: Armour x4, Vampiric: Only restore lost Health Points, Melee, Unique Disability: Only Affects Humans)	6	24
	-3	• Permanent		-3
6	6	Special Attack "Mist Blast" (60 / [[3d6+6]] Damage, Penetrating: Armour x4, Vampiric: Only restore lost Health Points, Short Range, Unique Disability: Only Affects Humans, Unique Disability: Blocked by Strong Winds / Water)	6	6
	-2	• Cursed (Special Attack; Automatically activates itself after five days without use, targeting anyone within range and superseding his Vulnerability)		-2
7	7	Special Defence (Ageing, Disease, Oxygen x2, Own Powers x2, Poison)	7	7
5	5	Special Movement (Balance, Light-footed, Swinging, Wall-crawling)	5	5
1	4	Superstrength	1	4

LVL	PTS	SKILLS	RANK
2	2	Animal Training (Rats)	2
1	3	City Knowledge (Empire City: Lower East Side)	2
2	4	Driving (Big Rigs)	2
3	9	Intimidation (Street)	3
1	4	Mechanics (Automotive)	1
1	2	Navigation (Highway)	1
1	3	Stealth (Silent Movement)	2
2	4	Street Sense (Influential Individuals)	2
1	3	Urban Tracking (Underworld)	1
2	20	Special Ranged Attack (Mist Blast)	2
2	16	Unarmed Attack (Holds)	2

PTS	DEFECTS	PTS
-3	Marked (Slate-gray skin, aura of shimmering mist)	-3
-2	Special Requirement (If Misthunter does not feed via his Draining Aura or Mist Blast within a week, he begins to suffer the effects of starvation)	-2
-2	Vulnerability (If Misthunter does not feed within 3 days, he loses all Powers except for Special Attack "Draining Aura" and Reincarnation)	-2
-3	Unappealing	-3
-2	Wanted (By law enforcement for several deaths, and by health officials for quarantining due to his condition)	-2

LIBERTY
JUSTICE
SECURITY
PEACE

CHAPTER FIVE
MOST WANTED

PAGE
109

REQUIEM (275 Character Points – Tri-Stat)

ADVENTURER LEVEL 8, POWERHOUSE LEVEL 1; 300 POINTS — d20 SYSTEM

IDENTITY: Kutta ("Dog") (Unknown)
OCCUPATION: Cosmic Nihilist
FIRST APPEARANCE: The Guard #101
FORMER ALIASES: Subject 24
PLACE OF BIRTH: Calcutta, India
AFFILIATION: None
TERRITORY: Operates universe-wide
HEIGHT: 7'0" (213 cm)   **EYES:** Violet voids
WEIGHT: 400 lbs. (181 kg)   **HAIR:** None

It is a hard thing, to be a saviour for those who do not want saving. Fortunately for Requiem, he has both the patience and the time.

Once, he was one of Calcutta's "Untouchables:" nameless, penniless, and starving. When addressed at all, he was merely called Kutta — the Hindi word for dog. The emerging revival of Buddhism gave him life, almost literally — food, education, purpose. Ironically, the shelter was run by British expatriates; he thought they did it as penance for their ancestors' crimes. He was right.

Their government backers, however, had other ideas.

British and Indian scientists had been studying the results of Project Anodyne and Operation Red Star. They believed they could create beings more powerful than Sentinel or Muzhik. First, they needed test subjects. Expendable ones. In an unholy alliance, neo-imperialists and Hindu fundamentalists "collected" suitable subjects. He was shanghaied, imprisoned, and given a new identity: Subject 24, one of twenty-five specimens to be used in Project Lotus.

Subject 24 preferred British philosophy over Hindu religious beliefs. When solar flame tore through him and became a pyre for his fellow victims, he thought of Robert Louis Stevenson's "Requiem" and waited for death with serenity ... except he did not die.

The gaping scientists were ecstatic at first. They had a successful test subject, and enough data for a much higher survival rate. Subject 24, once a wreck of a man, was now an obsidian behemoth seething with nearly limitless power. It was perfect, until they saw his eyes....

Subject 24 looked at them with sadness but an ironic smile. "This be the verse you grave for me: Here he lies where he longed to be," he quoted. Before the scientists could even scream, the entire building was engulfed in a star's flame.

Now, he was free, not only of his pain, but of all human need — hunger, sleep and even breathing were all frailties he had left behind. What was he to do with such transcendence?

Like the Enlightened One himself, Subject 24 meditated and thought, in the centre of the glass crater that was once a research centre and a place of pain. On the 49th day, his musings were interrupted by an Indian military strike. They could not hurt him, though. Fear, pain, and desperation were all around him. With a thought, it was all gone, turned to ash by his inescapable star-power. In that moment, enlightenment was his. He had realised the pain that was life, and knew the way to Nirvana.

Death.

Mere killing would not end the cycle of suffering, though. As long as there was life — any life — souls would be reborn into this world of struggle and caught in its sadistic web. There was only one solution.

He could not abandon infinite souls to suffering any more than the Buddha could after 49 days of contemplation. He would have to wait for

BODY	11	ATTACK COMBAT VALUE	14
MIND	10	DEFENCE COMBAT VALUE	13
SOUL	15	HEALTH POINTS	130

STR	46	DEX	22	CON	24	INT	20	WIS	32	CHA	28
REF	+8	FORT	+11	WILL	+13			BASE TO HIT MODIFIER		+7	
BASE AC MODIFIER		+10						HIT POINTS		108	

TRI-STAT				d20 SYSTEM	
LVL	PTS	CHARACTERISTIC ATTRIBUTES		RANK	PTS
2	6	Attack Combat Mastery		2	(3)
3	6	Defence Combat Mastery		4	(6)
4	4	Divine Relationship		1	1
7	7	Highly Skilled			

LVL	PTS	POWER ATTRIBUTES		RANK	PTS
3	30	Damage Absorption		3	30
3	11	Cosmic Engineer* (Duration 2; See Designer's Note)		3	11
	-1	• Detectable (Cosmic Engineering; Cosmic/reality detection)			-1
10	120	Dynamic Powers (Fusion plasma, minor; Area 5, Duration 3, Range 6, Targets 6)		10	(80)
	-1	• Detectable (Dynamic Powers; Radiation)			-1
2	12	Sixth Sense (Cosmic "Fault Lines," Stellar Energy; Area 10)		2	12
8	8	Special Defence (Ageing x2, Oxygen x2, Hunger x2, Sleep x2)		8	8
3	12	Superstrength		3	(8)

LVL	PTS	SKILLS	RANK
5	10	Cultural Arts (Metaphysics)	12
3	3	Etiquette (Upper Class)	5
2	4	Foreign Culture (British, Chinese)	5
3	9	Intimidation (Sheer terror)	10
4	4	Language (Hindi, English, Mandarin, Punjabi, Sanskrit)	4
5	40	Power Usage: Cosmic Engineering	15
3	24	Power Usage: Dynamic Power	10
3	6	Social Sciences (Theology)	10

PTS	DEFECTS	PTS
-3	Marked (Obsidian body, displaying star fields within)	-3
-2	Nemesis (Dark Queen, the Guard)	-2
-3	Unappealing (Wants to destroy all existence; strange form)	-3
-3	Wanted (Every major enforcement organisation in several galaxies)	-3

COSMIC ENGINEER

Cosmic Engineer is essentially a variant on Gadgeteer; rather than allowing a character to redesign a technological device, however, it allows Requiem to sense the very structure of reality and rewrite it for a time.

The Attribute follows the Time Progression Chart Reversed, to determine the amount of time required to set up the field, or activate the change, starting at one year (Level 1) and decreasing to 5 rounds (Level 10). The Duration PMV indicates how long the change remains in effect. Therefore, it takes Requiem a full month to create a change that will only last five rounds. Not very useful if he is trying to make a hero fall up instead of down, but this suits Requiem's philosophy. He attempts to find places in the universe which will crack easily, much like finding the flaws in a diamond that will make it shatter.

his own death until all of creation was annihilated. Only then would the pain of the extant be transcended.

Kutta and Subject 24 are gone; now he is Requiem, the joyful dirge for existence itself. If only they did not all fear him so.

It is a hard thing, to be a saviour....

SILVER AGE SENTINELS

SEAWOLF (200 Character Points – Tri-Stat)

COSTUMED FIGHTER LEVEL 3, POWERHOUSE LEVEL 3; 230 POINTS — d20 SYSTEM

IDENTITY: Charles D. Dagon (Publicly known)
OCCUPATION: Rebel leader, Captain of the Nemo
FIRST APPEARANCE: The American Sentinel #75
FORMER ALIASES: None
PLACE OF BIRTH: Groton, Connecticut
AFFILIATION: Metahuman movement, Seawolf's Get
TERRITORY: North Atlantic
HEIGHT: 6'9" (206 cm) **EYES:** Blue-Gray
WEIGHT: 275 lbs. (125 kg) **HAIR:** Black

Charles D. Dagon, child of the Golden Age.

Project Speargun: the Navy's dirty little secret. Anodyne wasn't supposed to be repeated, and the Dagons were living proof why. Hank was always sick, and their son was born … different.

Charles D. Dagon, test subject.

The Navy scientists were ecstatic. While other kids played, however, Charles was being studied. His one childhood joy was when they let him dive as long as he could. The Dagons did their best with the time they had, and their honest patriotism rubbed off on Charles to an extent.

Charles D. Dagon, Naval officer.

He enlisted on his 18th birthday, to nearly everyone's delight. But what other life did he know? For five years, Charles was the pride of the service. Then his parents died — of simultaneous heart attacks.

Charles was crushed. His father was never in good health, but both of them at once? It made no sense … until he did a little digging. Speargun had created a symbiosis between his parents as well as crippling his father. Hank's collapse had literally killed Martha. Charles' grief turned into rage.

Dagon looked at his life, and saw a laboratory specimen. Worse, the government's treatment of his parents was effectively murder in pursuit of metahuman agents. Well, if Charles D. Dagon was going to be a weapon, it would be a weapon for the freedom his parents held dear.

Charles D. Dagon. Seawolf.

Seawolf tried to steal the Nemo, a prototype submarine, but Sentinel and Caliburn arrested him. Kept drugged, he was convicted in a mockery of a trial. Seawolf had allies, though, and the dosage was reduced by court order. Even so, he knew the Navy would not permit a fair trial. Escape was simplicity itself. Passage of the Super Crime Act, which seemingly declared metahumans "weapons of mass destruction," cemented his philosophy.

Seawolf's next run on the Nemo was a success, and it became his base of operations. Ever since, he has fought for metahuman rights. Though he does not attempt to impose global metahuman rule, he does believe in metahuman superiority. Seawolf rules his bandit kingdom absolutely, albeit benevolently. His charismatic, anarchistic variant of *noblesse oblige* attracts hackers, gearheads, transhumanists and more, including several women of whom he is quite fond. With their help, Dagon has founded Seahaven, a private data resource that funds his movement. Seawolf's aquatic fortress is the ultimate in information security and anonymity, easily outstripping all competition as an interference-free Internet hub. Prices are exorbitant, but Dagon is a

BODY	14	ATTACK COMBAT VALUE	15
MIND	10	DEFENCE COMBAT VALUE	14
SOUL	10	HEALTH POINTS	120

STR 100	DEX 28	CON 28	INT 20	WIS 22	CHA 22

REF +10 FORT +12 WILL +8 BASE TO HIT MODIFIER +11
BASE AC MODIFIER +11 HIT POINTS 91

TRI-STAT				d20 SYSTEM	
LVL	PTS	CHARACTERISTIC ATTRIBUTES		RANK	PTS
4	12	Attack Combat Mastery		3	(6)
5	10	Defence Combat Mastery		4	(6)
1	8	Extra Attacks		1	8
1	3	Extra Defences		1	(0)
7	7	Highly Skilled			
10	10	Organisational Ties (Seahaven)		10	10
2	6	Wealth (Datahaven credit)		2	6

LVL	PTS	POWER ATTRIBUTES	RANK	PTS
1	1	Adaptation (Underwater)	1	1
6	18	Armour	6	18
1	3	Armour (Optimised vs. Cold)	1	3
1	3	Armour (Optimised vs. Heat)	1	3
		Enhanced Constitution	1	2
3	3	Features (Appearance x2, Nictating Membranes / Streamlined)	3	3
2	2	Heightened Awareness	2	2
3	3	Heightened Senses (Sight x2, Ultravision)	3	3
1	6	Regeneration	1	6
	-2	• Restriction (Regeneration; Only underwater)		-2
1	1	Special Defence (Ageing)	1	1
9	36	Superstrength	9	(32)
5	10	Water Speed	5	10

LVL	PTS	SKILLS	RANK
2	2	Boating (Submarines)	2
2	8	Computers (Databases)	2
3	3	Controlled Breathing (Cyclic Breathing)	3
2	4	Cultural Arts (History)	2
2	8	Electronics (Computers)	2
1	3	Intimidation (Personal)	2
2	2	Language (English, French, Spanish)	2
2	2	Management & Administration (Rebellion)	2
2	8	Mechanics (Aquatic)	2
3	9	Seduction (Female)	3
3	7	Social Sciences (Metahuman "movement," Sociology)	3
3	9	Stealth (Silent Movement)	4
5	5	Swimming (Deep-Sea)	7
2	2	Writing (Political)	2
1	12	Ranged Defence (Personal)	1
2	16	Unarmed Attack (Strikes)	3

PTS	DEFECTS	PTS
	Incomplete Training (No Combat Technique or Immovable)	-2
-2	Marked (Unusual appearance)	-2
-3	Nemesis (Guard)	-3
-3	Wanted (US Government)	-3

man of his word — all transactions are completely private and secure. Seahaven has become the top "data haven" in the world.

Meanwhile, Seawolf does his best to recruit metahumans to his cause. The number of metas who follow him flows like the tide. Sometimes, he has a veritable army following in his wake, while other times he swims alone. Currently, only a few of Dagon's "enhanced brothers" follow him, including Beholder, Blaze, Lash, Songbird, and Tempest (see Chapter 3, page 73). Charles hopes to bring Kaleidoscope into the fold, as she has expressed dissatisfaction in working alone. At last, the time for change has come.

SINNAPSE (125 Character Points – Tri-Stat)
PSYCHIC LEVEL 2; 120 POINTS — d20 SYSTEM

IDENTITY: Reginald Wagner (Publicly known)
OCCUPATION: Information trader
FIRST APPEARANCE: Caliburn #282
FORMER ALIASES: "Reggie"
PLACE OF BIRTH: Greenwich, Connecticut
AFFILIATION: Limited ties to organised crime
TERRITORY: Empire City
HEIGHT: 5'6" (168 cm) **EYES:** Brown
WEIGHT: 155 lbs. (70 kg) **HAIR:** Dark Brown

There are few villains so truly vile that they have no redeeming features, but if Reginald Wagner has one, none of his enemies have found it yet. The·man has no excuse for what he has become. He was not poor, or abused, or even picked on in school. Reggie was able to have pretty much anything he wanted ... except the respect of women.

Reginald didn't have trouble making friends (in spite of his slimy personality), earning good grades (although he never studied), having money to burn (without holding down a job), or even getting dates (even with his reputation as an octopus). Girls never took him seriously, though; they laughed at him, and would not do what he wanted. Reginald had a hard time dealing with this, since almost everyone did what he wanted.

During his junior year of college, in a class he'd hardly attended, Reggie began to have difficulty with a test. Panicking, he concentrated for the first time in what seemed like years. He got the answers ... right out of the teacher's head! The next quarter, he quickly signed up for a parapsychology class, and really buckled down for once. The only person happier than his parents was Reggie himself. Suddenly, his whole life fell into place. He realised he was a telepath, and one of respectable power.

Reggie soon had three girlfriends, all of whom seemed to compete to be his most subservient companion. Then Caliburn suddenly appeared, and took his life apart in a matter of days. Reginald's powers slid off the faceless hero, and he woke up in jail after a severe beating from his former servants.

Deliberate telepathic violation is a serious offence in the modern world. Reginald's previous, unconscious uses of power were easily excusable, but the young man clearly needed a lesson in responsibility. On the other hand, talented telepaths were rare and valuable, so a deal was brokered with the government by his parents, who intervened on his behalf. Reginald would go through an intensive prototype program teaching him the proper, accepted uses of his powers. When complete, he would have a number of government opportunities waiting for him.

Reggie had other ideas.

In spite of the precautions, escape was all too easy for the newly self-christened Sinnapse. Likewise, it was simplicity itself to ingratiate himself to a number of criminal syndicates by providing free samples of information he can provide. Today, a number of "organisations" use his talents. He is set up nicely … when not in jail.

Although a relatively minor player, he is developing a reputation within the East Coast underworld. He's connected to several branches of the Empire City Cosa Nostra, including the Bonnano and Lucchese families. Recently, Luigi Saracino and Torque have contracted him for information gathering and interrogation work as part of the new Murder Incorporated. The money is great, but he fears facing Caliburn again.

BODY	5	ATTACK COMBAT VALUE	5
MIND	11	DEFENCE COMBAT VALUE	8
SOUL	8	HEALTH POINTS	65

STR 9	DEX 12	CON 10	INT 22	WIS 20	CHA 15
REF +1	FORT +0	WILL +8	BASE TO HIT MODIFIER		-1
BASE AC MODIFIER +3			HIT POINTS		9

TRI-STAT				d20 SYSTEM	
LVL	PTS	CHARACTERISTIC ATTRIBUTES		RANK	PTS
2	4	Defence Combat Mastery		2	4
1	1	Divine Relationship (Rake's Luck)		1	1
1	3	Extra Defences		1	3
5	10	Henchmen (Jock Goons)		5	10
4	4	Henchmen (Eurotrash — Decorative Slaves)		4	4
8	8	Highly Skilled			

LVL	PTS	POWER ATTRIBUTES	RANK	PTS
5	32	Mind Control (Range 6; Targets 1)	5	32
	-3	• Concentration (Mind Control)		-3
	-1	• Dependent (Mind Control, on Telepathy)		-1
	-1	• Detectable (Mind Control; Mental/psychic senses)		-1
	-3	• Restriction (Mind Control; Victims remember being controlled)		-3
5	5	Mind Shield	5	(4)
10	41	Telepathy (Area 3; Range 6; Targets 2)	10	(38)
	-1	• Detectable (Telepathy; Mental/psychic senses)		-1
	-9	• Restriction (Telepathy; LVLs 5+ only work on targets with a Soul / [[Wisdom]] of less than 6 / [[12]], and whom he has Mind Controlled at least once)		-9

LVL	PTS	SKILLS	RANK
1	3	City Knowledge (Empire City: Upper West Side)	2
1	1	Etiquette (Lower Class)	2
3	3	Gaming (Gambling)	5
2	8	Interrogation (Psychological)	3
2	16	Power Usage: Mind Control	4
3	24	Power Usage: Telepathy	6
2	6	Seduction (Female)	3
3	6	Social Sciences (Psychology)	5
1	3	Stealth (Silent Movement)	2
2	4	Street Sense (Gangs)	4
3	36	Ranged Defence (Personal)	4

PTS	DEFECTS	PTS
	Incomplete Training (No Illusion)	-2
-9	Inept Attack	-6
-2	Phobia (Physical Violence)	
-2	Wanted (Various crimes)	-2

Sinnapse has even done some work for the Ghost Shadows Triad, making contact through their street arm, the White Tigers. Although he successfully completed several missions, demonstrating his ability to deliver valuable information from their rivals, the gang was interrupted by the Lady of the Lantern. Rather than face her, Sinnapse ran.

Fixer, hedonist and coward, Sinnapse is an all-around rotten guy. He wants money and women, usually in that order, and likes having a few egotistical jocks to dominate as well. He is not the type to go after superheroes, though. That would be dangerous. On the other hand, since he mentally enslaves tough guys and beautiful women and makes a living selling his powers to the highest bidder, he just cannot seem to avoid them. Sinnapse is starting to plan for the future, however. The more he deals with crime lords, the greater he desires that kind of power and respect. Sinnapse has ambitions to rule over an underworld empire, but doesn't know if he has the guts to pull it off. NOTE: for details on Sinnapse's henchmen, see the Appendix (Decorative Slaves and Jock Goons; pages 120-121).

CHAPTER FIVE MOST WANTED

LIBERTY
JUSTICE
SECURITY
PEACE

TORQUE (150 CHARACTER POINTS – TRI-STAT)
COSTUMED FIGHTER LEVEL 2, SKULKER LEVEL 2; 170 POINTS — d20 SYSTEM

IDENTITY: Carl Yates
OCCUPATION: Mafia Hitman
FIRST APPEARANCE: Tales from the Street #128
FORMER ALIASES: None
PLACE OF BIRTH: Empire City
AFFILIATION: Genovese Family, Murder Incorporated
TERRITORY: Empire City
HEIGHT: 6'2" (188 cm)   **EYES:** Brown
WEIGHT: 203 lbs. (92 kg)   **HAIR:** Black

Growing up in Hell's Kitchen does not necessarily mean becoming a nasty person. Many are able to make good lives for themselves, escaping the violence and crushing poverty. Carl Yates never wanted to escape. Like a human shark, he grew up swimming through the cruelty and ignorance with terrible grace. His entire life — bullying other kids for their pocket money, raping and killing his way through two terms in Vietnam, torturing his way to the top of a gang back in the Kitchen — was about becoming a bigger and better thug. Anything was better than thinking about his life, or rather lack of one.

Eventually, he got the GenTech job that changed his life. It was a win-win situation — Mister Matthews could thumb his nose at heroes while adding a little protection, and Yates could run his protection racket while hiding behind GenTech security. It was an ordinary detective, however, who blew the lid off the racket, almost literally. The fumes released by the damaged barrel were from GenTech's mutagenics, meant for animals. Both cops and mobsters became sick, and a few died.

Yates got insanely lucky, though an acquaintance occasionally insists that Carl is more than a little animalistic himself. Although nauseated by the fumes, Carl hid until the coast was clear, then made a break for home. A rookie cop on patrol spotted him, but before he could act, Yates lashed out with his mind, tearing the kid's head off. It is rather ironic that his powers are mental, but the humour is lost on him. To Carl, the ability to be ever more brutal than ever is all that matters.

In a rare bout of imagination, on his first assassination he used his power to literally twist his victim in half, turning the poor man one way from the waist up and the other way from the waist down. Micky "the Saint" Saracinco appreciated this gruesome tactic for its effectiveness, and dubbed his newest hit man Torque as a result. Carl really liked the name, especially since it scared people half to death when they found out how he got it.

Today, Yates is a major up-and-comer working for Luigi Saracino and his new "Murder Incorporated," enjoying his growing power and prestige. Torque still isn't happy about the "professional wrestler" outfit he's been told to wear, though he tolerates it as part of the business. Carl doesn't yet have the authority to question his superiors, and it has the benefit of inspiring tremendous fear among the citizens.

Torque's activities often draw the attention of the Marvels Tactical Unit and Officer Prometheus, but he's also sparred with Caliburn, Archer Gold, and Corbae. The newest Archer Gold has hinted of a personal connection between them, but Torque never realised he helped create this hero, by killing his parents. Torque is in jail as often as not, but his Mafia connections ensure he's never locked up for long.

BODY	10	AGILITY	7	SPEED	4	ATTACK COMBAT VALUE	11
MIND	4					DEFENCE COMBAT VALUE	5
SOUL	7					HEALTH POINTS	145

STR	20	DEX	10	CON	20	INT	10	WIS	14	CHA	12
REF	+5	FORT	+9	WILL	+4	BASE TO HIT MODIFIER	+7				
BASE AC MODIFIER	+0					HIT POINTS	78				

TRI-STAT				d20 SYSTEM	
LVL	PTS	CHARACTERISTIC ATTRIBUTES		RANK	PTS
4	12	Attack Combat Mastery		3	(6)
1	8	Extra Attacks		1	8
3	3	Highly Skilled		1	(0)
2	4	Organisational Ties (Connected; Genovese Family)		2	2
3	6	Tough		3	6

LVL	PTS	POWER ATTRIBUTES	RANK	PTS
1	1	Adaptation (Extreme Pressure)	1	1
5	23	Force Field (Stops 60 / [[30]]; Blocks Teleport, Field-Penetrating; Area 3)	5	23
3	3	Immovable	3	3
	-2	• Dependant (Immovable, on Force Field)		-2
6	24	Special Attack "Razor Field" (60 / [[3d6+6]] Damage, Aura, Area Effect, 6 Penetrating: Force Field x3, Drop Shields, Melee)		24
5	5	Special Attack "The Torque" (60 / [[3d6+6]] Damage, Burning, Tangle, Unique Ability: TK-Powered, Slow, Unique Disability: Focus)	5	5
5	5	Special Attack "Smackdown" (40 / [[2d6+4]] Damage, Area of Effect x2, Knockback x2, Short Range)	5	5
2	2	Special Defence (Own Attributes x2)	2	2
5	25	Telekinesis (Area 3; Range 2)	5	25

LVL	PTS	SKILLS	RANK
2	8	Interrogation (Physical)	4
2	6	Intimidation (Street)	4
1	4	Mechanics (Automotive)	2
1	6	Powerlifting (Free Weights)	2
3	6	Street Sense (Influential Individuals)	6
1	12	Ranged Defence (Personal)	2
1	10	Special Ranged Attack ("The Torque")	2
1	8	Unarmed Attack (Strikes)	2

PTS	DEFECTS	PTS
	Incomplete Training (No Combat Technique or Extra Defenses)	-4
-1	Less Capable (Agility)	
-1	Less Capable (Speed)	
-2	Nemesis (Officer Prometheus)	-2
-2	Owned (Mafia, Genovese Family)	-2
-1	Red Tape (Mafia protocol)	-1
-2	Skeleton in the Closet (Evidence of assaults and murders)	-2
-1	Unappealing (Sociopath)	-1
-1	Wanted (Empire City PD for questioning)	-1

UNIQUE ABILITY: TK-POWERED

This ability is only appropriate for telekinetic-based Special Attacks. The character may add 5 / [[3]] points of Damage per Level of his or her Telekinesis Attribute. This counts as one slot.

UNIQUE DISABILITY: FOCUS

Effects that last more than one Round, such as Burning, Enduring, or Tangle, must be actively maintained. The character can still Defend normally, but must spend a combat action focusing on the power. If he or she is distracted (takes Damage, for example), the focus is broken and all Abilities are broken. Focus counts as one slot.

LIBERTY

JUSTICE

SECURITY

PEACE

CHAPTER FIVE MOST WANTED

SILVER AGE SENTINELS

MOTIVE

The archetypes of villainy have already been covered in earlier chapters. That is an excellent place to start with any adversary, but each villain is unique (or should be). When dealing with existing villains, the core of the character is already provided. The GM's job is to expand on that core to make the villain a living part of the campaign, even if that part is peripheral. Though the Silver Age is often described as "four-colour," many characters created in that time have great depth. Motivation is what gives them that richness, and by looking at different motivations, any character can come alive in a game.

VILLAIN EX MACHINA

Sometimes, creating a villain to challenge a character from scratch can seem easier than using a pre-generated character. While writing up a villain from the ground up is considerable work, the results can be tailored to a specific hero or group. Trying to tie the group to Miolnir, for example, may be more difficult.

Perhaps the most important thing to remember is that the presented villains' personalities, histories, and even powers are not written in stone. While they are designed to be useful in a variety of campaigns, no one villain is going to be perfect for every game as written. A group of talented urban investigators, for example, should not be faced with Requiem, nor should Heartbreaker be trading punches with a goddess. Then again, if Requiem has subtle magic instead of vast solar power, he could be reduced to the point of being a viable street-level opponent while retaining the same basic motivation. Likewise, Heartbreaker could become a powerful psychic in a high-level campaign, shattering the will of mighty heroes foolish enough to give her the slightest quarter.

Such enormous changes aren't necessary, though. Even slight changes can give a villain more of a connection to a hero. The Dark Queen is not hiding behind her cool alabaster veneer; she really doesn't have any interest in romance ... until she does. Seawolf is an only child, as far as anyone knows, but the scientists behind Project Speargun were quite willing to ignore the basic ethics of society. It is not too much of a stretch to

REQUIEM LAYS WASTE TO THE INDIAN ARMY

imagine that another child quietly disappeared somewhere along the way. Perhaps the aquatic heroine with the mysterious background is also a Dagon. Superheroics allow for some wild coincidences, so the imagination can run wild. It takes a lot to destroy suspension of disbelief in a Silver Age world.

THE BREATH OF LIFE:
SUB-PLOTS AND THE WELL-ROUNDED VILLAIN

There is more to comic-book villainy than just pounding on Sentinel. Heroes and villains can obsess over each other, respect one another, form temporary alliances, and even fall in love. Villains can care about heroes and sometimes find purer desires than their old criminal intent. In all cases, however, something drives a villain, whether a higher ideal fallen into fanaticism or simple hunger for wealth, love or respect.

Traditionally, many supervillain characters get into a rut, particularly second-string criminals. They start out with as much of a rational excuse as anyone is likely to have to dress up in outlandish costumes and break the law in broad daylight. Once they start getting kicked around by the heroes, though, overblown egos and obsessions with revenge start to set in. The character's original purpose often gets lost in the search for bigger fights.

To be honest, there is nothing wrong with this at times. It can be fun to take a break from saving the world to knock a few heads together fighting Slipstream's Rogues (who are doing nothing more than trying to get the jump on him), but villains do not have to fall into this trap. It could be argued that any villain will be more interesting if his or her goals remain an important focus during most appearances. By using the villain in appropriate sub-plots, or perhaps by using sub-plots with the appropriate villains, the heroes' enemies remain engaging characters rather than punching bags in colourful costumes.

BELOVED ENEMY

Ah, love! Romance between a hero and villain has considerable precedent and enormous potential. The obvious starting point is whether the villain really loves the hero or is just using him or her. A simple date can be fraught with intrigue if neither knows the other's secret identity, particularly if both characters are trying to get away from the spandex for the night. Even if the villain genuinely loves the hero, he may not feel that what he is doing is wrong, or may be trapped in a villain's life for whatever reason.

A hero-villain romance can start in any number of ways. In the midst of heated battle, the characters lock in a clinch, their eyes meet, and sparks fly ... while rushing to that big meeting in his secret identity, he bumps into a lady who fascinates him, and the feeling is mutual, but she's running off as often as he is ... trapped by a villain they both oppose, they start talking while the death-trap moves ever closer to murder, and something clicks ... the possibilities are endless. The basic question is whether secret or masked identities are involved, but there are many permutations that can also be applied. Who knows whose identity, the civilian lives they lead, family ties, duties and obligations, and many more factors can add complications to an already complex relationship.

In game mechanic terms, a Beloved Enemy is a Significant Other. The truly masochistic can take Significant Other and Nemesis and apply both to the same character, but unless the Nemesis Defect is taken at 1 BP, the relationship is going to be very one-sided. Instead, the GM might consider allowing the Significant Other Defect to be worth an extra BP considering the frequency of its impact on the game. Being in love with someone that may be on the other side of the fight some day is certainly enough of a complication to warrant it.

In general, however, such romances should be restricted to adversaries who really are not that bad. Red Phoenix is not likely to start dating Kreuzritter in any identity, no matter what situations they end up in. Characters especially appropriate for this sub-plot include Alice, Queen of Hearts; Green Ronin; Kaleidoscope; and Seawolf.

FEAR AND LOATHING

Evoking anger is easy. Fear, especially in players, is another matter entirely. They never expect to lose against the big threats, since that would put a quick end to the campaign. Even a thing as simple as revulsion can be tough to induce. Many players prefer their heroes unflappable, others are only concerned with a desire to pound some bad guys, but even heroes without fear can find themselves repelled by a truly monstrous adversary.

CRIMINAL INTENT INTRODUCTION	CRIMINAL INTENT ANATOMY OF A VILLAIN	CRIMINAL INTENT THE LONE VILLAIN	CRIMINAL INTENT SUPERVILLAIN TEAMS	CRIMINAL INTENT ORGANISATIONS	CRIMINAL INTENT MOST WANTED	CRIMINAL INTENT APPENDIX
INTRODUCTION	CHAPTER 1	CHAPTER 2	CHAPTER 3	CHAPTER 4	CHAPTER 5	APPENDIX

LIBERTY

JUSTICE

SECURITY

PEACE

Perhaps the most effective way of going about creating a mood of uncertainty is by working with the players. Killing a few characters might instill some actual worry in battle, but that may completely ruin a four-colour campaign style. Players actually interested in the heroes they create, however, will have at least a few hooks in their background. Creating a memorable rivalry is valuable (see "The One You Love To Hate," page 117), but an epic rival can still be respected. For a villain to truly shake the characters to their core, more than mere theft and greed must be involved. Another quality must be cultivated: inhumanity.

Sinnapse and Torque perform different tasks for their vicious employers, but they share a taste for sadism and cultivate a complete lack of empathy. Bloody Mary and Doc Cimitière are magical, literally inhuman beings devoted to pain and suffering. Requiem, while not cruel, has traded the quest of life for a devotion to oblivion.

Even if the players enjoy pounding on such monsters, showing them the evil these characters inflict can help in role-playing the appropriate revulsion. Turning scenes into the gaming equivalent of a Quentin Tarantino sequence is not necessary, either. Watching Sinnapse pat a quivering slave on the head like a pet, hearing Miolnir rant about the "proper place" of the races, or seeing Requiem contemplate a flower placidly just before reducing it to subatomic particles are all examples of how less can be more.

Honour Among Thieves

Not all villains are utterly heartless monsters who torture innocent victims and live for the downfall of all that is noble and good. Many, in fact, see themselves as heroes, albeit realistic ones. Such characters often cultivate redeeming personality traits, and can be much more interesting than the cackling psychopaths.

The most important of these traits is a sense of honour. When the Dark Queen gives her word to the heroes that they are safe while under a truce, they can eat the food and sleep in the guest rooms without employing tasters or posting guards. While this is a valuable tool in establishing a character, its real use in an adventure is to allow the heroes to spar verbally with the villain (and vice-versa) without fear of a fight breaking out. They can try to convince the conqueror that democracy and negotiation are better ways, while the scoundrel

challenges every ideal the heroes cherish. An entire session can go by with all the dramatic tension of a battle to save the universe ... without a single punch thrown or eye-beam fired. Such lulls in the action also allow the villain to show off a sense of flair, whether a gallery of the finest art or her patronage of a master violinist.

Another valuable facet to be exploited is an adversary's ability to respect the opposition. When trying to establish a mood of noble conflict, nothing can ruin it faster than derisive quips or righteous contempt. In general, the best way to establish such respect is by having the villain show it first. That does not guarantee reciprocation, but the heroes are unlikely to give respect without getting it first. Such a feel can make otherwise difficult scenes, such as when hero and villain have battled to a draw, go more smoothly.

Regardless, trustworthy adversaries can allow adventures that other villains simply will not fit. Appropriate characters include Kreuzritter, General Winter, Green Ronin, and the Dark Queen, and in some situations characters like the Artificer or Seawolf.

The One You Love to Hate

In direct contrast to the Beloved Enemy, the truly unforgettable confrontations of sentinels and conquerors are between the most bitter of foes. Even if they respect one another, the enmity between the two can make every battle an epic one. Such rivalries often define both hero and villain, making legends of both.

As with many other aspects of translating a genre to gaming, this can be tricky. Obviously, a character with the Nemesis Defect has a powerful hook on which to hang this sub-plot, but regular appearances alone will not create a legend. Perhaps more than any other sub-plot (even Beloved Enemy), this one requires the player's help.

A great deal has already been said about creating such memorable conflicts. Using one of the villains presented above can present further difficulties, since they've already been defined, but can also create many opportunities. Perhaps most importantly, villains created for an RPG setting are not as inviolate as those from the comics. A certain armoured monarch from Eastern Europe simply does not feel right if he turns into a serial killer. If it suits a campaign better for the Dark Queen to be a cruel, sadistic monster, there aren't thirty years

worth of issues telling the players that the campaign is wrong. Tweaking the villain to reflect a hero's outlook should not be difficult in most cases.

For the player without a solid concept, however, it is possible to come at the issue from the opposite direction and base a hero on being opposed to a villain's archetype. Heroes and villains are sometimes born from the same origin story, or are linked by events and powers. Perhaps Sinnapse tries to mentally enslave a feminist, accidentally awakening her own latent telepathy. Requiem does not know of any other survivors from Project Lotus, but that doesn't mean there could not be any — one of them might have taken the Vishnu archetype to heart, devoting himself to life and hope. A youngster from Europe whose parents lost everything when Thule rose might be rescued by Sentinel and thus gain the power to oppose the hated Miolnir. The villains presented above and in previous books can provide endless opportunities for the interested player.

REDEMPTION

Why do heroes believe in saving lives, even those of the vilest villains? Hope.

The potential for good, for greatness, exists in everyone. Supercriminals may use their powers selfishly, but any one of them could change the world for the better. All they need is a reason.

This sub-plot is not appropriate for some villains, except as a way to drive the heroes crazy — they know their old enemy is lying, but cannot prove it. Many others, however, are victims of circumstance or their own powers. Still more believe themselves heroes, and in fact don't walk too far from the light. Regardless, all are separated from the heroes by a thin but clear line: the law. If the villain can be convinced that legal channels are a better way to get what he or she wants or needs, then the heroes may have a new ally. At the very least, it is better in the long run to convert foes than to keep sending them to jail.

One major obstacle to a good redemption sub-plot is that the heroes' efforts are often central to an enemy's change of heart. If the story involves a true redemption, then the heroes' actions should play a major part in the balance. The players, however, may have more interest in battling villains than debating with them. Establishing sympathy for the villain is the first step.

There are three types of villains that are most likely to have a genuine change of heart.

The first is the reluctant villain. Many supercriminals are trapped in a life of crime by circumstance, or even their own powers. They long for a normal life, and will take the first opportunity they can get to have one. This can be used against the heroes, such as when another villain provides such an opportunity. In general, though, the reluctant villain would vastly prefer the aid of the heroes. Such a villain might even become a hero if circumstances allow, but in general the solution or cure leaves the former victim normal. Some comic-book villains have even been saved in this fashion more than once, only to be afflicted again by another villain. Misthunter is an example of such a villain.

The second type could be argued to not be a villain at all. Characters like Pan, Rain Killer and Kaleidoscope walk a fine line between doing good and lawbreaking, and the right nudge can move such a character into full-blown heroism. This sub-plot works well in tandem with Beloved Enemy and Reluctant Allies. The trick with such characters is they can be difficult to nudge, which is where the plot comes in. A complication that can be enjoyable (if frustrating) occurs when a true villain is seducing the borderline character towards the dark side, even as the hero tries to complete the redemption.

The last type is the typical Silver-Age villain who was out for respect, attention or both, and discovers that all those old desires are much better filled by heroism rather than villainy. Even truly dangerous adversaries, like Iron Duke and Seawolf, can fit into this pattern. Characters in this last category can give the heroes fits. Are they really trying to change, or is it yet another devious plot? The wrong answer will have dire repercussions either way. Another way to involve the heroes is by having a villain come to them with the desire to reform. This could be an excellent way to introduce a new player to the group, if the GM does not mind adding some tension to the campaign.

RELUCTANT ALLIES

Some threats are so great that even the most vicious adversaries may be required to join forces against something greater than both. Coldstone would side with Sentinel in a heartbeat if they were the only ones capable of stopping Requiem. Red Phoenix could easily count on

SILVER AGE SENTINELS

Green Ronin if Kreuzritter were trying to shatter Excalibur in an effort to absorb its magical power. Even the Artificer could be trusted in the face of imperiled knowledge, if an alien probe were trying to return Earth to the Dark Ages and only he and Slipstream could stop it. Few villains are so monstrous that there isn't something worse out there, and the resultant alliance can force bitter foes to trust each other ... however much they might not want to.

Such collaborations would, of course, be extremely dangerous for the hero. Green Ronin could be trusted to keep her word as long as Excalibur was in danger ... but the moment the sword was safe, Red Phoenix would not be. Coldstone would not dare risk the entire universe while battling Requiem, but once the omnicidal madman was gone, Sentinel had better not be off guard. Villains being what they are, heroes need to be ready to defend themselves at a moment's notice.

Even more dangerous is a situation where a hero and villain who cannot trust each other are forced to work together. Coldstone is not the type to take risks with the universe, but Kreuzritter is both arrogant and treacherous enough to believe he can betray Sentinel in the middle of a fight and still destroy Requiem himself. All the same, if the threat is great enough the hero must take the risk, especially if the villain has some power or ability vital to victory.

On the other end of the spectrum is the situation where the hero can trust the villain, even after the main foe is vanquished. If the Untouchables and Seawolf were trying to save a group of kidnapped metahuman children from Bloody Mary, the only thing Anasazi would have to worry about regarding Seawolf is his silvery tongue. In these situations, the tension comes from opposing philosophies in conflict rather than the threat of betrayal. See Honour Among Thieves for further details (page 116).

STALKER

Another reflection of Beloved Enemy, this situation revolves around heroes in love with "civilians." More than once, villains have come to desire the same person as their heroic adversaries. NOTE: This sub-plot should be handled with *extreme* care, but can be used effectively if applied with a light touch.

The most common variant involves villains who are truly mirror images of the hero, to the point of nearly identical powers and some twisted reflection of the hero's purpose. This can range from the comical (a bizarre clone tries to "rescue" the hero's beloved) to the frightening (an obsessive adversary learns the hero's identity and tries to become the hero, complete with romance). As a rule, severe physical or emotional abuse to the Significant Other should be avoided. Villains who try to savage a Significant Other have occasionally succeeded ... and many of the resulting stories have ruined series and heroes for years. On the other hand, if handled delicately and well, such stories can enrich a character (albeit tragically), as in Caliburn's case. Perhaps the most important thing to do before embarking on such a potentially traumatic sub-plot is to talk with your player.

In the case of comic relief, the Significant Other should never be in any real danger, unless an injured dignity counts. In more serious circumstances, it is probably best if an aura of menace is all that is applied most of the time, with the occasional direct threat.

A less common variant, but perhaps one with more potential, is a more mundane romantic triangle. In this case, the villain is not trying to break the Significant Other, but is actually using normal methods to romance him or her. A fun date is more likely to win someone over than being strapped to the neuro-reverser anyway. This can be even more interesting if the entire triangle takes place between secret identities. If Johnny Smith has been romancing Katja Jacobs, and a wealthy charmer named Jefferson Walker cuts in, none of them may realise that the rivals tried to kill each other last week at a secret Haud base.

Nevertheless, some villains are more likely to get involved in this sort of sub-plot than others. Sinnapse, Torque, and Miolnir are possibilities for the obsessive variant, while Heartbreaker, Green Ronin, Seawolf, and Coldstone are potential rivals in the latter case.

CUSTOM SUB-PLOTS

The possibilities presented above are hardly exhaustive, of course. There are endless variations available when weaving the lives of heroes and villains together. The one important thing to remember is that

LIBERTY

JUSTICE

SECURITY

PEACE

CHAPTER FIVE
MOST WANTED

PAGE
118

at the end of the game, they're just that — sub-plots. They round out characters and add spice to a player's adventures, but they should never overrun the adventure itself. Of course, when a sub-plot reaches its climax, it can become a full adventure in of itself.

OPPORTUNITY

Villains do not do the game much good just sitting around the royal chambers in Thulestag playing poker. Sooner or later, that enemy of freedom and justice has to go out and threaten freedom and justice, either personally or by proxy. The pieces have been presented for creating villains with strong goals, appropriate resources, and the willingness to defy society. Creating adventures can be as simple as putting those pieces together.

POWERS AND VILLAINS

Not every Attribute in a villain's arsenal must be dedicated to hero-bashing. In particular, high-end villains are often capable of frightening levels of power, but heroes must still be able to fight them. Hence, the "plot device" power.

For example, Requiem was specifically designed to be able to alter reality itself for short periods of time. His Cosmic Engineering is very inexpensive for what it does, but it is also extremely limited. Essentially a variant on Gadgeteering, Cosmic Engineering allows him to sense the very structure of reality and rewrite it for a time. His power will take a great deal of time to activate, but when he uses it in the right time and place, he can theoretically create a wave that will destroy an entire universe.

That the power's effect is temporary is irrelevant; the force of a blow on the diamond only lasts a moment, but the damage it does remains. This is also why he cannot simply meditate for a month and destroy everything. He must find the "flaw in the diamond," or the blow glances off harmlessly.

Fortunately, his power also has the Detectable Defect, allowing a hero who can sense changes in the cosmos or disturbances in reality to find Requiem and presumably gather a force to stop him. Thus, the power does not ever really do anything, though its design gives it the potential power to obliterate everything.

In a similar vein, he controls stellar plasma instead of fire because in superheroic physics, it justifies the ability to mimic Hyperflight as well as Flight. In exchange, he cannot control mundane fire, but if he finds a cosmic flaw in the Horsehead Nebula, he can get there.

It is important to note that a power like Cosmic Engineering should never actually be used except to advance the plot. Heroes do not get powers like this, because the plot never requires them to have the ability to destroy the universe — at least not in a standard four-colour style game.

Game Masters, on the other hand, are encouraged to come up with their own such powers. The Point Cost can be low, so long as the Attribute itself has very little practical use in the campaign. Such powers are like the superweapons that villains such as Kreuzritter build. They look awesome, create an aura of menace, and always fail at the last second. The only difference is, these powers don't blow up in the final act.

LIBERTY

JUSTICE

SECURITY

PEACE

CHAPTER FIVE
MOST WANTED

UNSEELIE SHADOW KNAVES
35 CHARACTER POINTS — TRI-STAT ADVENTURER LEVEL 1; 35 POINTS — d20 SYSTEM

BODY	7	ATTACK COMBAT VALUE	7
MIND	3	DEFENCE COMBAT VALUE	3
SOUL	5	HEALTH POINTS	50

STR 12	DEX 11	CON 11	INT 8	WIS 10	CHA 6

REF +0   FORT +0   WILL +0   BASE TO HIT MODIFIER +0

BASE AC MODIFIER +0   HIT POINTS 8

TRI-STAT			d20 SYSTEM	
LVL	PTS	CHARACTERISTIC ATTRIBUTES	RANK	PTS
2	6	Attack Combat Mastery	2	6
2	8	Item of Power (Nightlance)	2	8

LVL	PTS	ITEM OF POWER'S ATTRIBUTES (NIGHTLANCE)	RANK	PTS
1	3	Armour	1	3
1	4	Flight	1	4
1	1	Mind Shield	1	1
1	4	Special Attack "Nightlance" (40 / [[2d6+4]] Damage, Affects Incorporeal, Hand-Held, Short Range)	1	4
	-2	• Restriction (Special Attack; Does not work in sunlight)		-2

LVL	PTS	SKILLS	RANK	
2	6	Burglary (Breaking-and-Entering)	3	
2	6	Disguise (Costume)	3	
1	2	Foreign Culture (Any)	1	
3	9	Stealth (Silent Movement)	4	
1	7	Melee Defence (Nightlance)	1	

	PTS	DEFECTS	PTS
	-2	Achilles Heel (Light-based attacks)	-2
	-1	Bane (Pure gold)	-1
	-2	Marked (Spectral, shadowy humanoids)	-2
	-1	Not So Tough	-1
	-3	Owned (Dark Queen)	-3

DECORATIVE SLAVES
15 CHARACTER POINTS — TRI-STAT ADVENTURER LEVEL 1; 20 POINTS — d20 SYSTEM

BODY	6	ATTACK COMBAT VALUE	3
MIND	3	DEFENCE COMBAT VALUE	1
SOUL	3	HEALTH POINTS	15

STR 6	DEX 10	CON 10	INT 8	WIS 8	CHA 8

REF +0   FORT +0   WILL -1   BASE TO HIT MODIFIER +0

BASE AC MODIFIER -1   HIT POINTS 8

TRI-STAT			d20 SYSTEM	
LVL	PTS	CHARACTERISTIC ATTRIBUTES	RANK	PTS
1	1	Features (Attractive)	1	1

LVL	PTS	SKILLS	RANK	
1	6	Acrobatics (Flexibility)	1	
2	6	City Knowledge (Empire City: Upper West Side)	2	
3	3	Domestic Arts (Cooking)	2	
1	3	Disguise (Make-up)	1	
2	2	Etiquette (Upper Class / Serving Sinnapse)	2	
2	4	Performing Arts (Dance)	2	
2	6	Seduction (Opposite Gender)	2	

	PTS	DEFECTS	PTS
	-1	Less Capable (Strength)	
	-3	Not So Tough	-3
	-3	Owned (Mentally enslaved)	-3
	-3	Phobia (Disobeying Sinnapse)	-3

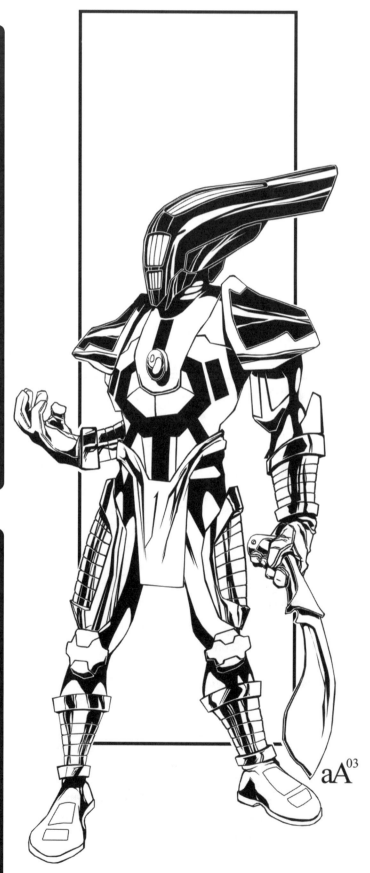

aA03

UNSEELIE SHADOW KNAVE

KREUZRITTER'S SECRET SERVICE

KREUZRITTER'S SECRET SERVICE
55 CHARACTER POINTS – TRI-STAT SKULKER LEVEL 2; 60 POINTS — d20 SYSTEM

BODY	8	ATTACK COMBAT VALUE	9
MIND	8	DEFENCE COMBAT VALUE	4
SOUL	4	HEALTH POINTS	55

STR 14	DEX 16	CON 15	INT 15	WIS 9	CHA 9

REF +6   FORT +4   WILL +1   BASE TO HIT MODIFIER +3

BASE AC MODIFIER +3   HIT POINTS 18

TRI-STAT			d20 SYSTEM	
LVL	PTS	CHARACTERISTIC ATTRIBUTES	RANK	PTS
3	9	Attack Combat Mastery	2	6
3	12	Item of Power (Thulian Military Armour)	3	12
	-2	• Conditional Ownership (Item of Power; Thulian Army)		-2
4	4	• Organisational Ties (Thulian Secret Service)	4	4

LVL	PTS	ITEM OF POWER'S ATTRIBUTES (THULIAN MILITARY ARMOUR)	RANK	PTS
2	6	Armour	2	6
1	2	Flight (Glider)	1	2
1	3	Invisibility (Blur Field — Sight)	1	3
1	4	Special Attack "Thulian Blaster" (40 / [[2d6+4]] Damage, Accurate, Hand-Held, Limited Shots: 1 action to reload)	1	4

LVL	PTS	SKILLS	RANK	
2	2	Boating (Hovercraft)	3	
3	9	City Knowledge (Thulestag; Government palace)	4	
2	8	Military Sciences (Any)	3	
1	3	Urban Tracking (Corporate)	2	
1	8	Gun Combat (Any)	2	

PTS	DEFECTS	PTS
	Incomplete Training (No Highly Skilled)	-1
-1	Famous (Thulian Secret Service)	-1
-1	Marked (Identifying tattoos)	-1
-3	Owned (Kreuzritter)	-3
-1	Red Tape (Thulian Government)	-1
-2	Skeleton in the Closet (Hushed activities)	-2

JOCK GOONS
15 CHARACTER POINTS – TRI-STAT ADVENTURER LEVEL 1; 20 POINTS — d20 SYSTEM

BODY	5	ATTACK COMBAT VALUE	4
MIND	3	DEFENCE COMBAT VALUE	1
SOUL	2	HEALTH POINTS	25

STR 12	DEX 10	CON 10	INT 7	WIS 3	CHA 6

REF +0   FORT +0   WILL -2   BASE TO HIT MODIFIER +1

BASE AC MODIFIER +0   HIT POINTS 8

TRI-STAT			d20 SYSTEM	
LVL	PTS	CHARACTERISTIC ATTRIBUTES	RANK	PTS
1	3	Attack Combat Mastery	1	3

LVL	PTS	SKILLS	RANK	
1	1	Driving (Cars)	1	
1	4	Mechanics (Automotive)	1	
1	1	Sports (Any)	1	
3	24	Unarmed Attack (Tackles)	1	

PTS	DEFECTS	PTS
-1	Not So Tough	-1
-3	Owned (Mentally enslaved)	-3
-3	Phobia (Disobeying Sinnapse)	-3
-1	Wanted (Various crimes)	-1

LIBERTY

JUSTICE

SECURITY

PEACE

CRIMINAL INTENT INTRODUCTION	CRIMINAL INTENT QUALITIES OF THE VALIANT	CRIMINAL INTENT THE HERO TEAM	CRIMINAL INTENT RULES OF ENGAGEMENT	CRIMINAL INTENT THREATS & DANGERS	CRIMINAL INTENT HEROIC PERSONAE	CRIMINAL INTENT APPENDIX
INTRODUCTION	CHAPTER 1	CHAPTER 2	CHAPTER 3	CHAPTER 4	CHAPTER 5	APPENDIX

LIBERTY

JUSTICE

SECURITY

PEACE

APPENDIX

SILVER AGE SENTINELS

LIBERTY

JUSTICE

SECURITY

PEACE

APPENDIX

CRIMINAL INTENT INTRODUCTION	CRIMINAL INTENT QUALITIES OF THE VALIANT	CRIMINAL INTENT THE HERO TEAM	CRIMINAL INTENT RULES OF ENGAGEMENT	CRIMINAL INTENT THREATS & DANGERS	CRIMINAL INTENT HEROIC PERSONAE	CRIMINAL INTENT APPENDIX
INTRODUCTION	CHAPTER 1	CHAPTER 2	CHAPTER 3	CHAPTER 4	CHAPTER 5	APPENDIX

LIBERTY

JUSTICE

SECURITY

PEACE

SILVER AGE SENTINELS

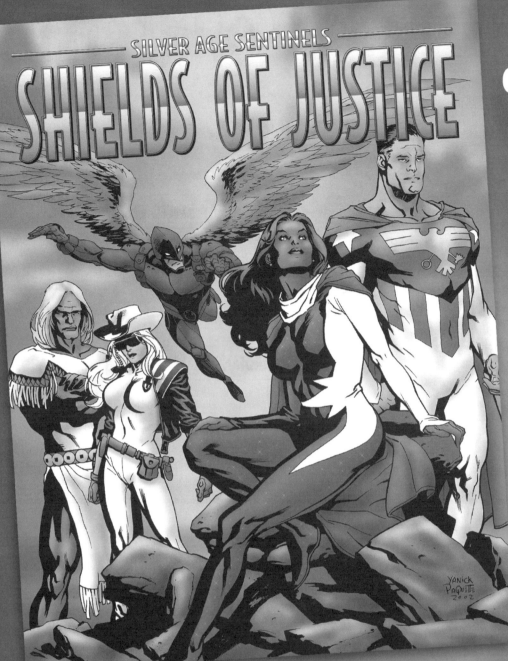

OPEN GAME LICENSE VERSION 1.0A

The following text is the property of Wizards of the Coast, Inc. and is Copyright 2000 Wizards of the Coast, Inc ("Wizards"). All Rights Reserved.

1. Definitions: (a)"Contributors" means the copyright and/or trademark owners who have contributed Open Game Content; (b)"Derivative Material" means copyrighted material including derivative works and translations (including into other computer languages), potation, modification, correction, addition, extension, upgrade, improvement, compilation, abridgment or other form in which an existing work may be recast, transformed or adapted; (c) "Distribute" means to reproduce, license, rent, lease, sell, broadcast, publicly display, transmit or otherwise distribute; (d)"Open Game Content" means the game mechanic and includes the methods, procedures, processes and routines to the extent such content does not embody the Product Identity and is an enhancement over the prior art and any additional content clearly identified as Open Game Content by the Contributor, and means any work covered by this License, including translations and derivative works under copyright law, but specifically excludes Product Identity. (e) "Product Identity" means product and product line names, logos and identifying marks including trade dress; artifacts; creatures characters; stories, storylines, plots, thematic elements, dialogue, incidents, language, artwork, symbols, designs, depictions, likenesses, formats, poses, concepts, themes and graphic, photographic and other visual or audio representations; names and descriptions of characters, spells, enchantments, personalities, teams, personas, likenesses and special abilities; places, locations, environments, creatures, equipment, magical or supernatural abilities or effects, logos, symbols, or graphic designs; and any other trademark or registered trademark clearly identified as Product identity by the owner of the Product Identity, and which specifically excludes the Open Game Content; (f) "Trademark" means the logos, names, mark, sign, motto, designs that are used by a Contributor to identify itself or its products or the associated products contributed to the Open Game License by the Contributor (g) "Use", "Used" or "Using" means to use, Distribute, copy, edit, format, modify, translate and otherwise create Derivative Material of Open Game Content. (h) "You" or "Your" means the licensee in terms of this agreement.

2. The License: This License applies to any Open Game Content that contains a notice indicating that the Open Game Content may only be Used under and in terms of this License. You must affix such a notice to any Open Game Content that you Use. No terms may be added to or subtracted from this License except as described by the License itself. No other terms or conditions may be applied to any Open Game Content distributed using this License.

3. Offer and Acceptance: By Using the Open Game Content You indicate Your acceptance of the terms of this License.

4. Grant and Consideration: In consideration for agreeing to use this License, the Contributors grant You a perpetual, worldwide, royalty-free, non-exclusive license with the exact terms of this License to Use the Open Game Content.

5. Representation of Authority to Contribute: If You are contributing original material as Open Game Content You represent that Your Contributions are Your original creation and/or You have sufficient rights to grant the rights conveyed by this License.

6. Notice of License Copyright: You must update the COPYRIGHT NOTICE portion of this License to include the exact text of the COPYRIGHT NOTICE of any Open Game Content You are copying, modifying or distributing, and You must add the title, the copyright date, and the copyright holder's name to the COPYRIGHT NOTICE of any original Open Game Content you Distribute.

7. Use of Product Identity: You agree not to Use any Product Identity, including as an indication as to compatibility, except as expressly licensed in another, independent Agreement with the owner of each element of that Product Identity. You agree not to indicate compatibility or co-adaptability with any Trademark or Registered Trademark in conjunction with a work containing Open Game Content except as expressly licensed in another, independent Agreement with the owner of such Trademark or Registered Trademark. The use of any Product Identity in Open Game Content does not constitute a challenge to the ownership of that Product Identity. The owner of any Product Identity used in Open Game Content shall retain all rights, title and interest in and to that Product Identity.

8. Identification: If you distribute Open Game Content You must clearly indicate which portions of the work that you are distributing are Open Game Content.

9. Updating the License: Wizards or its designated Agents may publish updated versions of this License. You may use any authorized version of this License to copy, modify and distribute any Open Game Content originally distributed under any version of this License.

10. Copy of this License: You MUST include a copy of this License with every copy of the Open Game Content You Distribute.

11. Use of Contributor Credits: You may not market or advertise the Open Game Content using the name of any Contributor unless You have written permission from the Contributor to do so.

12. Inability to Comply: If it is impossible for You to comply with any of the terms of this License with respect to some or all of the Open Game Content due to statute, judicial order, or governmental regulation then You may not Use any Open Game Material so affected.

13. Termination: This License will terminate automatically if You fail to comply with all terms herein and fail to cure such breach within 30 days of becoming aware of the breach. All sublicenses shall survive the termination of this License.

14. Reformation: If any provision of this License is held to be unenforceable, such provision shall be reformed only to the extent necessary to make it enforceable.

15. COPYRIGHT NOTICE

Open Game License v 1.0a Copyright 2000, Wizards of the Coast, Inc.

System Rules Document Copyright 2000, Wizards of the Coast, Inc.; Authors Jonathan Tweet, Monte Cook, Skip Williams, based on original material by E. Gary Gygax and Dave Arneson.

Silver Age Sentinels Copyright 2002, Guardians of Order, Inc.; Authors Stephen Kenson, Mark C. MacKinnon, Jeff MacKinnon, Jesse Scoble.

Silver Age Sentinels: Criminal Intent Copyright 2003, Guardians of Order, Inc.; Authors Dale Donovan, Jason Durall, Peter Flanagan, Michelle Lyons, Stan!

SILVER AGE SENTINELS OPEN CONTENT/PRODUCT IDENTITY

...n presented in Helvetica is Open Content.

...n presented in any font other than Helvetica, all images and graphics, and all fictional character names, ...s or objects, and locations are Product Identity. All rights reserved.